CiTY·SMaRT™
GUIDEBOOK

Cleveland /

Second Edition

Nancy Peacock

John Muir Publications
Santa Fe, New Mexico

John Muir Publications, P. O. Box 613, Santa Fe, New Mexico 87504

Printed in the United States of America.
Second edition. First printing February 1999.

ISBN 1-50201-450-0
ISSN 1092-4590

Editors: Peg Goldstein, Pamela Emsden, Heidi Utz
Graphics Editor: Tom Gaukel
Production: Marie J.T. Vigil
Design: Janine Lehmann
Cover Design: Suzanne Rush
Typesetting: Laurel Avery
Maps: Julie Felton
Printer: Publishers Press
Front cover photo: © Unicorn Stock Photos/B.W. Hoffman—Rock and Roll Hall of Fame
Back cover photo: © Unicorn Stock Photos/Andre Jenny—Heritage Park on the
   Cuyahoga River

Distributed to the book trade by
Publishers Group West
Berkeley, California

CONTENTS

MAP CONTENTS

See Cleveland the CiTY·SMaRT™ Way

The Guide for Cleveland Natives, New Residents, and Visitors
In *City•Smart Guidebook: Cleveland*, local author Nancy Peacock tells it like it is. Residents will learn things they never knew about their city, new residents will get an insider's view of their new hometown, and visitors will be guided to the very best Cleveland has to offer—whether they're on a weekend getaway or staying a week or more.

Opinionated Recommendations Save You Time and Money
From shopping to nightlife to museums, the author is opinionated about what she likes and dislikes. You'll learn the great and the not-so-great things about Cleveland's sights, restaurants, and accommodations. So you can decide what's worth your time and what's not; which hotel is worth the splurge and which is the best choice for budget travelers.

Easy-to-Use Format Makes Planning Your Trip a Cinch
City•Smart Guidebook: Cleveland is user-friendly—you'll quickly find exactly what you're looking for. Chapters are organized by travelers' interests or needs, from "Where to Stay" and "Where to Eat" to "Sights and Attractions," "Kids' Stuff," "Sports and Recreation," and even "Day Trips from Cleveland."

Includes Maps and Quick Location-Finding Features
Every listing in this book is accompanied by a geographic zone designation (see next page for zone details) that helps you immediately find each location. Staying in Playhouse Square and wondering about nearby sights and restaurants? Look for the Downtown label in the listings, and you'll know that statue or café is not far away. Or maybe you're looking for the Cleveland Metroparks Zoo and RainForest. Along with its address, you'll see a West Cleveland label, so you'll know just where to find it.

All That and Fun to Read, Too!
Every City•Smart chapter includes fun-to-read (and fun-to-use) tips to help you get more out of Cleveland, city trivia (Did you know that the first carbonated drink was made in Cleveland?), and illuminating sidebars (for the Best Used and Rare Bookstores, for example, see pages 136–137). And well-known local residents provide their personal "Top Ten" lists, guiding readers to the city's best wedding spots, cigar-friendly bars, and more.

CLEVELAND ZONES

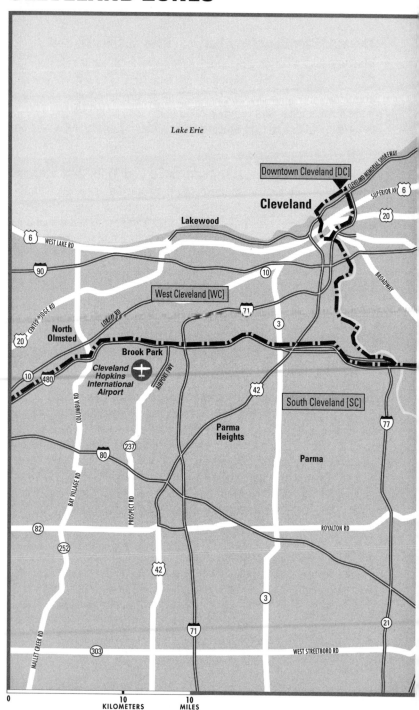

Lake Erie

Downtown Cleveland [DC]

Cleveland

Lakewood

West Cleveland [WC]

North Olmsted

Brook Park

Cleveland Hopkins International Airport

South Cleveland [SC]

Parma Heights

Parma

0   10 KILOMETERS   10 MILES

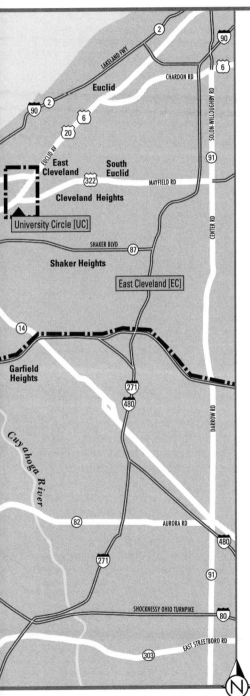

CLEVELAND ZONES

Downtown Cleveland (DC)
Downtown Cleveland, including Public Square, the Warehouse District, the Flats, and Playhouse Square. Boundaries are Lake Erie to the north, the west bank of the Cuyahoga River to the west, I-480 to the south, and I-90 to the east

University Circle (UC)
University Circle, including all the museums and buildings within Wade Oval, Carnegie Avenue to the south, Wade Park to the north, East 120th to the east, and East 105th to the west

East Cleveland (EC)
East Cleveland, including everything east of the Cuyahoga River and north of 480, except University Circle

West Cleveland (WC)
West Cleveland, including everything west of the west bank of the Cuyahoga River and north of I-480

South Cleveland (SC)
South Cleveland, including everything south of I-480

1

WELCOME TO CLEVELAND

After 200 years, Cleveland continues to remake itself in ways that, only a short time ago, even the locals could not have imagined. The city that began life as a transplanted New England village in 1796 has morphed itself through the Industrial Age of belching steel mills and ore freighters to a modern skyline that sports a glass tent dedicated to rock-and-roll music.

The city's location on the south shore of Lake Erie provides Cleveland with the ambiance of a coastal city. There are tradeoffs: the exquisite summer sunsets on the lake help to counterbalance the arctic blasts from "Alberta Clippers"—winds that blow off the water in winter. Cleveland is a city with grit.

Getting to Know Cleveland

Cleveland is a series of downtown districts. A good starting point for visitors is Public Square. Near the square you'll find the city's tallest skyscrapers: Terminal Tower (708 feet), the BP America Building (650 feet), and Key Center (888 feet).

Northwest of Public Square is one of the newer restored neighborhoods, the Historic Warehouse District. At one time, most of the products shipped in and out of the Port of Cleveland were stored in warehouses here. Now the warehouses are home to trendy restaurants, nightclubs, and loft apartments.

South of Public Square are the Gateway District and the Gateway sports complex. The complex includes Jacobs Field, home of the Cleveland Indians baseball team, and Gund Arena, home of the Cleveland Cavaliers

Local Heroes

The Soldiers and Sailors Monument on Public Square was built to honor those men from Cuyahoga County who served in the Union Army during the Civil War. Ohio-born president William McKinley was the main speaker when the monument was dedicated in 1894. The memorial chamber contains the names of 6,000 soldiers and sailors engraved in marble. Bronze sculptures on each side represent the infantry, artillery, cavalry, and navy. A 125-foot granite shaft atop the memorial features a 15-foot Statue of Liberty.

basketball team, the Cleveland Rockers women's basketball team, and the Cleveland Lumberjacks hockey team. Gateway is surrounded by great restaurants and sports bars to accommodate all the hungry fans.

To the east of Gateway is Playhouse Square, a series of restored vaudeville and movie palaces that now comprise the largest performance complex outside of New York's Lincoln Center.

On the north end of East Ninth Street is Northcoast Harbor, a park that juts out into Lake Erie. It is home to the Rock and Roll Hall of Fame and Museum, Cleveland's most high-profile museum, and the Great Lakes Science Center, a state-of-the-art museum with 300 hands-on exhibits. The museum's new next-door neighbor is a football stadium, home to the Cleveland Browns.

The Cuyahoga River is the western boundary of downtown Cleveland. Here you'll find an area known as the Flats. Once a rowdy place for sailors and dock workers, the Flats has been transformed into a restaurant, music, and nightclub district. A visit to Cleveland just isn't complete without a leisurely meal or beverage on one of the Flats' river patios.

West of the Flats is Ohio City, once an independent municipality that merged with Cleveland in 1854. The area still has a small-town feel, with residential neighborhoods that are now becoming gentrified. The West Side Market, an enormous indoor/outdoor collection of independent grocery vendors, has been a shopping tradition for generations of Clevelanders. The yellow-brick building that houses the market on West 25th Street is easy to find—just look for the large clock tower at the corner of Lorain and West 25th.

To the east of downtown is University Circle, a 488-acre campus of museums, concert halls, and educational institutions. The area includes Case Western Reserve University and University Hospitals. To the east of University Circle is Little Italy, a neighborhood known for its Italian restaurants, art galleries, and Italian religious festivals.

Shaker Square is easy to recognize. Located southeast of downtown on Shaker Boulevard, it is a village green surrounded by an octagonal, Georgian-style, red-brick shopping center. Built in the late 1920s, it was one of the first planned surburban shoppping centers in the United States. The Van Swearingen brothers, who also built Terminal Tower, created the shopping area, and the surburb of Shaker Heights, for affluent commuters of the 1920s.

Tremont, south of downtown, is experiencing rebirth. Its first settlers came from New England in 1818. When a university was established here in 1851, the area was named University Heights. The university is no longer here but the street names remain: Literary, College, Professor, and University. African American, Eastern European, Greek, Polish, and Appalachian immigrants were the next wave of Tremont residents. It is now a hot spot for art galleries, trendy restaurants, and coffee shops. Artists live here for the affordable housing and studio space.

A Brief History of Cleveland

The founder and namesake of Cleveland didn't hang around very long. Moses Cleaveland (with an "a") was a director of the Connecticut Land Company, a group of investors who bought 3 million acres of a chunk of land called the Western Reserve in the 1790s. The state of Connecticut had chosen to sell this land bordering Lake Erie to raise money for its public school system.

It was Moses Cleaveland's mission to establish a capital city for the Western Reserve. In Buffalo, New York, Cleaveland met with the Six Nation Indian tribes and promised to settle only the east bank of the Cuyahoga River, as the west bank still belonged to the Native Americans.

Cleaveland's group arrived at the mouth of the Cuyahoga River in July 1796. On the eastern bank, they laid out a New England–style town with a 10-acre public square and 220 two-acre blocks surrounding the square. In October, Cleaveland and most of his entourage went back to Connecticut, never to return.

Although he didn't seem overly attached to his namesake, Cleaveland did rashly predict that "Cleaveland" might someday be the size of Old Windham, Connecticut,

Moses Cleaveland

Western Reserve Historical Society

Top Ten Inventions by Cleveland-area Inventors

from Inventure Place, the Inventors Hall of Fame, in Akron

1. Chewing gum

2. The glass fare box used in buses and streetcars, invented by Cleveland mayor Tom Johnson

3. The hydraulic shock absorber, invented by Cleveland-born Claude H. Foster. Foster also invented the Gabriel musical auto horn, which operated on car exhaust.

4. Automatic windshield wipers, developed and patented by brothers Fred and William Folberth. The brothers held more than 100 patents and were ace mechanics.

5. The aircraft de-icer, invented by B. F. Goodrich

6. The spacesuit, the design of which is based on the tomato worm's anatomy

7. The modern golf ball, invented by Coburn Haskell

8. The automatic traffic light, invented by Garrett Morgan

9. Day-Glo colors, invented by brothers Robert and Joseph Switzer. Day-Glo was used to brighten military signal flags in World War II.

10. Rolled oats. German immigrant Ferdinand Schumacher married in Cleveland, then became a grocer in Akron. He loved oatmeal but couldn't buy it locally. So he made and sold it himself. During the Civil War, the army couldn't order Schumacher's oatmeal fast enough. By 1870, he was the leading cereal manufacturer in the United States.

population 2,700. That may not sound like wild speculation now, but it certainly was back then.

The Connecticut Land Company wanted only to sell the land, not to settle it. So they made few civic improvements and many of the people who bought parcels ended up leaving. The remaining settlers moved inland to escape the sicknesses that came from the low-lying swampy flood plain at the mouth of the Cuyahoga. In 1797, a settler from Vermont named Lorenzo Carter arrived. Carter stayed, and by April 1800 he was the area's sole resident.

Eventually, the Carter cabin became a trading post, post office, school, and church. A reproduction of that cabin stands today on the original site, now dwarfed by the bridges and warehouses that surround it.

It was the Ohio and Erie Canal, built by the state between 1825 and 1832, that jump-started Cleveland's growth. State representative Alfred Kelley successfully lobbied to make Cleveland the northern terminus of the canal, which ran south to Portsmouth on the Ohio River. Dug by laborers using picks, shovels, and wheelbarrows, the canal quickly made Cleveland a commercial hub, with a population of 21,000.

By the mid-1800s, the railroads were the rising stars of transportation. Cleveland became a major rail and manufacturing center in the 1860s, producing munitions and uniforms for the Union army.

By 1870, the city was a bustling industrial center with 92,829 people, the 15th-largest city in the country. Wealthy Cleveland industrialists built mansions on Euclid Avenue, dubbed "Millionaire's Row." Their fortunes were made possible by laborers who immigrated to Cleveland from Germany, Ireland, England, and Bohemia. Those immigrants were followed by Czechs, Slovaks, Slovenes, Croats, Serbs, Italians, Greeks, Poles, and Russian Jews. By 1890, three-quarters of the city's population consisted of either first- or second-generation immigrants. Today these ethnic groups still flourish, as evidenced by a multitude of festivals and ethnic restaurants.

African Americans originally lived interspersed throughout many neighborhoods. In the early 1900s, racial discrimination worsened as more African Americans moved to Cleveland for the manufacturing jobs created by World War I.

One of Cleveland's most colorful politicians was Tom L. Johnson, who had made his fortune in streetcars and came to Cleveland in 1879 to establish his empire here. He quickly became involved in the politics of reform, however, and his four terms as mayor (1901–1909) stand out as the most progressive era in Cleveland history.

Tom Johnson served as Cleveland's mayor from 1901 to 1909.

Western Reserve Historical Society

Called a "traitor to his class," Johnson held tent meetings to take his reformist message to immigrants, women, and others left out of the political process. He argued against business monopolies (one of which he had come to Cleveland to establish) and for city-owned utilities and women's suffrage.

Johnson's greatest legacy may be the city's Group Plan, or Mall. Under the plan, a run-down area northeast of Public Square was replaced with a symmetrical grouping of French Baroque buildings laid out in a rectangular promenade. The Mall includes the county and federal courthouses, public library, city hall, public auditorium, and school administration buildings. A statue of Johnson stands in Public Square, a testament to the man known as "the best mayor of the best governed city in America."

The post–World War I boom brought more urban amenities to Cleveland. The district on East 14th and Euclid Avenue that is now called Playhouse Square became an enclave of spectacular vaudeville and movie palaces. The Cleveland Indians baseball team, founded in 1901, won the World Series in 1920. That same year, the city (originally the capital of the automotive industry) was still producing a half dozen brands of automobiles, second only to Detroit.

The prosperity of the 1920s was taken to new heights in Cleveland by two reclusive bachelor brothers named Oris Paxton and Mantis James Van Swearingen. As young boys, who went by their initials O.P. and M.J., the brothers had shared a paper route in a rural area once inhabited by Shakers. When their adult partnership expanded into real estate, O.P. and M.J. bought the land and set about designing an exclusive residential community called Shaker Heights.

To connect this community with downtown, "the Vans" bought the Nickel Plate Railroad and constructed the massive $150 million Cleveland Union Terminal complex, complete with a train station, hotel, bank, department store, and restaurants, and topped by a 52-story office tower. Terminal Tower became the tallest building in the world outside of New York City. Cleveland's most recognizable landmark was called "the greatest peacetime engineering feat since the digging of the Panama Canal."

Six days after the first passenger train entered the downtown terminal, the stock market crashed. The Great Depression of the 1930s hit Cleveland hard. The police department became so corrupt that the mayor

---

Mr. Cleveland

When it comes to describing the people of Cleveland, no one does it better than Dick Feagler. A news reporter and columnist for nearly 40 years, Feagler writes for the Cleveland Plain Dealer. *On occasion, his news commentaries can be seen on Cleveland TV. To read a wonderful collection of his columns, pick up his book,* Feagler's Cleveland.

---

hired Chicago crimefighter Eliot Ness to do some housecleaning.

Fortunately, the cultural expansion of previous eras continued. In 1931, Severance Hall, the resplendent $4 million home of the Cleveland Orchestra, opened. And after nearly a decade of difficulties, the Cleveland Cultural Gardens opened in 1939.

World War II called for the building of telescopes, artillery, tanks, and B-29 bombers, which generated boom times for Cleveland factories. But even before the war began, the city's population began to drain as people moved to outlying areas.

The 52-story Terminal Tower

The decline continued after the war, as young families began moving to new suburbs. Shopping centers in the suburbs also began to devitalize downtown. A 1955 article in *Architectural Digest* warned, "Every metropolitan area is plagued by the paradox of suburbs siphoning off tax income. In Cleveland this parasitic situation reaches an extreme."

The 1950s and 1960s became a textbook study in "white flight." Cleveland's east side gradually shifted from a white majority to an African American majority. While politicians and developers concentrated on an urban renewal plan for downtown, east side neighborhoods continued to erode. In July 1966, the Hough neighborhood exploded into four days of riots.

The following year, Carl B. Stokes was elected mayor—the first African American mayor of a major American city. In spite of the positive national image the election generated and Stokes's hard work, Cleveland's Glenville neighborhood erupted in riots a year later.

By the early 1970s, Cleveland was losing 20,000 people a year. The vitality of downtown had vanished, the transit system was in financial trouble, and the city became known as "the Mistake on the Lake." The Cuyahoga River was so polluted that it caught fire, making national headlines. Cleveland was a laughingstock.

When populist Dennis Kucinich became mayor in 1977, he promised to stop the sale of the city-owned electric utility and to give more help to the neighborhoods. But financial problems and political infighting created what is arguably the city's most embarrassing moment: Cleveland was the first city to default on its finances since the Great Depression.

At that time, Cleveland typified the Rust Belt, a series of midwestern and northeastern industrial cities locked in a downward spiral. But like a boxer who refuses to stay down for the count, Cleveland began to rise, slowly and steadily, during the 1980s.

A downtown building boom began with new office towers for BP America, Ohio Bell, the Eaton Corporation, and the Society Key Corporation. In the last two decades, Cleveland has successfully remade itself.

The massive restoration of Playhouse Square and its theaters is nearing completion. The Flats has become a colorful, ever-expanding restaurant, comedy club, and nightclub scene on the Cuyahoga River. The North Coast Harbor waterfront features the Rock and Roll Hall of Fame and Museum and the Great

Statue of Moses Cleaveland on Public Square

Lakes Science Center. The Depression-era Municipal Stadium has been replaced by Jacobs Field and Gund Arena. A new football stadium is under construction, and a brand-new Cleveland Browns expansion team will begin play in 1999.

With a razzle-dazzle 200th birthday celebration in 1996, Cleveland has returned to the unbridled optimism of the 1920s. Realists also see a challenge ahead: the funding and upgrading of the Cleveland school system.

The People of Cleveland

Diverse is an overused word, but it is the only one that accurately describes Cleveland's people. John Grabowski, director of resources and planning for the Western Reserve Historical Society, echoes this description: "When you're introduced to someone in other cities, they may ask what you do. But when you're introduced to someone in Cleveland, they are more likely to ask what you are."

Whenever Cleveland enjoyed periods of economic development, it also experienced mass migration. Within the municipality, the largest ethnic ancestry is African American, followed by German, Irish, Italian, Polish, Slovenian, Hungarian, Yugoslavian, and Czech. According to local accounts, Cleveland was once home to more Hungarians than any other city except Budapest and more Slovenians than any other city except Ljubljana. The demographic mix results in a bountiful array of ethnic restaurants, markets, and year-round festivals.

Cleveland's Weather

The dean of Cleveland weather forecasters, Dick Goddard, explains Cleveland's weather best: "From November through April, we are one of the cloudiest places in the whole country because of Lake Erie and the air that flows across it. In June, July, and August, on the average, we get more sun than Miami, New Orleans, San Diego, or Hawaii. Cleveland is a place of dramatic weather changes."

Climatologically speaking, Cleveland sits within busy weather traffic patterns. The summers can be hot, but, thanks to the air-conditioning that Lake Erie provides, the city is spared the unbearably humid heat that southern Ohio endures. The warmth of the lake also extends the growing season into late fall.

Although folks in Cleveland talk about the "lake effect" as any weather event influenced by the lake, Goddard says the term actually refers to the snow that Lake Erie helps to produce from late autumn until the lake freezes over in winter (note, however, that the lake doesn't always freeze in winter).

The northeast Ohio snowbelt starts in the eastern suburbs and is centered over Geauga County, east of Cleveland. The lake effect can turn Cleveland into "one of the snowiest places on earth," according to

Cleveland Weather

	Average Daily High/Low Temps (degrees Fahrenheit)	Average Monthly Precipitation (in inches)
January	33/19	2.47
February	35/20	2.20
March	49/28	2.99
April	59/38	3.32
May	69/48	3.30
June	78/57	3.49
July	82/61	3.47
August	80/61	3.38
September	74/54	2.92
October	63/44	2.45
November	49/35	2.76
December	38/25	2.75

Source: *Weather of U.S. Cities*, Gale Research, Inc.

Goddard—a winter wonderland that delights cross-country and downhill skiers, tobogganers, and snowman-builders.

Dressing in Cleveland

Business in Cleveland is conducted in suits, and many people attend after-work activities such as cocktails or dinner in their business attire. But downtown shoppers, students, and tourists tend to dress more casually and comfortably, and no one begrudges them. Theater patrons at Playhouse Square, orchestra patrons at University Circle, and dance-club patrons in the Flats

Larchmere Antique Fare

enjoy looking as elegant as their surroundings, so it's wise to bring something classy for such occasions.

For the most part, however, Cleveland is a casual city. On a summer's day when the sun glitters off the lake, roomy shorts and a short-sleeved shirt is the outfit of choice—maybe it's because the Cleveland Indians play baseball in a downtown stadium, or maybe it's because much of the lakefront and Cuyahoga River are devoted to recreation and tourism. Conversely, when those winter winds howl across the icy lake, people hunker down and bundle up. Winter travelers should pack a warm coat and boots that can handle a slushy puddle. Fall and spring travelers should bring layers to peel off or pile on as needed.

When to Visit

Every season offers something memorable for visitors to Cleveland. Summers are warm but, thanks to the breezes off Lake Erie, humidity is usually not a problem. With the city's abundance of rivers, lakes, and pools, sports such as boating, fishing, sailing, waterskiing, Jet Skiing, and swimming are extremely popular.

Bicycling is popular year-round in Cleveland. Cleveland Metroparks has 60 miles of paved bike paths that take riders through breathtaking scenery. The Cuyahoga Valley National Recreation Area has a bike path on the towpath of the Ohio and Erie Canal.

In autumn the greater Cleveland area comes alive with color. Former residents plan return trips to coincide with the spectacular display of gold, orange, red, and brilliant yellow leaves. Many communities organize fall foliage tours through the countryside. On warm fall weekends, people drive to area farms to pick just the right pumpkins for Halloween jack-o'-lanterns and stop at roadside stands for fresh-squeezed jugs of apple cider.

Cleveland winters can bring blankets of snow, particularly in the "Snow Belt"—the city's far eastern and southeastern suburbs. Cross-country skiing is popular here in parks and golf courses.

Indoor activities keep people busy no matter what the weather. The I-X Center hosts a full calendar of shows that feature autos, sports, home and garden activities, and even an indoor amusement park.

Clevelanders celebrate in the middle of March, when buzzards make their annual return to the small town of Hinckley. Buzzard Sunday means a pancake breakfast and a chance to spot turkey vultures—the real name for buzzards—returning to their summer home.

Calendar of Events

The special days celebrated in Cleveland represent a composite of the city's ethnic and cultural communities. From neighborhood festivals and parades to the string of shows and activities at the I-X Center, there is never a lull in the action.

JANUARY
Martin Luther King Jr. Day Celebration, Western Reserve Historical Society; Winter Expo, Cleveland Metroparks Chalet; Winterscape, Public Square

FEBRUARY
Black History Month, Karamu Performing Arts Theatre; Cleveland Indians Winterfest, Cleveland State University Convocation Center; Cleveland International Rod and Custom Auto-Rama, Cleveland Convention Center; National Home and Garden Show, I-X Center

MARCH
Cleveland International Film Festival, [location]; The Sportsman Show, I-X Center; Greater Cleveland Auto Show, I-X Center; I-X Center Indoor Amusement Park; St. Patrick's Day Parade, downtown

APRIL
I-X Center Indoor Amusement Park; Tri-C JazzFest, Cuyahoga Community College

MAY
Finast Friendly Market's Great American Rib Cook-Off, Burke Lakefront Airport; CVS-Cleveland Marathon & 10K Race, downtown; Urban League Black and White Gala Celebration, Renaissance Hotel

JUNE
The Marilyn Bianchi Kids' Playwriting Festival, Dobama Theatre; Parade the Circle Celebration, University Circle

JULY
Cleveland Orchestra Concert, Public Square; Festival of Freedom, Edgewater Park; GTE Wireless KidsFest, Nautica Entertainment Complex

AUGUST
Cuyahoga County Fair, Berea; NAACP/Urban League Family Picnic Day, Luke Easter Park; Vintage Ohio Festival, Lake Farmpark

SEPTEMBER
Cleveland National Air Show, Burke Lakefront Airport; Taste of Cleveland, Nautica Entertainment Complex; Hispanic Heritage Month, Cleveland City Hall and various locations; Johnny Appleseed Festival, Mapleside Farm, Brunswick; Old World Oktoberfest, Geauga Lake

OCTOBER
Cleveland Ski & Winter Sports Fair, I-X Center; Hale Harvest Festival, Hale Farm & Village; Cleveland Family Pet Show, I-X Center

Cleveland Free Times

Cleveland's news, arts, and entertainment weekly comes out every Wednesday. Founded in the early 1990s, the Cleveland Free Times *is a top-notch, freewheeling collection of work by local writers and columnists. Although it was recently bought by the owners of the* Village Voice *in New York, the* Free Times *is very much a Cleveland entity. Roldo Bartimole, a well-known veteran journalist in this city, serves as the paper's political columnist and gadfly. Editor Eric Broder is also the humor columnist, recording his own skewed perspective on life through "The Great Indoors" column. Amy Braken Sparks is a senior writer and film critic who covers Cleveland's lively film scene. As its name suggests, the* Cleveland Free Times *is free of charge. Check out the paper's Web site at www.freetimes.com.*

The Cleveland skyline from the banks of the Cuyahoga River

NOVEMBER
Downtown Holiday Lighting Program, Public Square; Thanksgiving Polka Weekend, Marriott Key Center

DECEMBER
Black Nativity, Karamu Performing Arts Theatre; ice skating on Public Square; MAJIC Sings For Cleveland, Public Square; Medieval Feasts and Spectacles, Trinity Cathedral; Rock and Roll Shoot Out, Gund Arena

Business and Economy

By the end of the Civil War, Cleveland had become one of the country's first manufacturing centers. The city has long had a strong manufacturing base in steel, automobiles, and machine tooling. Manufacturing jobs still make up about 21 percent of the economy, about 4 percent higher than the national average.

Automotive manufacturing is a huge presence in the eight counties that make up the Cleveland market. All major automotive companies operate production or assembly plants in the area. Outside of Detroit, Cleveland is the largest employment area for the Ford Motor Company. Yet Cleveland's economy is not dominated by automotive manufacturing; steel and metal working continue to be manufacturing giants.

Smaller companies in the printing and plastics industries have grown significantly. Medical manufacturing companies such as Picker International represent another growth industry. Research and teaching

CLEVELAND TIME LINE

1796 Moses Cleaveland founds the city.

1800 The Western Reserve is declared part of the United States.

1803 The state of Ohio is admitted to the Union.

1825 Cleveland is selected to be the northern terminus of the Ohio and Erie Canal.

1837 The Panic of 1837 and ensuing depression halt development.

1845 Cleveland is revitalized and canal traffic reaches its peak.

1851 A celebration marks the arrival of the first railroad.

1861 President-elect Abraham Lincoln visits cheering crowds on Public Square.

1865 More than 100,000 mourners pay tribute to Lincoln, whose body lies in state on Public Square.

1870 Cleveland is a major manufacturing center, with a "Millionaire's Row" along Euclid Avenue to prove it.

1877 Standard Oil, owned by John D. Rockefeller, announces wage cuts to 56 cents a day. Strike leaders announce a citywide walk-out of everyone earning less than $1 a day. The strike fails after a riot with police.

1882 The organization that is to become the American Federation of Labor is born.

1884 The electric streetcar debuts in Cleveland.

1891 In an effort to create more efficient government, the city adopts the Federal Plan, replacing the city manager with a mayor.

1893 The Panic of 1893 brings unemployment to an estimated 8,000 to 20,000 people.

1895 Robert McKisson is elected mayor. His abuse of power leads to his ouster four years later.

1896 Cleveland celebrates its centennial by erecting a log cabin and a huge white arch on Public Square.

1901 Cleveland's progressive era of politics begins with the election of Tom L. Johnson. The Cleveland Indians baseball team is created.

1910 The city's population grows from 381,768 in 1900 to 560,663 in 1910. Cleveland is the sixth-largest city in the country.

1917 The Cleveland Metropolitan Park District is established by park engineer William Stinchcomb.

1918 The Cleveland Orchestra is born.

1930 The Cleveland Union Terminal is dedicated as Cleveland slips into the Great Depression.

The Great Lakes Exposition turns a former public dump into a lakefront fairgrounds filled with exhibits and entertainment.	**1935**
Cleveland begins to lose population to the suburbs. Appalachian whites and southern African Americans move to the city for manufacturing jobs.	**1940**
War manufacturing escalates as factories produce bombers, tanks, jeeps, and artillery.	**1941**
The city proclaims itself "the best location in the nation," with half of the U.S. and Canadian populations living within 500 miles.	**1944**
The Cleveland Indians win the World Series.	**1948**
The largest urban renewal program in the country is established, improving seven inner-city neighborhoods covering 6,000 acres.	**1955**
University Circle Development Corporation is founded and implements a 20-year plan for improving parking, roads, transportation, and security.	**1957**
I. M. Pei & Associates prepares the Erieview Plan, a 163-acre stretch of new office buildings, houses, and hotels downtown.	**1960**
Hough riots last four days, leaving four dead and destroying millions of dollars in property.	**1966**
Carl B. Stokes becomes the first African American mayor of a major American city.	**1967**
Greater Cleveland Regional Transit Authority (RTA) is founded.	**1975**
Cleveland is the first major American city to default on its debts since the Great Depression.	**1978**
Time magazine announces that "Cleveland is making a comeback." A downtown building boom brings new office towers.	**1980**
The *Cleveland Press*, flagship of the Scripps-Howard newspaper chain, folds. The *Plain Dealer* becomes Cleveland's only major daily newspaper.	**1982**
The first construction phase of North Coast Harbor, a lakefront promenade at the end of East Ninth Street, is completed.	**1988**
Tower City Center opens.	**1990**
Gateway Sports Complex, which includes Gund Arena and Jacobs Field, opens.	**1994**
The Rock and Roll Hall of Fame and Museum opens.	**1995**
The Great Lakes Science Center and RTA's Waterfront Line open.	**1996**
Cleveland Browns resume play in Cleveland in a new stadium.	**1999**

facilities at University Hospitals, the Cleveland Clinic, and Veteran's Hospital have created a strong economy not only in health care and medical equipment but also in administration and insurance-claim processing.

The area unemployment rate is 5.2 percent, the lowest in 25 years. "One of our assets is that we have a productive labor force at a reasonable cost," says Charles Webb, vice-president of Economic Development for the Greater Cleveland Growth Association. "Employees here expect to give eight hours of work for eight hours of pay." Nearly 30 Fortune 500 companies have moved their headquarters to Cleveland, including KeyCorp, LTV, and Allen-Bradley.

In keeping with the national trend, eight of every 10 new jobs being created are in the service sector, including high- and mid-value jobs in finance, accounting, and banking.

The Port of Cleveland is the largest overseas general-cargo port on Lake Erie and the third-largest port on the Great Lakes. The port serves more than 50 countries, shipping and receiving 14 million tons of cargo from 120 ports around the world each year.

Upriver from the port of Cleveland is the Flats, where freighters steam up the Cuyahoga River with loads of sand, cement, and gravel for the concrete operations. The freighters also carry mineral deposits for making steel. People never seem to tire of sitting in Flats' riverfront restaurants and watching the huge freighters maneuver through the bridges and bends of the crooked Cuyahoga River. "The magic of the Flats is that it will always have this dose of reality, of the industrial world together with the new world of entertainment," says Webb.

Underneath all this activity in the Flats, unknown to many residents, is

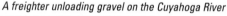

A freighter unloading gravel on the Cuyahoga River

© 1996 Jonathan Wayne

Top Ten Little-Known Spots in Cleveland
by T. S. Peric, Cleveland-area writer

1. The benches in Lakewood Park facing Lake Erie

2. The John G. White Collection at the Cleveland Public Library. Part museum, part library, it houses the largest collection of chess books in the world.

3. The upper floors of the Old Arcade, where you can sit in solitude and enjoy an eagle's-eye view of Cleveland

4. Huntington Beach in Bay Village. Known only to westsiders, this is the best beach around, located in a villagelike setting.

5. The hidden-away smoking section of Tower City. Bring along a Monte Cristo (if you can find one) and, between puffs, watch the ore boats squeeze by. A smoker's delight.

6. The John D. Rockefeller Monument in Lake View Cemetery. A towering reminder that no matter who we are, we all end up occupying about the same amount of space when we leave.

7. The main reference room at the main branch of the Cleveland Public Library. Why? Look up.

8. Any elementary school in Cleveland. Look at those young, yearning faces as they leave their classrooms and remember your own youth.

9. The Lobby Court Bar at the Renaissance Hotel. What better place to sip a gin and tonic or a full-bodied burgundy while playing the people-watching game on Public Square?

10. Any Cleveland Metropark, where you can discover your own private preserve. You can't wear this "emerald necklace," but it certainly belongs to you.

the largest domestic underground salt mine in the country. The mine stretches for miles under Lake Erie. Currently, salt mining is taking place beneath Burke Lakefront Airport on the city's North Coast Harbor. "There's a whole city down there," Webb says.

Housing

Clevelanders spend an average of 28 percent of their income on housing, considerably less than the 40 percent that people spend in Miami, Phoenix, and New York City. The suburbs to the west, south, and east

Recommended Reading

The Best Things in Life: 236 Favorite Things About Cleveland, *edited by Christopher Johnston. Quotations by famous and not-so-famous Clevelanders.*

Cleveland: A Concise History, 1706 1990, *by Carol Poh Miller and Robert Wheeler. An enjoyable history by two local experts.*

Cleveland Discovery Guide, *by Jennifer Stoffel and Stephen Phillips. Two Cleveland journalists review the scope of family recreation in Greater Cleveland.*

Cleveland Ethnic Eats, *by Laura Taxel. The definitive book on the multitude of ethnic restaurants and markets in Cleveland.*

Cleveland Golfer's Bible, *by John H. Tidyman. All you need to know for great golf outings, from the golf guru of Cleveland.*

The Cleveland 200: The Most Noted, Notable and Notorious in the First 200 Years of a Great American City, *by Thomas Kelly. The title explains it best; this collection is written by Kelly along with a handful of the city's best journalists.*

Cleveland: Where the East Coast Meets the Midwest, *by Peter Jedick. Wonderfully entertaining, well-written essays about places, events, and people in Cleveland.*

Guide to Cleveland Architecture, *by the Cleveland chapter of the American Institute of Architects. A treasure trove of information about Cleveland architecture. Includes walking tours of historic neighborhoods, illustrated by easy-to-follow maps.*

Neil Zurcher's Favorite One Tank Trips and Tales from the Road, *by Neil Zurcher. This local news reporter has made a lifestyle out of finding out-of-the-way places to visit close to Cleveland.*

Open Shelves and Open Minds: A History of the Cleveland Public Library, *by C. H. Cramer. Chronicles the people and events that shaped this groundbreaking library system.*

They Died Crawling, And Other Tales of Cleveland Woe, *by John Stark Bellamy II. Fifteen stories, including the Sam Sheppard murder case, the 1944 East Ohio Gas Company explosion, genius inventor Garrett Morgan's gas-mask rescue, and stranger-than-fiction true crime stories from Cleveland history.*

Spirit of '76 by Archibald Willard is one of America's most famous patriotic paintings. Willard was born in 1836 near Cleveland and lived most of his life here. He created as many as 14 versions of the painting, each time trying to improve it. There are obvious variations in the paintings. The one that hangs in City Hall he called his "Masterpiece Version." Another version hangs in the Western Reserve Historical Society on University Circle, and another hangs in the public library in the village of Wellington, southwest of Cleveland. Willard died in Cleveland in 1918 and is buried in Wellington.

continue to move outward into the surrounding farmland, expanding the area's already plentiful supply of new housing. Older neighborhoods such as Ohio City and Tremont are also finding new life as young business professionals and artists discover the appeal of period architecture at affordable prices.

Schools

Cuyahoga County has 31 school districts, including the Cleveland Municipal School District, the largest in the state. The district includes 77,000 students in 118 buildings throughout the city.

The Cleveland Municipal School District has undergone dramatic changes in the last two years. First, the district has been decentralized in an attempt to give each school more authority and autonomy. At each school, a core team of teachers, administrators, parents, and often students are creating Academic Achievement Plans that define goals and objectives for improving student performance.

Recently, the Ohio Legislature turned control of the district over to Cleveland Mayor Michael White. The mayor has appointed a new school board as well as a chief executive officer, chief financial officer, and chief operating officer. Yearly reports will be made to the community.

© 1996 Jonathan Wayne

2

GETTING AROUND CLEVELAND

Cleveland's location on the southern shore of Lake Erie guarantees at least one thing: there will never be a neighborhood called North Cleveland, except perhaps for the bluegill population. Greater Cleveland is mostly contained within Cuyahoga County, but continued growth has pushed the city's suburban reach into Lorain County to the west; Medina and Summit Counties to the south; and Portage, Lake, and Geauga Counties to the east.

City Layout

Surveyors who laid out the town in 1796 used the model of a New England agricultural village. They designed the town around a 10-acre public square. The original public square was divided in half by Ontario Street, a 90-foot-wide street running north and south. The east-west axis is Superior Street. The surveyors made it 130 feet wide because it ran westward down to the Cuyahoga riverbank.

All of Cleveland's numbered streets run north and south. Those east of Ontario bear the designation "East" before their number; those west of Ontario assume the designation "West."

The main east-west streets in downtown begin east of the Cuyahoga River. Some of the streets end in the downtown area, but a handful continue as far east as University Circle, providing an easy link between the two areas. Those downtown-to-University-Circle arteries are St. Clair, Superior, Payne, Chester, Euclid, Prospect, and Carnegie. Strictly speaking, none of the downtown streets run truly north-south or east-west, because the surveyors laid out the streets relative to the shore-line. If that troubles you, just think of Lake Erie as north and take it from there.

Interstates 71 and 77 both begin in downtown Cleveland. From that point, I-71 winds southwest, bisecting Ohio as it passes through Columbus, the state capital, and through Cincinnati to Louisville, Kentucky. I-77 goes almost straight south through Ohio, West Virginia, Virginia, and the Carolinas, where it ends in Columbia, South Carolina.

I-271 branches off I-71 south of Cleveland and goes northeast. On a map, I-271 forms the unofficial eastern border of metropolitan Cleveland. Crossing and linking up with those north-south highways are the east-west highways. I-90, which is at times part of the Ohio Turnpike, follows the Lake Erie coastline from west of Cleveland to the Pennsylvania state line. I-80 is the Ohio Turnpike from the Indiana Toll Road in the west to Youngstown in the east, near the Pennsylvania line. I-480, running east- west through the lower Cleveland suburbs, is a god-send to Cleveland's commuters.

Neighborhoods

Even if they master the lay of the land downtown, some visitors are reluctant to venture beyond Moses Cleaveland's original city limits. That's a shame, because Cleveland is fairly easy to navigate. Below are some of the areas worth cruising.

Heading east from downtown, take Chester Avenue and pass block after block of older retail and residential neighborhoods until it dead-ends

Aerial view of downtown Cleveland, showing the Cuyahoga River and Lake Erie

James Blank/Nu-Vista Prints

The First Mailman

In 1863 Clevelander Joseph Briggs dreamed up the idea of free home mail delivery. Prior to that, people stood in line at the post office for their letters and packages. (Junk mail had not yet been invented.) Briggs somehow convinced the government that home delivery was a good idea and subsequently became the first letter carrier. He even designed the first letter carrier's uniform. In the lobby of the Cleveland Post Office on Public Square is a plaque dedicated to Joseph Briggs and his visionary ideas.

Postscript: In 1899, Cleveland automobile pioneer Alexander Winton built the first mail truck.

on Euclid Avenue. You are now on the southernmost tip of University Circle. This area contains the vast majority of Cleveland's cultural museums, the University Hospitals complex, and the campus of Case Western Reserve University. Turn north and cruise Wade Oval or, better yet, park the car, get out, and wander the parklike grounds that surround these institutions. University Circle began as a wealthy neighborhood, and the area still retains a residential layout.

Directly east of University Circle is Little Italy. Mayfield Road cuts through the middle of this neighborhood of Italian restaurants and art galleries just east of Case Western Reserve University and southwest of Lake View Cemetery.

From Little Italy, take Mayfield Road east to Coventry Road and turn right. The Coventry Road shops are located between Mayfield and Euclid Heights. The area is also known as Coventry Village. If you've got an itch to see Cleveland's counterculture, this is it. Described as "a little Greenwich Village," Coventry Road includes one-of-a-kind restaurants, plus toy, gift , pet , clothing, and craft stores.

To reach Shaker Square, continue south on Coventry Road and turn west on Shaker Boulevard. Shaker Square shopping district is full of coffee shops, restaurants, and great boutique-style stores.

Heading west from downtown, take the Lorain-Carnegie bridge west on Lorain Avenue to West 25th Street. The West Side Market is a destination unto itself. Look for the Italian clock tower on one corner of the huge yellow-brick building.

This neighborhood west of West 25th Street is known as Ohio City. Once its own city, Ohio City was separated from Cleveland by the Cuyahoga River. The two cities were fierce competitors for the canal

DOWNTOWN BUS LOOPS

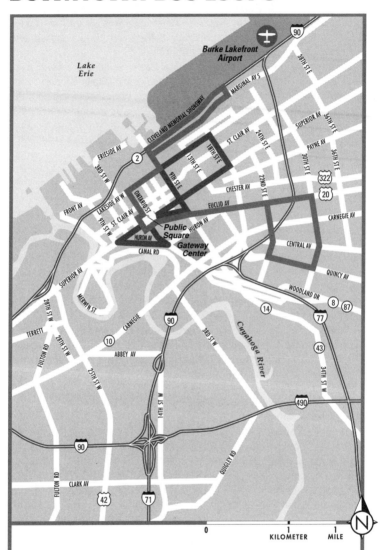

Downtown Bus Loops

The Cleveland Rapid Transit Authority serves all of Cleveland with a variety of public transit options. This map shows the two convenient downtown bus loops that take riders to many of downtown Cleveland's popular sights. For current fares and schedules, call the Regional Transit Authority at 216/621-9500.

boat business. Ohio City was annexed to Cleveland in 1854. The city was originally home to German, Hungarian, and Irish immigrants. More recent immigrants include Hispanic Americans and Asian Americans. Many stately old homes in the historic district have been restored, and many trendy restaurants have sprouted here.

Farther west on the Lake Erie shoreline is an area called the Gold Coast. This enclave of upscale highrise apartments in Lakewood affords its residents an enviably magnificent view of the Cleveland skyline. At the western end is a residential neighborhood filled with beautiful homes and winding streets.

Public Transportation

The Greater Cleveland Regional Transit Authority (RTA) is a countywide system that includes rapid-transit rail routes and more than 100 bus routes. At the heart of the RTA is Tower City on Public Square. Back in the golden age of passenger train travel, it was the main terminal for all passenger trains going through Cleveland. Today the underground station is a sleek new terminus for the RTA trains. Passengers disembark at the Tower City Center Station and ride up the escalators to The Avenue, an enormous, skylit shopping arcade with a massive food court, movie theaters, and a mall-like array of stores.

"Riding the Rapid," as locals call the RTA, is simple. The western Rapid actually goes southwest to Cleveland Hopkins International Airport. To the east, the Rapid travels through Shaker Square, Green Road, Van Aken Boulevard, and East Cleveland. A new RTA Waterfront line, opened in 1996, is a wonderful addition for getting around downtown. Riders from Tower City can get off in the Flats, at the many government offices, the Rock and Roll Hall of Fame and Museum, and the Great Lakes Science Center. Fare is $1.50 one way.

Cleveland Hopkins International Airport

Hopkins Int. Airport

There is 24-hour cab service to any destination within Cuyahoga County. Notable local companies include Americab, Inc. (6200 Roland Ave., 216/429-1111) and Yellow Cab Company of Cleveland (2069 W. 3rd St., 216/623-1550).

At Hopkins Airport, cabs can be found on the baggage claim level at

Become a Seasoned RTA Rider in No Time Follow These Tips:

1. *Got a question? You can get an answer by phone or online. To talk to a customer service representative about routes and schedule information, call the RTAnswerline, 216/621-9500, an automated service, Monday through Friday 6 a.m. to 7 p.m. and 8 a.m. to 4:30 p.m on Saturday. RTA's Web page carries schedules and maps, at http://little.nhlink.net/~rta.*
2. *When boarding, have exact change ready. Fare for the rapid or express bus is $1.50; for the local bus, $1.25; for the downtown loop bus, 50 cents.*
3. *RTA's family fare is a great way to save money. When an adult pays full fare ($1.50), up to three children ages 6 to 15 can ride for $1. That's a 58 percent savings. Up to three children under age 6 ride RTA for free with each full-fare adult.*
4. *An all-day pass for one individual is $4. Families pay $6 (one adult and three kids ages 6 to 15).*
5. *Save big bucks on park admission when you take RTA to Geauga Lake, Sea World, and the Metroparks Zoo and Rainforest. By presenting an operator-issued transfer at the parks' ticket windows, riders receive a $4.50 discount at Sea World on every admission or a $3 discount at Geauga Lake on each adult admission.*

exits 2 and 4. Phones for taxis are at each end of the exit vestibule. Many of the large hotels provide shuttle services to and from the airport. Ask your hotel for details.

Driving in Cleveland

Although traffic is heavy at traditional rush hours, actual gridlock occurs only during traffic accidents and horrendous weather conditions— or when you see those dreaded orange barrels that signify a

Auto Pioneer

Alexander Winton was an innovator in transportation. Moving to Cleveland in 1884, he created the Winton Bicycle Company. After selling bicycles for 10 years, Winton created the first successful automobile company in the United States with the first production-line assembly.

To promote his product, Winton and Cleveland Plain Dealer reporter Charles Shanks undertook the arduous journey of driving from Cleveland to New York City in 1899. During the historic trek, Shanks sent dispatches to local media, using the French term automobile *in reference to their vehicle. The exciting stories were gobbled up by an eager public, and* automobile *replaced the previously used* horseless carriage. *In New York, Winton's vehicle was greeted by a million people. Shanks became the first automotive editor of a newspaper, and Winton set the standard for automobiles.*

Winton built the first diesel engine and the first eight-cylinder motorcar in the United States. In the 1920's, he sold his automobile interests and began building boat engines. Two years before his death in 1932, Winton sold his successful engine business to what later became General Motors Marine Division.

construction job. People from Atlanta, Boston, and other large cities with real rush hours laugh scornfully at Cleveland's version. Still, if you hate the brake-roll-brake-roll of rush-hour driving, be prepared for several chronically slow spots.

The Metro curve on I-71 is notorious among Cleveland drivers. As I-71 goes south out of downtown, the first big bend to the southwest is located near MetroHealth Medical Center. Traffic can really stack up here.

Dead Man's Curve, where I-90 going north through downtown makes a sharp right at the lake, is a dangerous spot in bad weather. Trucks sometimes lose control here.

The ramp where I-77 branches off south from I-90 in downtown also confounds. It seems like all the commuters who use this artery synchronize their watches to travel this road at the exact same time.

Officially, there are two important driving tips in Cleveland: seatbelts are mandatory, and turning right on red is allowed, except where posted. Unofficially, Clevelanders are highly opinionated drivers. Cleveland publisher and veteran Cleveland driver David Gray describes what he calls the Cleveland Creep: "You're waiting behind a car at a red light. The driver in front of you eases his foot off the brake pedal and the car slowly creeps forward into the intersection. The car creeps so far forward that it is under the stoplight, so now the driver can't see it when the light turns green. So instead of being the first one off the block, he is now the last one. He is so eager to get out there that he ends up being slower than anyone else."

Another Cleveland driving tip from Gray: "Don't stop suddenly on a yellow light or charge forward immediately after the light turns green." Why? "Because there are people in this town who tend to run red lights. So if you stop suddenly at a yellow light, the person behind you could rear-end you. And if you're the first person across the intersection on a green light, someone might T-bar you, in other words, hit you sideways."

Hopkins and Aviation History

Cleveland established the world's first city-owned airport, Hopkins International, in 1925. The airport is credited with many more aviation firsts:

- *Hopkins had the world's first air-traffic control tower furnishing radio contact with planes in flight. The huge light and cab of that control tower are preserved in the Smithsonian Museum.*

- *Cleveland had the first system of lights for nighttime flying and the first airport beacon. The beacon was developed by Westinghouse, which pioneered other lighting systems and used the airport to test new inventions.*

- *Cleveland pioneered the first airport landing mat, after planes were having trouble landing in the crosswinds. The airport's first commissioner, Major Jack Berry, is reported to have said, "Let's pave the whole damn field and they can land any direction they want to." From then on, Cleveland pilots landed into the wind from any direction. The design has since been copied by many other airports.*

Cleveland drivers tend to be hurried (and sometimes harried) but courteous. Driving downtown is relatively easy because there are so few one-way streets. The only complicating factor is the "No Left Turn" signs at some major intersections. Those signs do keep traffic flowing, but they also may force you into some creative backtracking to get to your destination.

Biking in Cleveland

With 60 miles of paved bike paths in Cleveland Metroparks, it is possible to bicycle all the way around the greater Cleveland area. In terms of popularity, bicycling in Cleveland is second only to swimming. In the Cuyahoga Valley National Recreation Area, bike paths follow the towpath of the old Ohio and Erie Canal. In the downtown area, cyclists can ride the Lakefront Bikeway from East Ninth Street to Edgewater Park and the Harrison Dillard Bikeway that starts at Gordon Park on Lake Erie and runs south along Rockefeller Drive to the museums of University Circle.

For more information about area bike clubs and organizations, write to the Cleveland Area Bicycling Association, P.O. Box 94226, Cleveland 44101-4226 or call Bill Trentel at 216/522-2944. The bicycling newsletter *Crankmail* has a Web site at www.crankmail.com. The site lists clubs and scheduled rides.

Air Travel

Cleveland Hopkins International Airport, the largest airport in Ohio and the second-fastest-growing major airport in the United States, is a hub for Con-

Cleveland Hopkins International Airport

B CONCOURSE

C CONCOURSE

A CONCOURSE

tinental Airlines and Southwest Airlines. More than a dozen major airlines offer 350 flights daily. Convenient short-term and long-term parking lots are located both on- and off-premises, with connecting shuttle buses. Flight information, paging service, and lost-and-found assistance are provided. Car and limousine rental agencies are located on the baggage-claim level. A Hotel Courtesy Phone Center provides information and reservations at each end of the baggage-claim level. Many hotels offer shuttle services to and from Hopkins.

Located 10 miles southwest of downtown where east-west I-480 meets north-south I-71, Hopkins is an easy drive on either highway. Train service to Hopkins is easy, too. RTA has a well-designed station that feeds departing passengers directly up the escalators to the ticketing level of the main terminal. Arriving passengers are directed to the RTA station from the baggage claim.

Burke Lakefront Airport provides commuter service to regional cities, operates a heliport, and maintains facilities for business jets. Located just to the right of North Coast Harbor on Lake Erie, the downtown airport is also a handy location for some of Cleveland's annual events, including the Cleveland Rib Cook-off on Memorial Day weekend, the Cleveland 500 Indianapolis-style road race in late June or early July, and the Cleveland Air Show each Labor Day weekend.

Train Service

Amtrak (800/872-7245) provides daily passenger train service to Detroit, Washington D.C., New York, Chicago, Buffalo, Montreal, and Toronto. The station, located on the south shoreway between West Third and East Ninth Streets, is open from midnight to 3:30 p.m. Monday through Saturday.

Interstate and Regional Bus Service

Greyhound Bus Lines terminal (1465 Chester Ave., 216/781-0521) is open 24 hours a day. Call 800/231-2222 for fares and schedule. Lakefront Lines (216/267-8810) is located at 13315 Brookpark Road. For information on charter buses and group tours, call 800/638-6338.

Renaissance Cleveland Hotel

3

WHERE TO STAY

Deciding where to stay in Cleveland is difficult only because so many choices exist. The downtown lodgings are fewer in number than their suburban counterparts, but they are more convenient to tourist and business destinations. Downtown hotels also offer shuttle service, cab service, and close proximity to the RTA's bus and rail service, especially the new Waterfront Line.

The vast majority of lodgings are not downtown but are scattered throughout the suburbs, usually near one of the city's main traffic arteries. For example, many of the hotels southwest of downtown are within a five- to ten-mile radius of Cleveland's airport. Other suburban hotels are located near exits off I-271, I-90, and I-77, offering easy access to the airport and downtown destinations.

But don't let interstate access be your only criterion for picking your digs. Off-the-beaten-path resorts, neighborhood bed-and-breakfasts, and country inns offer an ambiance and restfulness that the others can't replicate.

The following price-rating symbols reflect the nightly cost of one double room.

Price-rating symbols:
$ Under $50
$$ $51 to $75
$$$ $76 to $125
$$$$ $126 and up

DOWNTOWN CLEVELAND

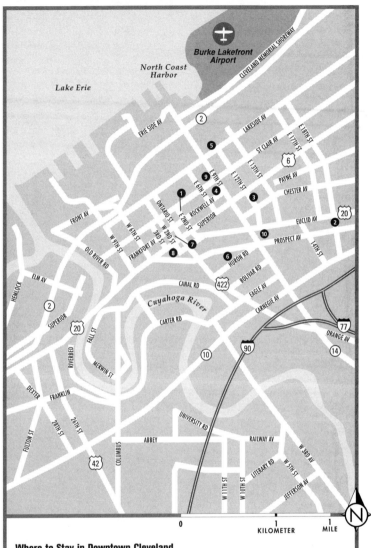

Where to Stay in Downtown Cleveland

1 Cleveland Marriott Downtown
  at Key Center
2 Comfort Inn Downtown
3 Embassy Suites Downtown
4 Hampton Inn Cleveland Downtown
5 Holiday Inn Lakeside

6 Radisson Hotel at Gateway
7 Renaissance Cleveland Hotel
8 Ritz-Carlton Cleveland
9 Sheraton Cleveland City Centre Hotel
10 Wyndham Cleveland Hotel

DOWNTOWN CLEVELAND

Hotels and Motels

CLEVELAND MARRIOTT DOWNTOWN AT KEY CENTER
127 Public Square
Cleveland
216/696-9200
$$$$

This 25-story hotel is part of Key Center, the tallest building in Cleveland (57 stories), so it is hard to miss. The hotel, which was completed in October 1991, has 401 rooms and 15 suites. All guest rooms have two telephones, fax and modem jacks, in-room bar, hair dryer, ironing board, and heat lamps. The hotel has a state-of-the-art fitness center with sauna and whirlpool. Valet parking is available in the 960-lot garage. Babysitting and concierge services are available. The 10,000-square-foot ballroom is available for meetings, and there are five smaller luxury meeting rooms including two boardrooms. Weekend packages include tickets to the Rock and Roll Hall of Fame and Museum. The hotel's grand front entrance is on West Mall Drive, in front of Memorial Plaza and across the street from Voinovich Park. David's is the hotel's 126-person full-service restaurant, Jake's Bar serves snacks and lunch, and the Lobby Piano Bar serves beverages and light meals. &. (Downtown Cleveland)

COMFORT INN DOWNTOWN
1800 Euclid Ave.
Cleveland
216/861-0001
$$$

Formerly Swingoes and the Keg and Quarter Hotel, this 130-room, five-floor hotel has been remodeled into a Comfort Inn. Located across from Playhouse Square, the Comfort Inn is within easy walking distance of Jacobs Field and other downtown attractions. The hotel has an exercise room and suites with whirlpool tubs. There are VCRs in all the rooms and movies for rent in the lobby. &. (Downtown Cleveland)

EMBASSY SUITES DOWNTOWN
1701 E. 12th St.
Cleveland
216/523-8000 or 800/362-2779
$$$$

The Embassy is downtown Cleveland's only all-suite hotel, and each of its 268 suites has a separate living room with sofa bed, armchair, and dining/work table. The kitchens have wet bars, refrigerators, coffeemakers, and microwaves. Other amenities include two computer data ports and voice mail–equipped telephones, two remote-control televisions with cable, in-room movies, and iron and ironing board. Lodging price includes a full, cooked-to-order breakfast. More than 2,160 square feet of meeting space, from boardrooms to ballrooms, are available. &. (Downtown Cleveland)

HAMPTON INN CLEVELAND DOWNTOWN
1460 E. Ninth St.
Cleveland
216/241-6600
$$$

The newest hotel in Cleveland is located at the corner of E. Ninth and Superior Streets, a half-mile from the Cleveland Convention Center, Jacobs Field, and the Rock and Roll Hall Of Fame. Kids under 18 stay free. This hotel has 14 floors, 194 rooms, and an exercise facility. Every room has voice mail, a coffeemaker, hair dryer, and iron. The room comes with a complimentary continental breakfast and free local phone calls. ♿ (Downtown Cleveland)

HOLIDAY INN LAKESIDE
1111 Lakeside Ave.
Cleveland
216/241-5100 or 800/425-3835
$$$

Built in 1974, this is the closest hotel to the Rock and Roll Hall of Fame and Museum. The 370-room hotel offers packages that include lodging, breakfast buffet, museum admission, and parking. The hotel has an indoor heated pool and saunas, and meeting rooms for groups up to 600. The 18-floor hotel has great views: Half of the rooms look out on the downtown skyline, the other half overlook Lake Erie. The hotel serves meals at Winners Bar & Grille. ♿ (Downtown Cleveland)

RADISSON HOTEL AT GATEWAY
651 Huron Rd.
Cleveland
216/377-9000
$$$–$$$$

Located in the historic Gateway neighborhood right across the street from Gund Arena and a block from Jacobs Field, this new Radisson hotel has 142 rooms on eight floors. The rooms are decorated with Mission-style furniture, and all have two-line phones, voice mail, computer modem data ports, coffeemakers, hair dryers, makeup mirrors, irons, and ironing boards. The hotel's library lounge is called the Amistad Room. Five meeting rooms accommodate from 12 to 200 people. This hotel is the official "home" for seven visiting ball clubs. Its restaurant is the popular

Diamond Back Brewery and Restaurant, which also provides banquet and room service. ♿ (Downtown Cleveland)

RENAISSANCE CLEVELAND HOTEL
24 Public Square
Cleveland
216/696-5600
$$$$

A charter member of the Historic Hotels of America, the Renaissance Cleveland Hotel has 491 guest rooms and 50 suites. Its designers clearly thought of everything: Every room has a remote-control TV, with a second TV in the bathroom, three telephones, 24-hour room service, a fully stocked refreshment center, and concierge service. A private Club Floor Lounge serves a continental breakfast and complimentary hors d'oeuvres every evening. There is an indoor swimming pool and sauna with a complete fitness center. The nearby health club provides indoor tennis, racquetball, squash, and a jogging track. The hotel has 62,000

Renaissance Cleveland Hotel

Renaissance Cleveland Hotel

square feet of meeting space, including three ballrooms and 27 meeting rooms. Sans Souci is the restaurant here, serving cuisine from Italy, Spain, Morocco, and Provence. The Brasserie serves lighter fare, Schuckers Tavern serves cocktails, and the Lobby Court Bar offers music and cocktails. ৬ (Downtown Cleveland)

RITZ-CARLTON CLEVELAND
1515 W. Third St.
Cleveland
216/623-1300
$$$$

"Puttin' on the Ritz" in Cleveland means staying at the Ritz-Carlton. The Mobil Four Star, AAA Four Diamond hotel opened in 1990, when the Terminal Tower complex was renovated and renamed Tower City. The Ritz-Carlton is connected to The Avenue at Tower City, which has theaters, restaurants, and 120 shops. Beneath The Avenue is the train terminal for the RTA Rapid lines. The Ritz-Carlton has 208 guest rooms and 27 suites, including three deluxe rooms for disabled guests. This luxury hotel has all the trimmings: marble bathrooms with

Ritz-Carlton Cleveland

telephones, maid service twice daily, evening turndown service, terrycloth bathrobes, computer access, babysitting, and 24-hour room service. The atrium-lit fitness center has an indoor pool. Meeting space is available for groups of 14 people in one of six smaller salons and for as many as 450 guests in the Ritz-Carlton Ballroom. The Riverview Room hotel restaurant offers diners a panoramic view of

TIP

Even kids get the royal treatment at the Ritz-Carlton. A Sunday Children's Tea is served from 1:30 to 5 in the Lobby Lounge, where kids enjoy special tea treats served on Royal Doulton Bunnykins China. Youngsters can also register in "Young Patrons" guest books at the front desk, and the concierge has children's videotapes, books, puzzles, and games to help keep little ones occupied. The concierge will also arrange babysitting services through the English Nanny and Governess School.

A Hotel with History

For more than 180 years, the Renaissance Cleveland Hotel has provided lodgings. Back in 1815, Phinney Mowrey bought the land for $100 and opened the city's first hotel, Mowrey's Tavern. In 1820, the log tavern became the city's first theater when "a comic opera, a farce, a drama and a variety show" were staged in the dining room. The tavern was later renamed the Cleveland House, until a new owner banned the sale of hard liquor and renamed it the Cleveland Temperance House. The hotel was destroyed by fire in 1845 and replaced with a four-story brick hotel called the Dunham House.

Enlarged and renamed the Forest City House, the hotel was the site from which William McKinley's presidential candidacy was announced in 1895. But a few years later the Forest City was razed, and the elegant, 14-story Hotel Cleveland opened in 1918. With 1,000 rooms, it was one of the largest hotels in the world. In 1934, a room cost $2 to $2.50 a night, dinner cost $1.25 in the main dining room, and breakfast could be had for 25¢.

In 1959, the hotel became the Cleveland Sheraton. Although it was a downtown landmark whose grand staircase appeared in scenes in several movies, the hotel closed in 1977 and went into receivership. Seven Cleveland corporations quickly banded together to restore it. In 1978, the hotel reopened as the Stouffer Inn-on-the-Square. A $40 million renovation in 1986 added the lobby's magnificent City of Culture Fountain. The fountain's white marble came from the same quarry as Michelangelo's David.

Renaissance Hotels International bought the structure in 1993 and renamed it the Stouffer Renaissance Cleveland Hotel. In 1995, the name was shortened to the Renaissance Cleveland Hotel.

GREATER CLEVELAND

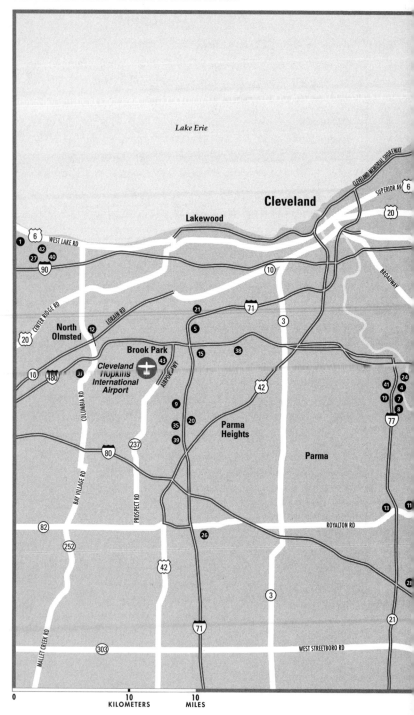

Lake Erie

Cleveland

Lakewood

North Olmsted

Brook Park

Cleveland Hopkins International Airport

Parma Heights

Parma

0   10 KILOMETERS   10 MILES

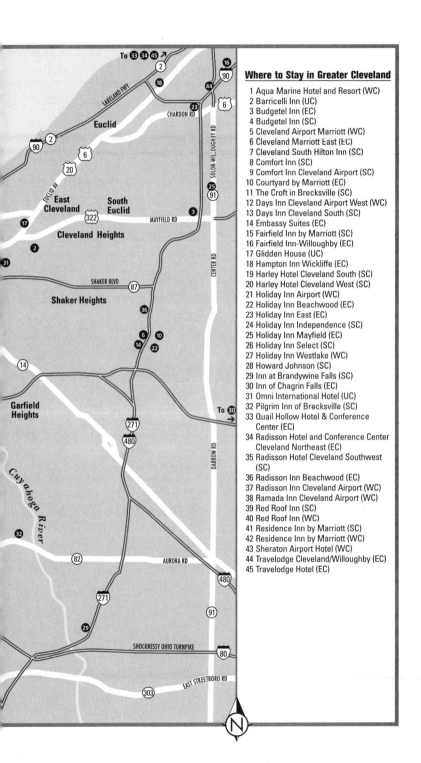

Where to Stay in Greater Cleveland

1 Aqua Marine Hotel and Resort (WC)
2 Barricelli Inn (UC)
3 Budgetel Inn (EC)
4 Budgetel Inn (SC)
5 Cleveland Airport Marriott (WC)
6 Cleveland Marriott East (EC)
7 Cleveland South Hilton Inn (SC)
8 Comfort Inn (SC)
9 Comfort Inn Cleveland Airport (SC)
10 Courtyard by Marriott (EC)
11 The Croft in Brecksville (SC)
12 Days Inn Cleveland Airport West (WC)
13 Days Inn Cleveland South (SC)
14 Embassy Suites (EC)
15 Fairfield Inn by Marriott (SC)
16 Fairfield Inn-Willoughby (EC)
17 Glidden House (UC)
18 Hampton Inn Wickliffe (EC)
19 Harley Hotel Cleveland South (SC)
20 Harley Hotel Cleveland West (SC)
21 Holiday Inn Airport (WC)
22 Holiday Inn Beachwood (EC)
23 Holiday Inn East (EC)
24 Holiday Inn Independence (SC)
25 Holiday Inn Mayfield (EC)
26 Holiday Inn Select (SC)
27 Holiday Inn Westlake (WC)
28 Howard Johnson (SC)
29 Inn at Brandywine Falls (SC)
30 Inn of Chagrin Falls (EC)
31 Omni International Hotel (UC)
32 Pilgrim Inn of Brecksville (SC)
33 Quail Hollow Hotel & Conference
   Center (EC)
34 Radisson Hotel and Conference Center
   Cleveland Northeast (EC)
35 Radisson Hotel Cleveland Southwest
   (SC)
36 Radisson Inn Beachwood (EC)
37 Radisson Inn Cleveland Airport (WC)
38 Ramada Inn Cleveland Airport (WC)
39 Red Roof Inn (SC)
40 Red Roof Inn (WC)
41 Residence Inn by Marriott (SC)
42 Residence Inn by Marriott (WC)
43 Sheraton Airport Hotel (WC)
44 Travelodge Cleveland/Willoughby (EC)
45 Travelodge Hotel (EC)

the Cuyahoga River. A harpist plays while afternoon tea is served every day. Weekend and special-event packages make this a popular getaway hotel for Clevelanders as well as out-of-towners. & (Downtown Cleveland)

SHERATON CLEVELAND CITY CENTRE HOTEL
777 St. Clair Ave.
Cleveland
216/771-7600
$$$–$$$$

Centrally located downtown, the Sheraton Cleveland City Centre Hotel is across East Sixth Street from the Cleveland Convention Center. Each of its 470 guest rooms and 45 suites has two phones, computer hookup, and an oversized desk. The Lane Suite is a Spanish-style bilevel suite with gorgeous views of Lake Erie. Abundant ballrooms and meeting rooms are named for such famous Clevelanders as Olympic runner Jesse Owens, comedian Bob Hope, actor Paul Newman, Terminal Tower and Shaker Heights creators the Van Swearingen brothers, Standard Oil founder John D. Rockefeller, and TV broadcaster Dorothy Fuldheim. Guests enjoy access to downtown health clubs. The Avenue St. Clair serves breakfast, lunch, and light evening buffet with jazz in the background. The City Centre Grill, located on the lower level, also serves breakfast, lunch, and dinner and is surrounded by Cleveland art and contemporary decor. & (Downtown Cleveland)

WYNDHAM CLEVELAND HOTEL
Playhouse Square
1260 Euclid Ave.
Cleveland

Wyndham Cleveland Hotel

216/615-7500
$$$$

Owned in part by the Playhouse Square Foundation, the Wyndham was designed to enhance the Playhouse Square district as well as to provide lodgings for the performers who fill the magnificently restored theaters on the square. So don't be surprised if you share an elevator ride with a Broadway tour cast member, an opera diva, or a pop music star. The hotel also attracts business travelers and theater patrons. The 205-room Wyndham offers packages that include dinner, theater tickets, and overnight lodging. The guest rooms have home-away-from-home touches such as coffeemakers, voice mail, data ports, hair dryers, and irons and ironing boards. & (Downtown Cleveland)

Extended Stay

BRIDGESTREET ACCOMMODATIONS

1395 W. 10th St.,
Suite 120
Cleveland
216/861-7850 (Cleveland)
330/650-2425 (Akron)
$$–$$$$

Whether you're in town for a few days or a few months, BridgeStreet Accommodations offers condos, townhouses, and apartments for short-term rental, with 22 locations throughout the Cleveland, Akron, and Canton areas. While many of the company's clients are corporate, an increasing number of tourists have been renting the fully furnished one- to three-bedroom apartments. Rates vary according to length of stay. The minimum is one night, but some guests have stayed as long as two years. Average length of stay is 30 days. & (Downtown Cleveland)

PRIVATE LODGINGS, INC.
P.O. Box 18557
Cleveland
216/321-3213
$$–$$$

Owner Jean Stanley says she has seen all the homes and looked under all the beds of the rooms she arranges for short-term housing. She offers several different services, including bed-and-breakfast arrangements in private homes and referrals to private residence accommodations. Stanley says people come to Cleveland to work, visit, or study. Many travelers who can afford a big hotel choose a private home instead. Most (but not all) of the homes are close to the museum and university network of University Circle. Fax her at 216/321-8707 or E-mail her at privatlodg@aol.com for information. & (Downtown Cleveland)

UNIVERSITY CIRCLE

Hotels and Motels

OMNI INTERNATIONAL HOTEL
Carnegie and 96th Sts.
Cleveland
216/791-1900 or 800/843-6664
$$$$

It is no coincidence that this luxury hotel is located next to the world-renowned Cleveland Clinic. In the 1920s the Bolton Square Hotel housed clinic personnel, but it wasn't spacious or modern enough. So in 1974, this 17-story hotel was constructed to serve patients and their families, who come from all over the world.

The 17th-floor penthouse boasts the most luxurious of the hotel's 16 suites, which have been temporary homes to sheiks, ambassadors, and an occasional emir or princess from the Middle East.

The hotel also boasts Classics, a AAA-rated Four Diamond restaurant. Another café has family-style dining with daily specials, including a daily Arabic dish prepared by the café's Arab cook. A cozy bistro is also located in the lobby.

Over the last two decades, the 300-room hotel has evolved into a general luxury hotel, attracting corporate and leisure guests. "We get a lot of people who prefer to stay here because it's less congested than downtown," says Omni's Tom Risk.

All guest rooms, meeting rooms, and lobbies have been recently remodeled. The hotel added voice mail ports, coffeemakers, and hair dryers in all guest rooms. The Oval Lobby, a 2½-story atrium with a central fireplace, has also been redecorated with silk sofas and lots of artwork by Ohio artists. Valet parking. ♿ (University Circle)

Bed-and-Breakfasts

BARRICELLI INN
2203 Cornoll Rd.
Cleveland
216/791-6500
$$$–$$$$
The Barricelli Inn is the former residence of the Barricelli family. The inn has seven guest rooms, four with queen-sized beds and three with king-sized beds. All rooms come with a breakfast of fruit, homemade pastries, muffins, croissants, coffee, tea, and juice. Paul Minnillo is the owner and chef of the Inn's restaurant, renowned for its fine continental cuisine and elegant decor. ♿ (University Circle)

GLIDDEN HOUSE
1901 Ford Dr.
Cleveland
216/231-8900
$$$–$$$$
Cleveland industrialist Frank Glidden, the eldest son of the founder of the Glidden Paint company, built this three-story French Gothic–style mansion in 1910. Eight Victorian-style suites, named after Glidden family members, occupy the second and third floors of the original mansion (all suites have their own baths). A guest wing built in 1988 houses 52 rooms with private baths. The Glidden House is a favorite place for weddings and corporate retreats. Around the corner from the garden-filled lawn is all that University Circle has to offer: most of Cleveland's cultural museums as well as Severance Hall, home of the Cleveland Orchestra. The continental breakfast buffet includes pastries, fruit, juices, and coffee. You can dine in either the dining room or the glass-enclosed loggia. ♿ (University Circle)

EAST CLEVELAND

Hotels and Motels

BUDGETEL INN
1421 Golden Gate Blvd.
Mayfield Heights
440/442-8400
$$–$$$
This Budgetel has 102 rooms and six suites, with complimentary coffee machines in rooms and complimentary continental breakfast; *USA Today* delivered upon request; and in-room cable TV with movies for rent. Nearby are a variety of restaurants and John Carrol University, Case Western Reserve University, and Notre Dame College. The hotel is within 20 minutes of downtown attractions. ♿ (East Cleveland)

CLEVELAND MARRIOTT EAST
3663 Park East Dr.
Beachwood
216/464-5950
$$$–$$$$
This Marriott has 403 rooms and six suites. Amenities include a Tuscan bistro called Christino's, a lounge called Capers offering nightly entertainment, indoor and outdoor pools, health facilities, room service, and concierge service. Offering easy access to Geauga Lake and Sea World, this hotel is within 25 minutes of downtown. The business center located off the main lobby has facilities for secretarial services, computers, laptops, photocopying, and faxing. The health club features 24-hour access and

a masseuse. In addition to its 16,000-plus square feet of banquet space, the hotel has a Hertz car rental agency on site and a gift shop selling Cleveland souvenirs. ૬ (East Cleveland)

COURTYARD BY MARRIOTT
3695 Orange Pl.
Beachwood
216/765-1900
$$–$$$
This inn has 113 rooms and four suites, plus the Courtyard Cafe restaurant, which is open for breakfast. Located in a business district with popular restaurants nearby, the hotel has a lounge, an outdoor pool, and health facilities. Access to downtown is easy via I-271 and I-480. A business center behind the front desk provides faxing, photocopying, computer data ports, and conference call facilities. ૬ (East Cleveland)

EMBASSY SUITES
3775 Park East Dr.
Beachwood
216/765-8066 or 800/362-2779
$$$–$$$$
This hotel has 216 suites, the full-service Boca restaurant and lounge, indoor pool, sauna and hot tub, and an all-new cardiovascular and fitness room. The four-story atrium is filled with tropical plants, and ducks and turtles live in the two ponds. A complimentary cooked-to-order breakfast is featured each morning, and complimentary cocktails are served from 5:30 to 7:30 p.m. The hotel is located about 18 miles from downtown, near Geauga Lake and Sea World. Located near I-271. Complimentary shuttle service runs within a three-mile radius of business and com-

mercial establishments. Gift shop. ૬ (East Cleveland)

FAIRFIELD INN–WILLOUGHBY
35110 Maplegrove Rd.
Willoughby
440/975-9922
$$–$$$
The inn has 134 rooms and a heated outdoor pool and provides access to the Scandinavian Health Spa across the street. A variety of restaurants are nearby, and it's about 40 minutes to Sea World and Geauga Lake. The hotel features complimentary continental breakfast and complimentary newspapers for Insider Club members. Also offered are Cable TV with ESPN, HBO, and CNN and Pay-per-view movies. Easy access to I-90, the Great Lakes Mall, and downtown Cleveland attractions. Airport limo service is available nearby. ૬ (East Cleveland)

HAMPTON INN WICKLIFFE
28611 Euclid Ave.
Wickliffe
440/944-4030
$$–$$$
The inn has 123 rooms, five suites, a restaurant and lounge called Arthur's, plus an indoor pool and health facilities. Guests receive complimentary continental breakfast. Newspapers are available at the front desk, with coffeemakers provided in all rooms. The Dock, a steak and seafood restaurant across the street, gives a 25 percent discount to hotel guests. Arthur's also gives a 10 percent discount to hotel guests. Located off I-90 about 15 minutes east of downtown Cleveland, the hotel is about a half-hour drive from the airport. ૬ (East Cleveland)

HOLIDAY INN BEACHWOOD
3750 Orange Pl.
Beachwood
216/831-3300
$$$
Completely renovated in 1996, the Holiday Inn has 173 rooms, Uno's restaurant and lounge, a combination indoor and outdoor pool, a new fitness center, and men's and women's saunas. Weekday guests enjoy complimentary *USA Today*. Guest rooms have irons, ironing boards, and 25-inch TVs with Nintendo games and video movies on demand. A video game room is located near the pool. During summer, the hotel offers packages for Sea World and Geauga Lake. Downtown Cleveland attractions are 16 miles away; the airport is 14 miles away. Business services, such as faxing and photocopying, are available at the front desk. ℅ (East Cleveland)

HOLIDAY INN EAST
28600 Ridgehills Dr.

Wickliffe
440/585-0600
$$–$$$
With 215 rooms, this inn features Patty's Pub restaurant and lounge, an indoor pool, and a fitness center with sauna and Jacuzzi. Eight conference rooms and three ballrooms are available for meetings or social events. Off I-90 and 15 minutes from downtown attractions, the hotel is about 45 minutes from the airport via I-90 west. Coffeemakers, hair dryers, irons, and ironing boards are placed in every room. Complimentary newspapers are also provided. The hotel is about 30 minutes away from Sea World, 10 minutes from University Circle. ℅ (East Cleveland)

HOLIDAY INN MAYFIELD
780 Beta Dr.
Mayfield Village
440/461-9200
$$$
This inn has 115 rooms, two suites, the Spaghetti Company restaurant

Quail Hollow Resort, p. 43

Quail Hollow Resort

and lounge, an indoor and outdoor pool, and fitness facilities. The 1,800-square-foot ballroom seats from 10 to 150 people. About 25 minutes from the airport and 20 minutes from downtown Cleveland attractions, the hotel offers in-room coffeemakers and complimentary newspapers in the lobby. It's close to University Circle museums and performance venues. & (East Cleveland)

QUAIL HOLLOW HOTEL & CONFERENCE CENTER
11080 Concord Hambden Rd.
Painesville
440/352-6201
$$$–$$$$

This resort has 167 rooms, two executive suites, four hospitality rooms, and a cabin (see tip on page 46). The Quail Wagon restaurant serves breakfast, lunch, and dinner. The Shot 'n' Shell Lounge features live weekend entertainment. The nearby Red Hawk Grille restaurant and lounge features outside dining and activities such as shuffleboard and bocce ball. The three-tiered pavilion overlooking the golf course serves Sunday brunch, with live piano entertainment. An indoor pool, two golf courses, fitness facilities, volleyball courts, two tennis courts, sauna, and whirlpool combine to make this a great getaway spot. & (East Cleveland)

RADISSON HOTEL AND CONFERENCE CENTER CLEVELAND NORTHEAST
35000 Curtis Blvd.
Eastlake
440/953-8000
$$$–$$$$

This hotel has 121 rooms and five Jacuzzi suites; its conference center features 11,164 square feet of meeting space. A business center is located off the hotel lobby, and Mantel's Restaurant offers full-service American cuisine. Off the restaurant is the lobby lounge. The hotel features an indoor pool and fitness facilities. Located at the intersection of Routes 2 and 91, the hotel is 30 minutes from the airport via I-90 and I-71. It's 15 minutes from downtown Cleveland attractions and about 40 minutes from Sea World and Geauga Lake. & (East Cleveland)

RADISSON INN BEACHWOOD
26300 Chagrin Blvd.
Beachwood
216/831-5150
$$$–$$$$

This Radisson has 196 rooms and six suites. Guest rooms have coffeemakers and full-size irons and ironing boards, on-demand movies, and Nintendo games. Refrigerators are also available. The hotel includes Bloom's restaurant and lounge, an outdoor pool, and fitness facilities. An on-site bakery features home-baked muffins, cookies, and cinnamon rolls. Banquet space is available for as few as two people and as many as 300, with in-house catering. A car rental agency is on site, along with a barbershop and gift shop. Complimentary newspapers are available in the lobby, and business services are available to hotel guests. & (East Cleveland)

TRAVELODGE CLEVELAND/WILLOUGHBY
34600 Maplegrove Rd.
Willoughby
440/585-1900
$$–$$$

Renovated in 1998, this Travelodge has 110 rooms and an indoor pool. A

Bob Evans Restaurant is on hotel grounds. Rooms include coffeemakers, complimentary continental breakfast, and cable TV with HBO, ESPN, and CNN. Complimentary *USA Today* can be found in the lobby, and the *Cleveland Plain Dealer* is delivered to each room daily. Hotel guests have free use of the Bally's Scandinavian Health Club across the street. ♿ (East Cleveland)

TRAVELODGE HOTEL
7701 Reynolds Rd.
Mentor
440/951-7333
$$–$$$
This Travelodge offers guests 141 rooms, two suites, complimentary continental breakfast, *USA Today* and the *Cleveland Plain Dealer*, an outdoor pool, and fitness facilities. The hotel also features the Bravo lounge and serves complimentary coffee in the lobby. Guest rooms have cable TV with Showtime. Airport shuttle service is available to guests. The hotel is about an hour from Cleveland Hopkins International Airport and about 20 minutes from downtown via I-90. It's also convenient to the Great Lakes Mall and Holden Arboretum. ♿ (East Cleveland)

Bed-and-Breakfasts

INN OF CHAGRIN FALLS
87 West St.
Chagrin Falls
440/247-1200
$$–$$$
This charming bed-and-breakfast has 15 guest rooms with private baths. Three of the rooms have Jacuzzi bathtubs, and 11 have working fireplaces. Two working

fountains adorn the inn's front yard, which is landscaped like an English garden. In warm weather, guests enjoy sitting outside with a book and a cup of tea, listening to the gurgling fountains. Room rates include breakfast. Attached to Gamekeeper's Tavern, which serves lunch Monday through Saturday and dinner every day, the inn is located one block off Main Street in picturesque Chagrin Falls. ♿ (East Cleveland)

WEST CLEVELAND

Hotels and Motels

AQUA MARINE HOTEL AND RESORT
216 Miller Rd.
Avon Lake
440/933-2000
$$–$$$
A half-hour drive from the airport but well worth the trip, the Aqua Marine Hotel and Resort is located two blocks south of Lake Erie in Avon Lake. The 249 oak-paneled rooms have inviting terraces that overlook an 18-hole golf course. The hotel restaurant features American cuisine. The hotel also offers guests a complete fitness center and indoor and outdoor swimming pools. Winter supersaver rates are a bargain. ♿ (West Cleveland)

CLEVELAND AIRPORT MARRIOTT
4277 W. 150th St.
Cleveland
216/252-5333
$$$–$$$$
The Marriott is located one exit north of the airport off I-71. It offers 375 rooms and four suites, an indoor pool, hotel restaurant, and

Aqua Marine Hotel and Resort, p. 44

Aqua Marine Hotel and Resort

lounge. Concierge service is also offered, and breakfast packages are available on weekends. All rooms have coffemakers, hair dryers, irons, and ironing boards. Three miles from the airport and 15 minutes to downtown attractions, the Marriott is close to Great Northern Mall and the I-X Center. ♿ (West Cleveland)

DAYS INN CLEVELAND AIRPORT WEST
24399 Lorain Rd.
North Olmsted
440/777-4100
$$–$$$
Five miles from the airport, the Days Inn has 73 rooms, the Nuevo Acapulco Mexican restaurant and lounge, and an outdoor pool. Off I-480, the inn is 14 miles west of downtown attractions and six miles northwest of the I-X Center. Guests enjoy complimentary continenetal breakfast, coffee, and tea in the hotel lobby. All rooms have cable TV. ♿ (West Cleveland)

HOLIDAY INN AIRPORT
4181 W. 150th St.
Cleveland
216/252-7700
$$$
Four miles from the airport off I-71, this hotel has 146 rooms and an indoor pool. Coffeemakers are in all rooms, along with cable TV with HBO, CNN, ESPN, Showtime, and pay-per-view movies. Irons, ironing boards, and hair dryers are available on request. Winner's sports bar and restaurant serves breakfast, lunch, and dinner. The inn is about 15 minutes from downtown, with an RTA rapid-transit train station across the street. Its billiards room features 16 pool tables, a Ping-Pong table, video games, and a bar. The hotel also has a fitness center with state-of-the-art equipment. Airport shuttle service is provided 24 hours daily. ♿ (West Cleveland)

HOLIDAY INN WESTLAKE
1100 Crocker Rd.
Westlake

440/871-6000
$$$–$$$$
Holiday Inn Westlake has 266 rooms and 20 suites and is located 12 miles from the airport. The hotel features Huntington's, a full-service restaurant; Corker's lounge, with piano entertainment; an indoor pool; health facilities; and room service. Located at I-90 exit 156, it's about 20 minutes from downtown. ♿ (West Cleveland)

RADISSON INN CLEVELAND AIRPORT
25070 Country Club Blvd.
North Olmsted
440/734-5060
$$$–$$$$
Five miles from the airport, the Radisson Inn has 139 rooms, including seven suites. All have coffeemakers, hair dryers, irons, and ironing boards. The hotel restaurant is Café Pierre, serving American-style cuisine with a living room–style lounge connected to the restaurant. This Radisson has an indoor pool with a workout room and room service. It's located across the street from Great Northern Mall and about 20 minutes from downtown. ♿ (West Cleveland)

RAMADA INN CLEVELAND AIRPORT
13930 Brookpark Rd.
Cleveland
216/267-5700
$$$
This recently renovated Gold Key hotel has a complimentary 24-hour airport shuttle. Guests also receive a free continental breakfast. The hotel has 152 rooms, and business-class suites are available. Harpo's Sports Café serves lunch and dinner. Other amenities include a fitness room and complimentary park-and-fly for hotel guests. ♿ (West Cleveland)

RED ROOF INN
29595 Clemens Rd.
Westlake
440/892-7920
$$–$$$
This Red Roof Inn has 99 rooms and is 10 miles from the airport. Wallaby's Grille and Brewpub, across the street, serves lunch and dinner. Cleveland Metroparks' Huntington Beach Reservation, with trails, picnic areas, and a beach, is one mile north of the hotel. The inn is located off I-90, about 12 miles from downtown. ♿ (West Cleveland)

RESIDENCE INN BY MARRIOTT
30100 Clemens Rd.
Westlake
440/892-2254
$$$–$$$$
This hotel has 104 suites and is 12 miles from the airport. All rooms have cable TV, fully equipped kitchens, and living rooms. Studio suites come with one or two queen-sized beds. Some rooms have fireplaces. The penthouses offer an additional bilevel loft with a queen-sized bed, TV, and bathroom. Amenities include continental breakfast every morning and a social hour Monday through Thursday evenings. Grocery shopping, laundry machines, and valet dry-cleaning service are available. In addition to free newspapers, the hotel has an outdoor pool, spa, and nearby health club. ෆ (West Cleveland)

SHERATON AIRPORT HOTEL
5300 Riverside Dr.
Cleveland
216/267-1500
$$$–$$$$
The only lodging actually on the property of Cleveland Hopkins Airport, this Sheraton contains 288 rooms and 29 suites. The hotel has a restaurant named Amelia's (in honor of the famous pilot); the Time Out sports bar and grill; an indoor pool; fitness room with sauna, whirlpool, and Nautilus equipment; room service; and concierge service. It also provides a complimentary 24-hour airport shuttle service. Each business suite has a conference table, two-line speaker phones, TV and VCR, and wet bar. The hotel's 26,000 square feet of meeting rooms and can accommodate groups of up to 500 people. Complimentary shuttle service runs to Great Northern Mall. ෆ (West Cleveland)

SOUTH CLEVELAND

Hotels and Motels

BUDGETEL INN
6161 Quarry Ln.
Independence
216/447-1133
$$–$$$
With 105 rooms and seven suites, this Budgetel is 10 miles from the airport via I-480 and six miles from downtown via I-77. Several restaurants are nearby. The hotel provides coffeemakers in rooms, free local phone calls, and a complimentary, room-delivered continental breakfast. It's about 17 miles from Sea World and Geauga Lake. ෆ (South Cleveland)

TRIVIA

During the 1960s, when the biggest names in music came to Cleveland to perform, they stayed in Swingoes and the Keg and Quarter Hotel, which are now the Comfort Inn Downtown. Stars included Elvis Presley, the Beatles, the Rolling Stones, and Frank Sinatra. Owner Ted Sahley Sr. reports that the hotel is still a favorite with musicians and actors who perform in Cleveland.

CLEVELAND SOUTH HILTON INN
6200 Quarry Ln.
Independence
216/447-1300
$$–$$$

This Hilton is perched on a hill near the I-77 and I-480 interchange. The hotel has 195 rooms, including three suites, and is 12 miles from the airport. Its full-service restaurant and bar is Shula's Steak 2 (named for Don Shula, the winningest coach in the NFL), which has special themes each night. The hotel has indoor and outdoor pools, health facilities, room service, concierge service, and a complimentary 24-hour airport shuttle. & (South Cleveland)

COMFORT INN
6191 Quarry Ln.
Independence
216/328-7777
$$$

Of this hotel's 90 rooms, 42 are equipped with Jacuzzi bathtubs. Located 20 minutes from the airport via I-480 and eight miles from downtown via I-77, the inn has an outdoor swimming pool and serves a complimentary continental breakfast between 6 and 10 a.m. All rooms have TVs and VCRs, and movie rentals are available at the front desk. & (South Cleveland)

COMFORT INN CLEVELAND AIRPORT
17550 Rosbough Dr.
Middleburgh Heights
440/234-3131
$$$

Just three miles from the airport, this Comfort Inn has 136 rooms, one suite, and an outdoor pool. Complimentary deluxe continental breakfast is served, with dinner room service provided by the Olive Garden Restaurant. Guests receive free *USA Today* and *Wall Street Journal* papers, and there is a coffeemaker in each room. The hotel is located about 15 minutes from downtown. & (South Cleveland)

DAYS INN CLEVELAND SOUTH
4501 E. Royalton Rd.
Broadview Heights
440/526-0640
$$$

Located 17 miles from the airport, this hotel has 108 rooms and an outdoor pool. The adjacent Country Kitchen restaurant serves breakfast, lunch, and dinner 24 hours a day. The King rooms have king-sized beds, coffeemakers, extra-large bath towels, TV remotes, and clock radios. Weekly and monthly rates are available. Downtown is about 15 minutes away via I-77. Complimentary morning coffee is brewed in the lobby. (South Cleveland)

FAIRFIELD INN BY MARRIOTT
16644 Snow Rd.
Brookpark
216/676-5200
$$–$$$

TRIVIA

Some Glidden House guests report that the ghosts of the Glidden family still pay an occasional visit to their French Gothic homestead.

Just one mile from the airport, the inn has 135 rooms. Amenities include an outdoor pool and complimentary continental breakfast. It's located about 12 miles from downtown. ♿ (South Cleveland)

HARLEY HOTEL CLEVELAND SOUTH
5300 Rockside Rd.
Independence
216/524-0700
$$$
Offering 184 rooms and two suites, this hotel is located eight miles from the airport. It features the Pavilion restaurant and lounge, tennis courts, indoor and outdoor swimming pools, whirlpool, and saunas. Guest rooms on the Ambassador Row concierge floor include in-room steam baths, complimentary continental breakfast, and evening cocktails and hors d'oeuvres. Room service is available. It's a 10-minute drive to downtown Cleveland via I-77. Package rates include tickets to the Rock and Roll Hall of Fame and Museum. ♿ (South Cleveland)

HARLEY HOTEL CLEVELAND WEST
17000 Bagley Rd.
Middleburgh Heights
440/243-5200
$$$
This Harley Hotel has 220 rooms and two suites. It offers both a restaurant and a lounge called the Sundial, featuring entertainment on the weekends and Sunday brunch. Ballroom and meeting room facilities can accommodate up to 300 people. The hotel has indoor and outdoor pools, room service, and an airport shuttle service. Saunas, game room, and free parking are provided. The hotel is located about 20 minutes from downtown, only minutes from the

Holiday Inn Select

Holiday Inn Select, p. 50

Ohio Turnpike and I-480, and four miles from the airport. ♿ (South Cleveland)

HOLIDAY INN INDEPENDENCE
6001 Rockside Rd.
Independence
216/524-8050
$$$
This Holiday Inn has 364 rooms and five suites, a full-service restaurant called Maxie's, the Impulse lounge with nightly entertainment, an on-site gift shop, and a jewelry store. The hotel also boasts an indoor pool, room service, and concierge service. On the Holiday Inn Priority Club floor, members can earn frequent flyer miles with participating airlines and also receive complimentary continental breakfast, appetizers, and a newspaper. The conference center is mammoth—10 conference rooms in the convention facility and three adjoining ballrooms that open into one enormous ballroom. Hotel guests pay a nominal fee to use a nearby fitness center from 6 a.m. to 8 p.m. weekdays and 9 to 3 on

Saturday. The hotel is centrally located 15 minutes from downtown Cleveland and 12 miles from the airport and is near many family-style restaurants. & (South Cleveland)

HOLIDAY INN SELECT
15471 Royalton Rd.
Strongsville
440/238-8800
$$$

This Holiday Inn underwent a $5 million renovation in 1996. The hotel is six miles south of the airport and a half-mile from the enormous Southpark Mall. The inn's family restaurant, the Simmering Pot, serves hearty food made from scratch. The upscale lounge is called Vinnie's Place, geared toward the business traveler. Indoor and outdoor pools come with a sundeck, health facilities with sauna, and a game room with pool tables, Ping-Pong, and Foosball. The hotel has 305 rooms, an executive floor, and room service. All rooms have two phones, in-room coffeemakers, hair dryers, irons and ironing boards, makeup mirrors, in-room data ports, voice mail, and in-room movies. Both HBO and *USA Today* are free. A laundry room and bicycles are available. This Holiday Inn boasts one of the largest banquet facilities in the area, with 10,500 square feet of banquet space. & (South Cleveland)

HOWARD JOHNSON
5171 Brecksville Rd.
Richfield
330/659-6116
$$–$$$

This hotel, 20 miles from the airport, has 61 rooms . Lodging includes free continental breakfast and cable TV with HBO and ESPN. The hotel has a lounge called the Valley Forge. Full meals are served next door at the Demetrios family restaurant, which offers senior-citizen discounts. Less than 500 feet away from Ohio Turnpike Exit 11, this hotel is only about 20 minutes from Sea World and the Geauga Lake amusement park. & (South Cleveland)

The Croft in Brecksville, p. 51

The Croft Bed & Breakfast

PILGRIM INN OF BRECKSVILLE
8757 Brecksville Rd.
Brecksville
440/526-4621
$$–$$$

The inn has 67 rooms and is 20 miles from the airport. Eddie's Creekside restaurant, next door, offers lunch and dinner every day and breakfast on Saturday and Sunday. Some rooms have cable TV. The hotel is convenient to Blossom Music Center and is 13 miles from downtown Cleveland attractions. ⅃ (South Cleveland)

RADISSON HOTEL CLEVELAND SOUTHWEST
7230 Engle Rd.
Middleburgh Heights
440/243-4040
$$$

Just three miles from the airport, this Radisson has 240 rooms and two suites. Complimentary shuttle service to and from the airport runs Monday through Friday 5 a.m. to 11 p.m., Saturday and Sunday from 6 a.m. to 11 p.m. The inn has a restaurant and lounge called Signatures, and room service is available until 11 p.m. Guests can enjoy an indoor pool, outdoor pool with sauna and hot tub, and 24-hour access to a new health facility. The hotel has a gift shop and a video game room. There are coffeemakers in all rooms plus free cable TV. Located 15 miles from downtown, the hotel was completely renovated in 1997. Its executive level has upgraded guest rooms with added amenities. ⅃ (South Cleveland)

RED ROOF INN
17555 Bagley Rd.
Middleburgh Heights
440/243-2441

$$–$$$

The inn has 117 rooms and is two miles from the airport. All rooms have cable TV with with Showtime, ESPN, and CNN. Guests enjoy complimentary coffee and newspaper in the morning. A variety of restaurants are nearby. ⅃ (South Cleveland)

RESIDENCE INN BY MARRIOTT
5101 W. Creek Rd.
Independence
216/520-1450
$$$–$$$$

This 118-suite hotel is located 10 miles from the airport. The studio suite has a full kitchen and living room with TV, one queen-sized bed, and a sofa bed that converts into a single bed. The two-bedroom suite has a centrally located kitchen and living room. Both bedrooms have a queen-sized bed, a TV, and a full bath. All rooms have ironing boards and irons and free cable TV with HBO, ESPN, VH-1, CNN, Discovery Channel, and Cleveland area stations. The hotel also has an outdoor pool and an exercise room. Grocery shopping and daily laundry service are available. Complimentary continental breakfast is served in the dining room. ⅃ (South Cleveland)

Bed-and-Breakfasts

THE CROFT IN BRECKSVILLE
6760 Old Royalton Rd.
Brecksville
440/526-1465
$$–$$$

This antique-filled 1904 farmhouse is now a bed-and-breakfast—just 20 minutes from downtown. A night's stay includes a full sit-down breakfast. The Croft has no air-conditioning but does have flower gardens, a screened-in front porch, and a large patio. The bath comes with bubbles and candles. Guests are welcome to play badminton or croquet on the lawn. ♿ (South Cleveland)

INN AT BRANDYWINE FALLS
8230 Brandywine Rd.
Sagamore Hills
330/650-4965
$$–$$$

On the National Register of Historic Places, the Inn at Brandywine Falls was originally a farmstead in 1848, then became a B&B in 1988. Own-ers George and Katie Hoy offer three bedrooms and three suites. The inn provides breakfast, then encourages guests to try one of 17 above-the-cut restaurants within easy driving distance. "Since we opened, we have had 9,300 guests stay 23,000 times, and 85 percent travel less than 40 minutes to get here," Hoy says. "This is a destina-tion." The inn is located in the Cuyahoga Valley National Recre-ation Area, 38 minutes from down-town Cleveland on I-77. ♿ (South Cleveland)

Hyde Park Restaurants

4

WHERE TO EAT

Since the early days of the Ohio and Erie Canal, when much of Ohio's agricultural bounty passed through Cleveland, this has been a town that loves to eat.

The immigrant groups that came to Cleveland over the years have made a good living by creating an impressive array of ethnic restaurants. Little Italy is an oasis of Italian cuisine, but such restaurants can be found in almost every neighborhood in the city. Cleveland also has a wealth of restaurants offering Eastern Asian, Mediterranean, Eastern European, Continental, Greek, and Latin American cuisine. There is an impressive array of Middle Eastern restaurants and even a marvelous Ethiopian restaurant.

But those who enjoy more traditional fare won't be disappointed. There are good breakfast spots, burger places, and seafood and steak houses throughout the area. Vegetarian entrées, once found on only a few menus—and then almost by accident—are now a mainstay of casual and classy restaurants alike.

Like the city's revitalized neighborhoods, Cleveland's cuisine has been redefined and expanded to serve a new and bigger audience. Eating out in Cleveland has never been more enjoyable.

Listed on the next page are area restaurants organized by category, with zone designations in parentheses. Each individual restaurant description includes a price-rating symbol reflecting the cost of one meal (appetizer and entrée) for one person.

Price-rating symbols:
$ Under $10
$$ $11 to $20
$$$ $21 and up

American/Contemporary

City Centre Grill (DC), p. 57
Coaches (DC), p. 58
David's (DC), p. 58
Gatekeepers Inn (DC), p. 59
Goodfellas (UC), p. 59
Johnny's Downtown (DC), p. 61
Lincoln Inn (DC), p. 63
Lola (WC), p. 77
Miracles (WC), p. 78
Pufferbelly (SC), p. 80
Sammy's (DC), p. 64
Sweetwater Cafe Sausalito(DC), p.65
Taverne of Richfield, Cleveland Style (DC), p. 65
Terrace Club (DC), p. 68
Uptown Grille (UC), p. 70

Best Breakfasts

The Big Egg (WC), p. 76

Brazilian

Sergio's (UC), p. 70

Brewpubs

Diamondback Brewery (DC), p. 58

Burgers

Flat Iron Cafe (DC), p. 58
Heck's (WC), p. 77

Chinese

Bo Loong (DC), p. 57
Li Wah (DC), p. 62
Lu Cuisine (DC), p. 63
Sun Luck Garden (EC), p. 75

Continental

Baracelli Inn (UC), p. 68
Hickerson's at the Hanna (DC), p. 60
Parker's (WC), p. 79

Delis

Around the Corner (WC), p. 76
Corky & Lenny's (EC), p. 72
Max's Deli (WC), p. 78
Nate's Deli and Restaurant (WC), p. 79

Diners

Ruthie & Moe's (EC), p. 74

Ethiopian

Empress Taytu Ethiopian Restaurant (EC), p. 72

Eastern European

Balaton (EC), p. 71
Fanny's (EC), p. 72
Parma Pierogies (SC), p. 80
Sterle's Slovenian Country House (EC), p. 74

Fine Dining

Cabin Club (WC), p. 76
Classics (UC), p. 68
Johnny's Downtown (DC), p. 61
Sammy's (DC), p. 64

German

Hofbrau Haus (EC), p. 73

Greek

Greek Isles (DC), p. 60
Mad Greek (EC), p. 73

Indian

Cafe Tandoor (EC), p. 71
Mad Greek (EC), p. 73

Italian

Acappella (DC), p. 55
Amici's (WC), p. 75
Arrabiata's (EC), p. 71
Eddie's Place (EC), p. 72
Frank and Pauly's (DC), p. 59
Frankie's Italian Cuisine (WC), p. 76
Guarino's (UC), p. 69
Johnny's Bar on Fulton (DC), p. 61
La Dolce Vita (UC), p. 69
Mama Santa's (UC) , p. 69
Maria's (WC), p. 77
Massimo da Milano (WC), p. 77
New York Spaghetti House (DC), p. 64
Nido Italia (EC), p. 73
Piccolo Mondo (DC), p. 64

Pizzaz (EC), p. 73
Salvatore's (UC), p. 70
Sforzo's Family Restaurant (WC),
 p. 80
Spaghetti Warehouse (DC), p. 65
Trattoria on the Hill (UC), p. 70

Korean
Seoul Hot Pot & De Angelo's Pizza
 (EC), p. 74

Mediterranean
Ciao Cucina (DC), p. 57
Georgio's (WC), p. 76
Sans Souci (DC), p. 64

Mexican
Luchita's (WC), p. 77
Nuevo Acapulco (WC), p. 79

Middle Eastern
Aladdin's Eatery (EC and WC),
 pp. 71, 75
Ali Baba Restaurant (WC), p. 75
Nate's Deli and Restaurant (WC),
 p. 79

Ribs
Hot Sauce Williams (EC), p. 73

Seafood
Blue Pointe Grille (DC), p. 55
Don's Lighthouse Grille (WC), p. 76
Hornblower's (DC), p. 61
The Lancer (UC), p. 69
Landry's Seafood Restaurant (DC),
 p. 62
Pier W (WC), p. 79
Salmon Dave's (WC), p. 80
The Watermark (DC), p. 68

Soul Food
Soul Vegetarian (EC), p. 74

Spanish
Mallorca (DC), p. 63

Steakhouses
Cleveland Chop House & Brewery
 (DC), p. 57
Hyde Park Chop House Downtown
 (DC), p. 61
John Q's Steakhouse (DC), p. 61
Morton's of Chicago, The Steak-
 house (DC), p. 63

Vegetarian
Soul Vegetarian (EC), p. 74
Tommy's (EC), p. 75

DOWNTOWN CLEVELAND

ACAPPELLA
1621 Euclid Ave.
Cleveland
216/621-7212
This moderately priced bistro seats
46 people. Although there's no liquor
served, you'll enjoy cozy fine dining
here. Silk-screen art adorns the
walls, and fresh flowers fill the room
with color. The restaurant is on the
eastern end of Playhouse Square,
about 20 steps away from the Palace
Theater. It's a great place to eat
before or after a performance. Fresh
seafood, pasta, and salad are the
favorites here. Lunch weekdays. Call
for weekend and evening hours.
(Downtown Cleveland)

BLUE POINTE GRILLE
700 W. St. Clair
Cleveland
216/875-7827
Blue Pointe serves seafood with a
capital S in the Warehouse District.
The restaurant is named in honor of
the bluepoint oyster, and you can get
these oysters crispy fried, on the half
shell, or Rockefeller style. Both the
lunch and dinner menus are like
guided tours of the world's fresh- and
saltwater bodies. Entrees include

DOWNTOWN CLEVELAND

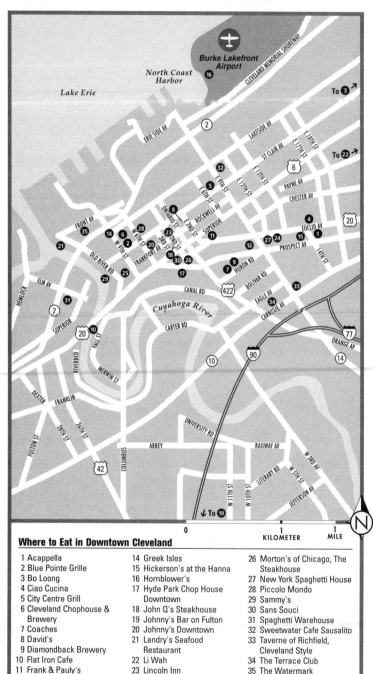

Burke Lakefront Airport

North Coast Harbor

Lake Erie

To 3

To 22

Cuyahoga River

0   1 KILOMETER   1 MILE

Where to Eat in Downtown Cleveland

1 Acappella
2 Blue Pointe Grille
3 Bo Loong
4 Ciao Cucina
5 City Centre Grill
6 Cleveland Chophouse & Brewery
7 Coaches
8 David's
9 Diamondback Brewery
10 Flat Iron Cafe
11 Frank & Pauly's
12 (Tom's) Gatekeepers' Inn
13 Goodfellas

14 Greek Isles
15 Hickerson's at the Hanna
16 Hornblower's
17 Hyde Park Chop House Downtown
18 John Q's Steakhouse
19 Johnny's Bar on Fulton
20 Johnny's Downtown
21 Landry's Seafood Restaurant
22 Li Wah
23 Lincoln Inn
24 Lu Cuisine
25 Mallorca

26 Morton's of Chicago, The Steakhouse
27 New York Spaghetti House
28 Piccolo Mondo
29 Sammy's
30 Sans Souci
31 Spaghetti Warehouse
32 Sweetwater Cafe Sausalito
33 Taverne of Richfield, Cleveland Style
34 The Terrace Club
35 The Watermark

Idaho ruby red trout, Atlantic salmon, Lake Superior walleye, Nags Head grouper, and South American tilapia. The dinner menu adds filet mignon and New York strip steaks to the lineup. Side dishes include lobster mashed potatoes and sweet potato puree. Blue Pointe is pricey, but seafood addicts don't seem to mind. Lunch weekdays, dinner daily. Reservations suggested. ♿ (Downtown Cleveland)

BO LOONG
3922 St. Clair Ave.
Cleveland
216/391-3113
$$

This is authentic Chinese cuisine—maybe a little too authentic for those who prefer a menu without fried chicken feet or beef tripe. But there is plenty of room (the place seats 400), and this restaurant has probably the best recommendation of all: Chinese Americans eat here on a regular basis. The casual atmosphere, Asian decor, and enormous menu add to the comfort level. There is something on the menu for everyone—from vegetarians to those willing to try the exotic. Dim sum, dumplings, and pastries can be ordered individually, or you can create your own combination platter. You can eat here from mid-morning until past midnight. Daily 10–2. Reservations recommended. (Downtown Cleveland)

CIAO CUCINA
1515 Euclid Ave.
Cleveland
216/621-8777

This Mediterranean trattoria is a new jewel in the Playhouse Square crown. Before or after a show at the Palace, Ohio, State, or Allen Theaters, try the fresh seafood,

pasta, veal, or pork entrées. Lunch offerings include gourmet sandwiches such as pastrami salmon club on foccacia bread, a variety of pizzas, salads, and entrées such as grilled tuna, tomato linquine with grilled chicken, and grilled pork tenderloin. Dinner is equally wonderful, with daily specials adding to the array of regular entrées. The waitstaff is quite savvy when it comes to getting you fed by curtain time. Lunch weekdays; dinner Tue–Sat. Open Sun on performance days. (Downtown Cleveland)

CITY CENTRE GRILL
Sheraton City Center Hotel
777 St. Clair Ave.
Cleveland
216/771-7600
$–$$

The City Centre Grille boasts a healthy menu and a contemporary atmosphere. The walls are filled with original Cleveland art. Breakfast, lunch, and dinner daily. (Downtown Cleveland)

CLEVELAND CHOPHOUSE & BREWERY
824 W. St. Clair
Cleveland
216/623-0909

A great addition to the Warehouse District, Cleveland ChopHouse & Brewery opened in May 1998. Owned by Rock Bottom Restaurants, this lunch and dinner spot is popular for many reasons. The onion rings and chicken tenders are made to order. Calamari with a sesame seed crust and apricot ginger glaze is a favorite. The mussels diavolo in a fresh herb-tomato vermouth sauce is a big draw. Lunch and dinner menus feature salads, sandwiches, gourmet pizzas, and "classics." Favorites include the salmon BLT and grilled romaine Caesar salad. The Iowa pork chop is a two-inch-thick center cut, and the 10-ounce salmon is served on an aromatic cedar plank. Try any entrée with the white cheddar mashed potatoes. Lunch Mon–Sat, dinner daily, Sun brunch. & (Downtown Cleveland)

COACHES
631 Huron Rd.
Cleveland
216/579-9700
$$$

Anyone who judges this restaurant from the outside is in for a nice surprise. For although it has the name, the look, and the location (across the street from Gund Arena) to suggest it's just another wings and potato-skins sports bar, Coaches offers much more. The 120-seat full-service restaurant has a French rotisserie offering pork chops, prime rib, and chicken. Yes, Coaches has the standard appetizers, but it also has a variety of upscale dishes such as Portobello mushroom strudel, lobster ravioli, and crab cakes. Lunch and dinner Mon–Fri, dinner only Sat and Sun. Bar open until 2:30 a.m. Sat. Reservations recommended, especially on game days. (Downtown Cleveland)

DAVID'S
Marriott Society Center Hotel
100 St. Clair Ave.
Cleveland
216/736-7080
$$$

David's emphasizes fresh ingredients in its simple but elegant cuisine. The à la carte menu allows diners to tailor meals around individual appetites. Seafood, the house specialty, is grilled over charcoal and served with a cream sauce or fresh fruit chutney. Chicken and beef entrées are equally well prepared. Breakfast, lunch, and dinner Mon–Sat, brunch and dinner Sun. Reservations recommended. (Downtown Cleveland)

DIAMONDBACK BREWERY
724 Prospect Ave.
Cleveland
216/771-1988
$$$

The Diamondback Brewery, which opened in 1996, brews six different types of beers, including an oatmeal stout, a Vienna red beer, a white diamond light, and a wheat beer. Appetizers include Spanish tapas. Artsy murals decorate the walls, and chandeliers hang from the ceilings. A mezzanine champagne bar overlooks the restaurant. The full-service menu includes steaks and seafood. Open daily. (Downtown Cleveland)

FLAT IRON CAFE
1114 Center St.
Cleveland
216/696-6968
$–$$

This comfortable Irish pub in the Flats serves American cuisine that includes burgers, chicken sandwiches, pasta specials, and fresh Lake Erie yellow perch. You can wash that food down with one of 100 varieties of beer, five on tap. Owner John Wasmer has been running the show for 10 years, but the Flat Iron has been around since 1910. On St. Patrick's Day, the Flat Iron becomes a popular destination point, with a big corned-beef-and-cabbage celebration. The regular crowd consists of mostly downtown businesspeople, 25 years and older. The Flat Iron offers a free shuttle service (minimum of four people) from Gateway, Playhouse Square, and downtown office buildings and hotels. The Flat Iron also has free parking. Lunch and dinner daily. Open until 1 a.m. Fri and Sat. (Downtown Cleveland)

FRANK & PAULY'S
200 Public Square
Cleveland
216/575-1000
$$–$$$

Located on the ground floor of the BP building on Public Square, Frank and Pauly's offers up great southern-style Italian cuisine. All tables, chairs, and photos date to the romantic era of Gershwin, Sinatra, and Billie Holiday. The southern Italian red pastas are deliciously filling, but save some room for the rich chocolate Vesuvio cake, apple crostata, or tiramisu for dessert. Lunch Mon–Fri, dinner daily. Reservations suggested. (Downtown Cleveland)

(TOM'S) GATEKEEPERS' INN
850 Euclid Ave.

Hyde Park Chop House, p. 61

Hyde Park Restaurants

Cleveland
216/687-0044
$

In a stroke of public relations genius, Tom Kohn has named almost everything on his menu for a Cleveland media celebrity. If you're new in town and don't know who these folks are, Tom makes it even easier by running their photos and a brief explanation next to the entrée. Try the chicken carbonara à la Otto Orf, goalkeeper for the Cleveland Crunch soccer team; or the Leon Bibb classic club sandwich, named for the veteran TV-5 newscaster and host of *Weekend Exchange*. Other specialties are gourmet pizzas, pastas, grilled seafood, chicken and beef entrées, and specialty salads. Lunch and dinner Mon–Fri. Open during Indian home games on Sat and Sun. Reservations recommended for dinner. (Downtown Cleveland)

GOODFELLAS
1265 W. Ninth St.
Cleveland
216/781-1500
$$$

Located in the historic Warehouse District, Goodfellas is fine dining without the stuffiness, a wax works without the wax. Owners Steve and Peter Boukis offer an eclectic menu and an eccentric decor. First the menu: seafood entrées like horseradish goat-cheese-crusted grouper and Carribean Grilled Halibut with clams, spinach, fresh lime juice, and coconut broth. Meat eaters can sample the Pork Tenderloin Pacifico with a fruit chutney or rack of lamb. The decor is even more memorable. Local artist Doug Manry has painted murals from the Golden Age of Hollywood, depicting such entertainment greats as Shirley Temple and

Late-night Eats Downtown

Every city needs a diner like Checkers (1225 W. Sixth St., 216/696-3310). After an enjoyable evening at Jacobs Field or Gund Arena, listening to music, dancing, or attending the theater, head to Checkers for some hearty diner food. This Warehouse District eatery serves breakfast all the time. Grilled items include burgers and daily specials. Soups, salads, and desserts round out the menu. Carry-out and delivery service are popular choices. The authentic stainless-steel diner has a marble-topped bar with stools. The place seats 39 people, many of whom are loyal regulars. Open Monday through Friday 6 to 3, Saturday 7 to 1. Then the diner closes down for a breather, reopening at 10 and staying open until 4 a.m. on Friday and Saturday.

Gene Kelly. To enhance the effect, the Boukis brothers ordered wax figures from a Hollywood production company and seated them strategically at the table facing the front window. So you will be dining with celebrities such as Clark Gable, Jimmy Cagney, John Wayne, and Marilyn Monroe. And if that isn't enough, the place has also become a hot spot for swing dancing to the music of Benny Goodman. Lunch Mon–Fri, dinner Mon–Sat. Rest rooms are not wheelchair accessible. (Downtown Cleveland)

GREEK ISLES
500 W. St. Clair
Cleveland
216/861-1919
$$
Many people accidentally discover the Greek Isles while strolling in the Warehouse District. At the corner of West St. Clair and Sixth Street,

the restaurant's exterior and large windows beckon invitingly. Inside, the spare white walls and sun-washed decor exude just the right ambiance for the cuisine. Spinach-feta pie with Phyllo crust, flaming cheese, calamari, salads—all the Greek entrées are nicely done. Save room for the baklava. Lunch and dinner daily. Reservations accepted only on weekends. (Downtown Cleveland)

HICKERSON'S AT THE HANNA
1422 Euclid Ave.
Cleveland
216/771-1818
$$$
Gene Hickerson provides Playhouse Square theatergoers with convenient, pricey dining before and after performances. Red meat classics such as chateaubriand and prime rib share the bill with a long list of seafood, pastas, and a

grilled vegetable platter. Lunch weekdays, dinner daily. (Downtown Cleveland)

HORNBLOWER'S
1151 N. Marginal Rd.
Cleveland
216/363-1151
$$$

What better place to eat seafood than on a barge next to the submarine USS *Cod* in North Coast Harbor? Hornblower's serves a great lineup from conch chowder and crab cakes to blue marlin and black-tip shark. And every dish comes with a great view. If you're not interested in shelling out for seafood, try the pasta dishes, steaks, or vegetarian ragout. Lunch and dinner Mon–Sat, brunch Sun. Reservations recommended on weekends. (Downtown Cleveland)

HYDE PARK CHOP HOUSE DOWNTOWN
123 W. Prospect Ave.
Cleveland
216/344-2444
$$$

You'll feel like a high roller dining at the Hyde Park Chop House Downtown. The restaurant was once a Cleveland Trust Bank, and the decor is still banklike, from its polished brass railings to its black granite floor and bar top. Private parties can be seated in the bank's enormous vault. On weekends, individual diners can eat in the vault. The impressive 20-ton door is still on its original hinges. Connected to Gund Arena, Tower City Center, and the Renaissance and Ritz-Carlton Hotels, Hyde Park Chop House serves steaks and chops and fresh seafood. Lunch weekdays, dinner Mon–Sat. Reservations recommended. (Downtown Cleveland)

JOHN Q'S STEAKHOUSE
55 Public Square
Cleveland
216/861-0900
$$$

Justifiably known for its great steaks, John Q's serves only certified Angus beef, in sizes from 10 to 28 ounces. The lunch menu offers shaved beef on a French-dip sandwich or on a salad. Kids are welcome and have their own menu. The restaurant is easy to find: look for the big "55" on the building northwest of Public Square. Lunch and dinner. Reservations recommended. (Downtown Cleveland)

JOHNNY'S BAR ON FULTON
3164 Fulton Rd.
Cleveland
216/281-0055
$$$

Don't let the name turn you off—the food is anything but standard bar chow. The menu includes masterfully rendered Italian cuisine and seafood. The Italian Feast is a thing of beauty: scallops and shrimp in a marinara sauce over linguini. The breads and desserts are all homemade and wonderful. Lunch weekdays, dinner Mon–Sat. Reservations are recommended for three or more. (Downtown Cleveland)

JOHNNY'S DOWNTOWN
1406 W. St. Clair
Cleveland
216/623-0055
$$–$$$

This, the second Johnny's, located in the Warehouse District, is an easy walk or quick ride from downtown hotels and offices. In fact, Clevelanders voted Johnny's Downtown one of the best places for a business lunch. But this restaurant is worth a

A Rich Recipe

At least two culinary fortunes have been made in Cleveland. In 1917, Hector Boiardi was brought to Cleveland by automobile manufacturer Alexander Winton to be the master chef at Winton's elegant downtown hotel. Boiardi's reputation for homemade pasta soared, and he was besieged with take-out orders. This eventually became a business unto itself, spawning the pre-packaged spaghetti dinner. When he hit the mass market, Boiardi changed his name to the white-bread spelling "Boy-ar-dee."

Vernon Stouffer also built a convenience-food empire in Cleveland. His father, Abraham, ran a lunch counter in the Arcade. Within 10 years, Vernon, a graduate of the Wharton School of Business, had turned the counter into a chain of restaurants. Stouffer was an early enthusiast of frozen food and began manufacturing in 1951. Today Stouffer's is a frozen-food giant, with corporate headquarters in the Cleveland suburb of Solon.

visit any time of day. The dining room has a classically swank atmosphere, with white tablecloths, low lighting, and high ceilings. The menu is a stylish lineup of seafood, beef, lamb, and other top-notch offerings. Lunch weekdays, dinner daily. Reservations recommended. (Downtown Cleveland)

LANDRY'S SEAFOOD RESTAURANT
1036 Old River Rd.
Cleveland
216/566-1010
$$–$$$
Landry's specializes in fresh fish: snapper, walleye, and perch. The shrimp platters are also very popular. Kids get their own menu, which features fried fish, shrimp, hamburg-

ers, and corndogs. Landry's also satisfies grownup tastes and will create an original dish on request. A crowd-pleaser for dessert is Bananas Foster: vanilla ice cream wrapped in crepes and topped with hot fudge, caramel, bananas, and whipped cream. Lunch weekdays, dinner daily. Reservations accepted for parties of eight or more. (Downtown Cleveland)

LI WAH
2999 Payne Ave.
Cleveland
216/696-6556
$$–$$$
The Asian Plaza east of downtown is an indoor mall of travel services and stores catering to Cleveland's

Asian American community. Li Wah is the anchor of this plaza. The large, attractive dining room is filled with busy waiters and happy diners, and why wouldn't those diners be happy? The food here is delicious and reasonably priced and kids are welcome. Dinner daily; lunch Mon–Sat. (Downtown Cleveland)

LINCOLN INN
75 Public Square
Cleveland
216/621-1085
$$–$$$

This inconspicuous (to the point of being hard to find without directions) downtown dining spot is where you'll find most of the legal community at lunch or dinner. That proves two things beyond a reasonable doubt: Lawyers and judges are creatures of habit, and lawyers and judges know and enjoy a quality restaurant with good prices when they see it. Formerly the Lawyers Club of Cleveland, the Lincoln Inn is an unpretentious, understated business lunch club. Cuisine is the star witness. Cross-examine the menu's variety of steaks, pastas, pizzas, seafood, and ultra-fresh salads. Be sure to save room for the appealing homemade desserts. Lunch and dinner on weekdays. Reservations are recommended. Case dismissed. (Downtown Cleveland)

LU CUISINE
Halle Building
1228 Euclid Ave.
Cleveland
216/241-0095
$$$

Considered by some to serve the best Chinese food downtown, Lu Cuisine is in the Playhouse Square

neighborhood, making it the perfect place for a pre-curtain dinner. Start with the appetizer platter of spring rolls, dumplings, chicken, and shrimp and pork pastry. The menu has a broad selection of such delights as a seafood bird's nest made of potatoes and filled with vegetables and seafood. Or try the escolar whitefish, barbecued in a wok. Daily specials round out the menu. The restaurant is one of the new tenants in what was once Halle's department store, and the restored building is a treat in itself. Lunch Mon–Fri; dinner Tue–Sat. (Downtown Cleveland)

MALLORCA
1390 W. Ninth St.
Cleveland
216/687-9494
$$$

For a quick escape to Spain, try lunch or dinner at Mallorca. The waiters are Spanish and Portuguese and are charmingly Old World in their tuxedoes and service. The menu is a wonderful selection of seafood, beef, and pork entrées. Mounds of paella and crisp vegetables complement the main dishes, and portions are generous enough to satisfy even the largest appetites. The dining room is cozy and softly lit. Lunch, dinner daily. (Downtown Cleveland)

MORTON'S OF CHICAGO,
THE STEAKHOUSE
W. Second and Prospect
Cleveland
216/621-6200
$$$

The big steaks here are the centerpiece, presented tableside for your approval. You can also order fresh seafood and shellfish. The dark paneled dining room sets the mood for a considerably "beefy" meal, which can include a 48-ounce porterhouse steak. Lunch Mon–Fri, dinner daily. Reservations recommended. (Downtown Cleveland)

NEW YORK SPAGHETTI HOUSE
2173 F. Ninth St.
Cleveland
216/696-6624
$$$
Hearty Italian cuisine and steaks in a cozy dining room that has long been a Cleveland landmark. Conveniently located just north of Jacobs Field, this makes a great spot in which to meet and eat before a game. Lunch, dinner Mon–Sat; open Sun on game days. (Downtown Cleveland)

PICCOLO MONDO
1352 W. Sixth St.
Cleveland
216/241-1300
$$–$$$
Here is Northern Italian ambiance with great food and a wonderful location at the corner of West St. Clair Avenue and West Sixth Street. Piccolo Mondo is a classy cornerstone of the historic Warehouse District. The roomy bar is a comfortable place for people-watching. A wood-burning brick oven and a large open grill create some wonderful entrées. Pasta and pizzas are popular. Try the avocado crab salad, too. Café-style outdoor seating is available in good weather. Lunch and dinner Mon–Sat. Reservations accepted. (Downtown Cleveland)

SAMMY'S
1400 W. 10th St.
Cleveland
216/523-5560
$$$
Sammy's has been a standard for cutting-edge cuisine since it opened. Owner Denise de Fuego has created a loft-style dining area that affords panoramic views of the Flats and the west side bridges. Fresh fish, pastas, pizza, beef, and lamb are staples here. Known as a great place to go on an expense account, Sammy's has redefined itself somewhat by offering a lunch menu of entrées under $10. Sammy's boasts the best seafood raw bar west of Boston and has nightly live music at 6. Reservations required. You can also find Sammy's cuisine at Gund Arena, where they offer a special summer buffet before each Indians home game; on the 21st floor of the Huntington Building; at the Keynote Restaurant in Severance Hall; and on the Manakiki Golf Course in Cleveland Metroparks. (Downtown Cleveland)

SANS SOUCI
Renaissance Cleveland Hotel
24 Public Square
Cleveland
216/696-5600
$$$
Tucked away off the elegant lobby of the Renaissance Cleveland Hotel, this Mediterranean-style restaurant offers such specialties from Provence as lobster bouillabaisse with shrimp, clams, and sea scallops. But the menu is broad enough to include Black Angus strip steak, lamb chops, pasta, and seafood. Dining in this Mediterranean decor is almost as good as an instant getaway to southern France. The look is upscale, but dress is informal and kids have their own menu. Lunch Mon-Fri; dinner daily. (Downtown Cleveland)

SPAGHETTI WAREHOUSE
1231 Main Ave.
Cleveland
216/621-9420
$$

Spaghetti is the main draw at this Flats eatery. Dinners include salad, fresh-baked sourdough bread, soup, or applesauce. The 480-seat restaurant's signature dish is a 15-layer lasagna of beef, sausage, pork, ricotta, and romano and provolone cheeses. Tiramisu, golden sponge cake with white frosting and a coffee liqueur flavor, is another favorite. Tuesday night is all-you-can-eat family night: $4.99 for adults and $1.99 for kids. Also, kids under age 10 with a paying adult eat free on Sunday. Lunches begin at $3.69. Lunch and dinner daily. Reservations accepted for parties of 10 or more. Call-ahead seating for smaller parties. Rooms for private parties, rehearsal dinners, bus tours, and schools. ♿ (Downtown Cleveland)

SWEETWATER CAFE SAUSALITO
Galleria at Erieview
1301 E. Ninth St.
Cleveland
216/696-2233
$$–$$$

This restaurant serves a combination of Mediterranean, Italian, and French cuisines. The house specialties are fresh seafoods and pastas. Kids are accommodated with pint-size burgers, grilled cheese sandwiches, or pastas. A piano bar keeps the restaurant pleasantly mellow on Friday and Saturday nights. Dinner/theater packages are offered for major shows at the Playhouse Square theaters, including free shuttle rides to and from the theater, free parking at the Galleria, and great seats. Lunch daily, late lunches served in the bar, dinner Mon–Sat. Sun hours vary. Reservations accepted. (Downtown Cleveland)

TAVERNE OF RICHFIELD, CLEVELAND STYLE
2217 E. Ninth St.
Cleveland
216/781-6556
$$–$$$

This is an especially busy place because it is conveniently located across the street from Gateway's Jacobs Field and Gund Arena. The menu includes prime beef, fresh seafood, and house specialties. The apple walnut pie is not to be missed. A word of explanation on the restaurant's name: when Gateway opened a few years ago, owner Mel Rose created this restaurant, using some popular items from the menu at his historic Taverne of Richfield. The result is a new menu featuring tried-and-true favorites such as the Taverne's New England clam chowder and a 24-ounce porterhouse

Sans Souci

GREATER CLEVELAND

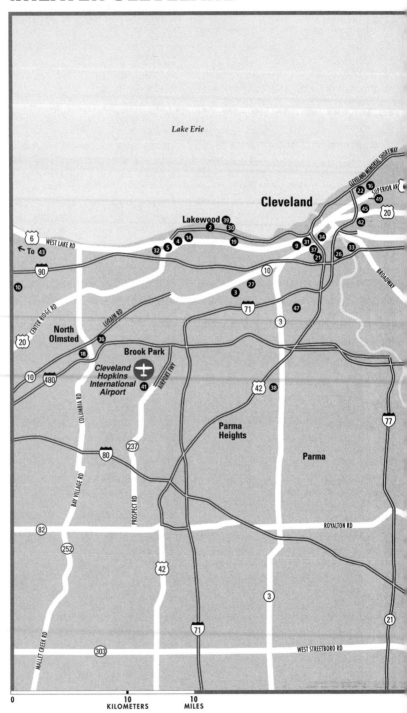

Lake Erie

Cleveland

Lakewood

West Lake Rd
← To 43

North Olmsted

Brook Park

Cleveland Hopkins International Airport

Parma Heights

Parma

Royalton Rd

West Streetboro Rd

0   10
KILOMETERS   10
MILES

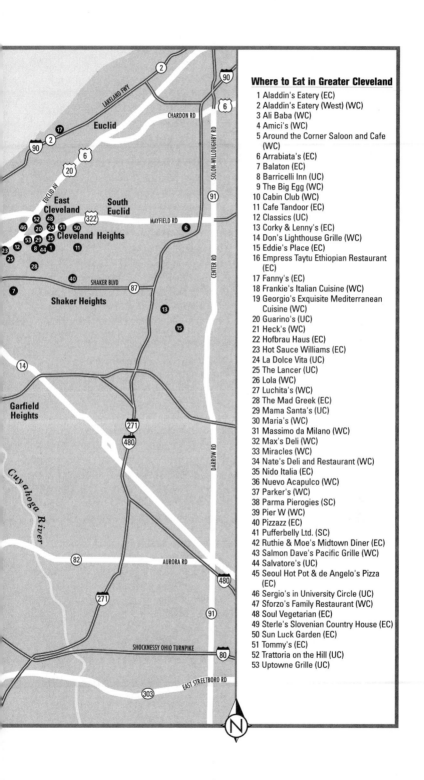

Where to Eat in Greater Cleveland

1 Aladdin's Eatery (EC)
2 Aladdin's Eatery (West) (WC)
3 Ali Baba (WC)
4 Amici's (WC)
5 Around the Corner Saloon and Cafe (WC)
6 Arrabiata's (EC)
7 Balaton (EC)
8 Barricelli Inn (UC)
9 The Big Egg (WC)
10 Cabin Club (WC)
11 Cafe Tandoor (EC)
12 Classics (UC)
13 Corky & Lenny's (EC)
14 Don's Lighthouse Grille (WC)
15 Eddie's Place (EC)
16 Empress Taytu Ethiopian Restaurant (EC)
17 Fanny's (EC)
18 Frankie's Italian Cuisine (WC)
19 Georgio's Exquisite Mediterranean Cuisine (WC)
20 Guarino's (UC)
21 Heck's (WC)
22 Hofbrau Haus (EC)
23 Hot Sauce Williams (EC)
24 La Dolce Vita (UC)
25 The Lancer (UC)
26 Lola (WC)
27 Luchita's (WC)
28 The Mad Greek (EC)
29 Mama Santa's (UC)
30 Maria's (WC)
31 Massimo da Milano (WC)
32 Max's Deli (WC)
33 Miracles (WC)
34 Nate's Deli and Restaurant (WC)
35 Nido Italia (EC)
36 Nuevo Acapulco (WC)
37 Parker's (WC)
38 Parma Pierogies (SC)
39 Pier W (WC)
40 Pizzazz (EC)
41 Pufferbelly Ltd. (SC)
42 Ruthie & Moe's Midtown Diner (EC)
43 Salmon Dave's Pacific Grille (WC)
44 Salvatore's (UC)
45 Seoul Hot Pot & de Angelo's Pizza (EC)
46 Sergio's in University Circle (UC)
47 Sforzo's Family Restaurant (WC)
48 Soul Vegetarian (EC)
49 Sterle's Slovenian Country House (EC)
50 Sun Luck Garden (EC)
51 Tommy's (EC)
52 Trattoria on the Hill (UC)
53 Uptowne Grille (UC)

marinated in Jack Daniels. Lunch, dinner daily. Reservations accepted. (Downtown Cleveland)

THE TERRACE CLUB
Jacobs Field, 2401 Ontario
Cleveland
216/420-4700
$$–$$$
You must have a Terrace Club membership to dine here when the Cleveland Indians play. But this glass atrium restaurant overlooking Jacobs Field is open for lunch Monday through Friday on non-game days. The restaurant is also open before the Cleveland NBA Cavaliers play their home games. (Downtown Cleveland)

THE WATERMARK
1250 Old River Rd.
Cleveland
216/241-1600
$$–$$$
The Watermark opened in 1985 and is a contemporary upscale seafood restaurant in the Flats. A bank of windows allows diners to watch the river traffic while enjoying fresh Maine lobster or Lake Erie walleye. Dessert favorites are crème brulée and chocolate torte. On the riverside deck, the outdoor umbrella tables make for pleasurable afternoon or evening dining. Lunch and dinner daily. Reservations accepted. (Downtown Cleveland)

UNIVERSITY CIRCLE

BARRICELLI INN
2203 Cornell Rd. at Murray Hill Rd.
Cleveland
216/791-6500
$$$
Continental dining at its most ele-gant, the Barricelli Inn occupies a fine old house near University Circle. The European-style specialties are in-house-made pastas, sautéed veal tenderloin, seared Ahi tuna, beef tenderloin, roast chicken, and sautéed duck. The appetizers are as tempting as the entrées: Tuscan bean soup with smoked shrimp, smoked pheasant ravioli in a chicken foie gras sauce, jumbo shrimp in a chili pepper marinade, and polenta with grilled Portobello mushrooms and reggiano parmi-giano. Dinner Mon–Sat, lunch during December holidays only. &
(University Circle)

CLASSICS
Omni International Hotel
Carnegie and E. 96th Sts.
Cleveland
216/791-1300
$$$
Classics features continental cuisine served up on fine china, crystal, silver, and linen. Clevelanders recently voted this restaurant both the most romantic and the one with the best service. Maybe it is the classical decor, the piano and harp music, or the waitstaff's meticulous attention to detail that make this restaurant the ideal spot for an anniversary dinner or Valentine's Day rendezvous. Appetizers include escargots, calamari, spicy shrimp, crabmeat fettucini, and two soups. Entrées include a variety of fish, veal, poultry, beef, and lamb. Flambé desserts (what could be more romantic?) include bananas Foster, cherries jubilee, and peaches cardinale. Other desserts include truffles, strudel, torte, and tarts. The Classics Assortment is an arrangement of bite-sized pastries that includes a chocolate marquise, dipped strawberry, pecan tart, petit four, and

Cleveland medical researcher James Henry Salisbury (1823–1905) was a Civil War physician who, as early as 1849, advanced the theory that germs cause disease. He later focused his research on the role that diet plays in health. Today we remember him for the invention that still bears his name: Salisbury steak.

chocolate éclair. Lunch weekdays, dinner Mon–Sat. (University Circle)

GUARINO'S
12309 Mayfield Rd.
Cleveland
216/231-3100
$$$

The anchor restaurant of Little Italy since it opened in 1908, Guarino's claims to be the oldest family-owned Italian eatery in Cleveland. The southern Italian cuisine, Victorian decor, and romantic garden setting make this a wonderful dining experience. Don't miss Mama Guarino's lasagna and her veal scallopini with homemade sauce and pasta. Lunch and dinner daily. Weekend reservations recommended. (University Circle)

LA DOLCE VITA
12112 Mayfield Rd.
Cleveland
216/721-8155
$$

This Little Italy eatery is a popular spot in a neighborhood where good Italian cuisine is taken for granted. Everything from the house salad dressing to the pasta, pizzas, and entrées is prepared with a sense of style and taste. Outdoor dining is available in spring and summer. Lunch Mon–Sat, dinner daily. Reservations recommended. (University Circle)

THE LANCER
7707 Carnegie Ave.
Cleveland
216/881-0080
$$–$$$

This restaurant is actually located in the midtown corridor between downtown and University Circle. Locals and out-of-towners alike rave about Lancer's fried red snapper and broiled scampi. Equally heavenly are the homemade peach cobbler and New Orleans–style bread pudding. On Thursday and Saturday evenings, live jazz makes this a great destination for a late snack. Lunch and dinner daily. (University Circle)

MAMA SANTA'S
12305 Mayfield Rd.
Cleveland
216/231-9567
$

With great Italian food at even better prices, Mama Santa's is the place to go when you want a casual atmosphere with good food—and lots of it. Pizzas have perfectly chewy crusts. All the standard favorites—manicotti, lasagna, ravioli, spaghetti, and fettucini—are hearty and well prepared. Adventurous eaters can try the noodles with faggioli (beans), lenticchie (lentils), or ceci (chickpeas). It's an extremely kid-friendly environment with comfy booths. Lunch, dinner Mon–Sat. (University Circle)

Paul Mette/Innovations

Guarino's Restaurant, p. 69

SALVATORE'S
2181 Murray Hill Rd.
Cleveland
216/231-7670
$$

The specialty of the house is sautéed calamari, risotto, and veal, but Salvatore's does wonderful things with many of its menu items. Hearth-baked pizzas come with combinations of Portobello mushrooms and sausage, plum tomatoes, spinach, mozzarella, olive oil, proscuitto, and carmelized onions. Pasta dishes include a daily ravioli selection, linguini with seafood in a spicy marinara sauce, and homemade potato dumplings with marinara and fresh basil. Veal, chicken, and fish round out the menu. Children are welcome in the earlier hours. Lunch Mon–Fri, dinner Tue–Sun. Reservations are recommended. No wheelchair access. (University Circle)

SERGIO'S IN UNIVERSITY CIRCLE
1903 Ford Dr.

Cleveland
216/231-1234
$$–$$$

Next to the Glidden House bed-and-breakfast in University Circle is a former carriage-house-turned-restaurant. Owner Sergio Abramof uses his Brazilian heritage and his culinary know-how to create an intimate, original destination for lunch or dinner. Lunch Mon–Fri, dinner Mon–Sat. Reservations recommended. (University Circle)

TRATTORIA ON THE HILL
12207 Mayfield Rd.
Cleveland
216/421-2700
$$

A favorite in Little Italy's colony of Italian restaurants, Trattoria's reputation for great pizzas and pasta make it a perennial favorite among Clevelanders. Slow down and enjoy one of the appetizers, such as the roasted red peppers or the antipasto platter of marinated eggplant, tuna bean salad, calamari salad, olives, cheese, and mushrooms. Chicken and veal entrées are prepared in several delectable ways, and the steaks and baby back ribs are grilled to your liking—with prices to your liking. In warm weather there is outdoor dining and entertainment most Saturdays. Children have their own menu with pint-sized versions of the Italian fare. Lunch Mon–Fri, dinner daily. Reservations accepted. (University Circle)

UPTOWNE GRILLE
11312 Euclid Ave.
Cleveland
216/229-9711
$$

This restaurant is a United Nations of specialties. The menu features

American, Italian, French, Greek, and Spanish culinary delights, as well as cuisine from that exotic country known as Eclectica. The hors d'oeuvres run the gamut from mussels diablo and baked mussels in a hot marinara sauce to French baked brie topped with honey and almonds.

Sandwiches range from the open-face prime rib to The Harvest, a vegetarian treat of broccoli, zucchini, onions, and peppers topped with cheese on sourdough. Dinner specialties include paella, couscous, Moroccan Tagine, tenderloin kebabs, and steak au poivre. Seasonal outdoor dining and jazz seven nights a week with no cover charge make this place a real find. Children are welcome, and the chef will create grilled cheese sandwiches, spaghetti, or other favorites in child-sized portions. Breakfast, lunch, and dinner daily. Reservations recommended. (University Circle)

EAST CLEVELAND

ALADDIN'S EATERY
12447 Cedar Rd.
Cleveland
216/932-4333
$
Here the fare includes soups, salads, pita pockets, rolled pitas, and Aladdin's special "pitza" pita pizzas. The tabouli and shish kebabs are like a wish granted by a genie. Healthy raw-juice combos provide energy and taste good too. Heavenly smoothie drinks are made from strawberries, bananas, honey, and your choice of eight fruit juices. Beer and wine are also served. The cake display is not to be missed—

cheesecakes, layer cakes, baklava, cookies, and chocolate-dipped pretzels. Lunch and dinner daily. Reservations not accepted. (East Cleveland)

ARRABIATA'S
6169 Mayfield Rd.
Mayfield Heights
440/442-2600
$$
Arrabiata's serves southern Italian cuisine that pleases. Lunch Mon–Fri, dinner Mon–Sat. Special late menu 11–1. Reservations suggested on weekends and holidays. (East Cleveland)

BALATON
13133 Shaker Square
Cleveland
216/921-9691
$–$$
Located in the Shaker Square shopping center, this is Hungarian food just like Grandma used to make, even if your grandma is not Hungarian. Try the goulash, stuffed cabbage, Wiener schnitzel, and homemade dumplings and gravy—not exactly a Weight Watcher's blue-plate special but very good Hungarian food. Desserts include apple strudel and *dobos* torte. Lunch, dinner Tue–Sat. Reservations accepted only for large groups. (East Cleveland)

CAFE TANDOOR
2096 S. Taylor Rd.
Cleveland
216/371-8500
$$–$$$
Indian cuisine here is geared to the novice as well as the seasoned diner. The 16 special curry dishes on the menu include lamb, chicken, shrimp, and fish; the tandoori specialties are

Carbonated beverages are here to stay, and for that we can thank Cleveland chemist Graham W. Clarke. Clarke was the first to liquefy carbonic acid gas, putting the fizz into soft drinks.

an array of lobster, chicken, lamb, and vegetables. More than a dozen vegetable specialties can be paired with a variety of breads, soups, and appetizers. Even the ice cream comes Indian-style, in mango, pistachio, and coconut flavors. Lunch Mon–Sat, dinner daily. Reservations recommended. (East Cleveland)

CORKY & LENNY'S
27091 Chagrin Blvd.
Woodmere
216/464-3838
$
The best deli in Greater Cleveland, provided you want to make the trip to Woodmere. You'll find dill pickles on the tables and an enormous menu that features every imaginable deli sandwich. Breakfast, lunch, and dinner daily. (East Cleveland)

EDDIE'S PLACE
28601 Chagrin Blvd.
Woodmere
216/591-1545
$$$
This southern Italian/Mediterranean restaurant offers three varieties of pane bello—ciabatta bread topped with a combination of mushrooms, cheese, and vegetables. Other lunch offerings are tuna, chicken, and salmon. Dinner specialties are veal, fresh seafood, and pasta dishes. On Friday and Saturday nights, dine to the strains of

soft jazz. Reservations recommended. Lunch, dinner Mon–Sat. ♿ (East Cleveland)

EMPRESS TAYTU ETHIOPIAN RESTAURANT
6125 St. Clair Ave.
Cleveland
216/391-9400
$$–$$$
No hamburgers here. This is real Ethiopian cuisine. Like an instant trip to the African continent, your dining experience at Empress Taytu's begins when you sit down under a grass hut on low woven seats with a large basket for a table. The food is served on sheets of *injera*, a soft flatbread that you break off to scoop up food. Although the menu includes spicy stews of beef, chicken, and lamb, vegetable lovers will enjoy the vegetable combination platter. The honey wine served with dinner resembles mulled cider. *Cleveland Magazine* readers voted this restaurant the "Most Adventurous Dining" experience in Cleveland. Lunch Mon–Fri, dinner Tue–Sun. Reservations recommended. ♿ (East Cleveland)

FANNY'S
3539 E. 156th St.
Cleveland
216/531-1231
$–$$

Fanny's prepares Slovenian cuisine such as *imuk* (stew), beef goulash served over spaetzles, and *ajmont* soup (chicken soup made Slovenian style with a dash of vinegar). But there are plenty of standards, too, for those who prefer more familiar fare. Lunch and dinner daily. Cash only. Reservations required for groups of six or more. ♿ (East Cleveland)

HOFBRAU HAUS
1400 E. 55th St.
Cleveland
216/881-7773
$$–$$$

The immense dining room features an all-you-can-eat German buffet offering schnitzel, potato pancakes, *rouladen* (thin slices of beef rolled around a stuffing), sauerbraten, Koenigsburger *klops* (meatballs), strudel, and more. Lunch Sun–Fri, dinner Tue–Sun. Reservations recommended on weekends. ♿ (East Cleveland)

HOT SAUCE WILLIAMS
7815 Carnegie Ave.
Cleveland
216/751-0440
$–$$

Jim Williams has taken a franchise restaurant building on Carnegie Avenue and filled it with the most delightful barbecue this side of heaven, including chicken, ribs, and shrimp dishes. Family dinners come with greens, cornbread, and macaroni and cheese. Williams's award-winning ribs have a national following. "We have people who call from Texas and California wanting us to send them our ribs," says Williams. Williams also does off-site catering. Lunch and dinner daily. ♿ (East Cleveland)

THE MAD GREEK
2466 Fairmount Blvd.
Cleveland Heights
216/421-3333
$$

Greek and Indian cuisine are offered on the same menu in this eastside eatery whose decor combines Greek and post-modern. But so what? The Greek food is wonderful, from the salads to the gyros and moussaka. The Indian cuisine has a curry rating scale from one to six, with the high numbers reserved for the hardiest taste buds. Lunch and dinner daily. Reservations are a good idea on weekdays and a must on weekends. (East Cleveland)

NIDO ITALIA
12020 Mayfield Rd.
Cleveland
216/421-0221
$–$$

Nido Italia is Italian for "Italian Nest," and people do flock like birds to this club in Little Italy. Plain on the outside but elegant on the inside, the Nido offers a simple but satisfying weekday lunch menu of four pasta dishes, four sandwich platters, three salads, and one soup. Tuesday and Thursday nights' offering is an eight-course dinner that includes two appetizers, soup, salad, pasta, entrée, dessert, and wine. Live entertainment on those nights may include singers or a dance orchestra. Tue–Fri lunch and dinner; Sat dinner only. No reservation required for lunch, but dinner reservations are a must. (East Cleveland)

PIZZAZZ
20680 N. Park Blvd.
Cleveland
216/321-7272

$$–$$$

This casual spot, in business since 1975, features an Italian American menu. Appetizers tempt the palate with chargrilled Portobello mushrooms, pesto tomato bruschetta, and Italian-seasoned chicken sausage sautéed with roasted red peppers. Pizzas come red, white, or pesto, with different combinations of toppings like fontinella cheese, smoked gouda, and artichoke. Calzones come in combinations of meats and vegetables. The menu includes dinner salads, subs and sandwiches, and a choice of pasta dinner. The charbroiled chicken and veal entrées can be accompanied by pasta, steamed vegetables, or french fries. Kids are welcome and have their own menu. Lunch and dinner daily. Live blues Thur–Sat 10 p.m.–2 a.m. Reservations accepted for eight or more. (East Cleveland)

RUTHIE & MOE'S MIDTOWN DINER
4002 Prospect Ave.
Cleveland
216/431-8063
$

Backed by a 60-year history of serving great food, this diner has enough local fans to swing a national election. The place not only makes great milkshakes, french fries, and sandwiches, it also offers great daily specials that are a cut above typical diner food. The pasta salads are worthy of a white tablecloth bistro, but your meal will sit atop a paper placemat and you'll enjoy it just as much. Friendly atmosphere. Breakfast and lunch Mon–Fri. & (East Cleveland)

SEOUL HOT POT & DE ANGELO'S PIZZA

3709 Payne Ave.
Cleveland
216/881-1221
$–$$

The only Cleveland eatery where you can get a pepperoni pizza, *jaeyook bokum* (marinated pork), and *twikim mandu* (fried dumpling), this 40-seat Korean/pizza restaurant is better looking inside than outside. Lunch and dinner Mon–Sat. Reservations accepted; encouraged for large groups. (East Cleveland)

SOUL VEGETARIAN
2240 Lee Rd.
Cleveland Heights
216/932-0588
$–$$

For those who enjoy deliciously seasoned, non-meat and non-dairy cuisine at its best, Soul Vegetarian is worth a visit. Sandwiches include the sunburger, made with ground sunflower seeds; the veggie gyros, made with a whole wheat flour product called kalebone; and the barbecue roast, a kalebone served in barbecue sauce on a whole-wheat pita. Popular drinks include the Boomerang, a papaya drink with protein powder, ginseng, wheat germ and brewer's yeast. Or try a little Strawberry Heaven, made with strawberries, coconut milk, honey, ice, and your choice of vanilla or ginseng. Seating is limited to three tables, but carryout is unlimited. Lunch and dinner daily. & (East Cleveland)

STERLE'S SLOVENIAN COUNTRY HOUSE
1401 E. 55th St.
Cleveland
216/881-4181
$$$

To sample authentic Slovenian

roast pork, paprikash, and stuffed cabbage, join the many Cleve-landers who enjoy this 300-seat restaurant. The Wiener schnitzel is the restaurant's biggest seller, and the strudel is authentic and deli-cious. Less adventurous types can order a few American standards. The restaurant features live polka music on Friday and Saturday evenings. Lunch and dinner daily. Reservations for five or more ap-preciated. ♿ (East Cleveland)

SUN LUCK GARDEN
1901 S. Taylor Rd.
Cleveland
216/397-7676
$$
Sun Luck Garden serves reasonably priced Chinese cuisine at its best—fresh and well-seasoned. Lunch and dinner daily. Reservations accepted. (East Cleveland)

TOMMY'S
1824 Coventry Rd.
Cleveland Heights
216/321-7757
$–$$
Although Tommy's does offer meat pies, beef, and ham, the art on the menu—happy, dancing vegeta-bles—says it all: this place is vege-tarian heaven. Where else could you order 11 different kinds of toasted cheese, including lactose-free cheese? Or 13 kinds of falafel pita sandwiches? The sandwiches include veggie hot dogs, tofu salad, and five kinds of tuna. Dozens of salads are named everything from Cindy to Jesse. Children are wel-come but they don't need their own menu to find a peanut butter entrée. The homemade desserts and milk-shakes are worth a try. Lunch and dinner daily. ♿ (East Cleveland)

WEST CLEVELAND

ALADDIN'S EATERY (WEST)
14536 Detroit Rd.
Lakewood
216/521-4005
$
See listing on page 71.

ALI BABA
12021 Lorain Ave.
Cleveland
216/251-2040
$
Ali Baba is the home of great Middle Eastern cuisine. The best choice is the "chef's choice," a combination platter of hummus, baba ghanoush, *labnee* (yogurt cream cheese), tabouli, and other hard-to-pronounce but easy-to-enjoy dishes. No alcohol. Lunch and dinner Tue–Sat. Reserva-tions accepted. No credit cards. (West Cleveland)

AMICI'S
18405 Detroit Ave.
Lakewood
216/221-1150
$$$
Here you'll enjoy Italian cuisine in a small but cozy dining room. The Ital-ian bread is homemade and delicious. The restaurant has a large menu with antipasti divided into hot and cold categories. The hot antipasto for two is a plate of fried mozzarella, stuffed clams Casino, artichokes, mussels marinara, eggplant rollatini, and shrimp Amici's with calamari. Entrées include a half-dozen offerings of chicken, calamari, fish, veal chops, and pasta dishes. Try the Chicken Murphy, chicken pieces sautéed with hot and sweet peppers in a wine and cheese sauce. Lunch Mon–Fri, dinner daily. Reservations recommended on weekends. (West Cleveland)

AROUND THE CORNER SALOON AND CAFE
18616 Detroit Ave.
Lakewood
216/521-4413
$

The café offers great wings in four varieties: mild, medium, suicidal, and nuclear. On Tuesday, Thursday, and Sunday, wings are only 15 cents each and the place is packed with wing lovers. The wings are served with celery and blue cheese dressing to soothe your taste buds. You can get hamburgers, hot dogs, and chicken sandwiches custom-made, or plates of appetizers like fried zucchini, nachos, and mozzarella sticks. Mon–Fri 3–11, Sat and Sun noon–11. No reservations accepted. & (West Cleveland)

THE BIG EGG
5107 Detroit Ave.
Cleveland
216/961-8000
$

True to its name, the Big Egg makes the biggest omelettes and egg dishes west of the Cuyahoga River. The fact that it is open 24 hours a day, every day, makes it a favorite place to grab eggs Benedict whenever the mood strikes. The lunch and dinner offerings of sandwiches and soups are just as hearty and huge. Breakfast, lunch, dinner. (West Cleveland)

CABIN CLUB
30651 Detroit Rd.
Westlake
440/899-7111
$$–$$$

This place is a log cabin in decor only—there is nothing backwoodsy about the Cabin Club's menu. Everyone raves about the peppercorn steak, although the pasta, chicken, lamb, and seafood are equally well prepared. The Cabin Club is far enough off the downtown beaten path to be a well-guarded secret. The rustic dining room seats only 55, which means reservations are a good idea. Worth the drive to Westlake. Lunch and dinner daily. & (West Cleveland)

DON'S LIGHTHOUSE GRILLE
8905 Lake Ave.
Cleveland
216/961-6700
$$$–$$$$

Don's prepares exceptionally fresh seafood from Foley's in Boston. The sea scallops come breaded in a light cracker meal and broiled in sherry and butter. Don's signature entrée is the English Blue Medallions—twin medallions of beef grilled and served atop whipped potatoes, then topped with blue cheese and fried leeks and served in a pool of red wine sauce. Lunch weekdays, dinner daily. Reservations recommended. & (West Cleveland)

FRANKIE'S ITALIAN CUISINE
4641 Great Northern Blvd.
Cleveland
216/734-8646
$$

Frankie's is known for its casual atmosphere and great Italian food in bountiful quantities. The garlic bread is as delicious as the sauce, meatballs, lasagna, and pizza. Lunch and dinner Mon–Sat, dinner Sun. Reservations taken for groups of six or more. Another West Cleveland location at 25930 Detroit Rd., Westlake, 440/892-0064. & (West Cleveland)

GEORGIO'S EXQUISITE MEDITERRANEAN CUISINE

11709 Detroit Ave.
Lakewood
216/226-6333
$$

The prices are as reasonable as the food is good. Georgio's lunch menu offers tapas, pizza, sandwiches, pastas, and entrées such as Mediterranean stew and pork chop al porto. The dinner menu features Italian, Spanish, French, and Greek cuisine. Lunch Mon–Fri; dinner Mon–Sat. (West Cleveland)

HECK'S
2927 Bridge Ave.
Cleveland
216/861-5463
$$–$$$

If you like burgers—juicy, giant burgers—take the time to visit Heck's. They have a dozen kinds of burgers to go, along with fountain milkshakes, malts, and floats. There are bountiful salads and seafood and vegetarian offerings too. The place is small but cozy. Lunch and dinner Mon–Sat, brunch Sun. Reservations recommended. (West Cleveland)

LOLA
900 Literary Rd.
Tremont
216/771-5652
$$$

In the regentrified near-west neighborhood of Tremont, Lola is a contemporary bistro that attracts diners from throughout greater Cleveland. Owner Michael Symon made a reputation for himself as the chef of Caxton Cafe, a former downtown hotspot. His loyal customers continue to enjoy the imaginative recipes he concocts in this new location. Dinner Mon–Sun. Reservations a must. ♿ (West Cleveland)

LUCHITA'S
3456 W. 117th St.
Cleveland
216/252-1169
$$

Luchita's specializes in traditional Mexican fare such as chile rellenos and offers weekly authentic Mexican specials. The decor is simple and the place is small, but the portions are *grande*. You can also try the pork or chicken and cactus simmered in your choice of sauce. For a cooler cactus, try the ensalada Mexicana, which teams lettuce with cactus and avocados in a vinaigrette dressing. Lunch Tue–Fri, dinner daily. (West Cleveland)

MARIA'S
11822 Detroit Ave.
Lakewood
216/226-5875
$$–$$$

Homemade pastas and cucina bread at this long-time Italian favorite on the west side keep the loyal clientele coming back for more. Traditional entrées such as veal, chicken, and eggplant parmigiana also live up to their reputations. The pizza will never be confused with a chain restaurant's; the crust and the seasonings in the sauce make it a memorable dish. A private party room in back seats up to 60 people. Outdoor dining in the summer. Lunch Mon–Fri, dinner daily. Reservations accepted. ♿ (West Cleveland)

MASSIMO DA MILANO
1400 W. 25th St.
Cleveland
216/696-2323
$$

This renovated bank building is the perfect setting for great regional Italian food. Dining among the pillars makes the well-prepared pasta dishes even better. The crusty bread, house salad, and dessert fare perfectly complement the first-rate entrées. Breakfast and lunch weekdays, dinner daily. Reservations recommended. (West Cleveland)

MAX'S DELI
19337 Detroit Rd.
Rocky River
440/356-2226
$

A New York–style deli with high- and low-cholesterol foods such as corned beef on rye, potato pancakes, salads, vegetarian sandwiches, and cures-what-ails-you chicken soup with matzo balls. Desserts include a wonderful selection of cheesecakes, including the delectable Oreo cheesecake. Lunch and dinner daily, breakfast Sat and Sun. Reservations not accepted. &
(West Cleveland)

MIRACLES
2399 W. 11th St.

Tremont
216/623-1800
$$

In the near-westside neighborhood of Tremont, Miracles serves such specialties as potato pancakes and fresh fish. A few of the sandwiches come on a kaiser roll or Jewish rye, but the featured sandwiches are a complete meal served between potato pancakes, with such delectables as corned beef, steakburgers, meatless "unBurgers," turkey with cucumber dill sauce, and potato cake melts with either chicken or tuna salad and melted cheese. Finer dining in the evening features certified Black Angus steaks, fresh salmon, and long-bone pork chops with apple chutney. The Sunday brunch features such delicacies as carrot cake waffles, an assortment of hearty breakfast platters, and (what else?) a potato pancake platter. Desserts are topped with Euclid Beach–style frozen custard, so save room for the hot fudge brownie sundae or purpleberry pie.

Pier W, p. 79

Massery Photography

Kids are welcome to order off the regular menu. Outdoor dining in warmer weather. Lunch Mon–Sat, dinner Tue–Sat, brunch Sun. Reservations accepted for five or more. & (West Cleveland)

NATE'S DELI AND RESTAURANT
1923 W. 25th St.
Cleveland
216/696-7529
$

The Middle Eastern food in this restaurant near the West Side Market is one of the best bargains around. Bring your appetite for lunch or dinner because the portions are large. Loyalists have crowned Nate's the best place in town for creamy hummus and crisp falafel, but the tabbouleh, gyros and baba ghanoush are equally popular. Lunch Mon–Sat. Reservations preferred for four or more. & (West Cleveland)

NUEVO ACAPULCO
24409 Lorain Rd.
North Olmsted
440/734-3100
$$$

This Mexican restaurant caters to the whole family but is clearly a notch above the chains. Decorated with Mexican artwork, the restaurant serves a nice balance of the familiar tacos, burritos, and quesadillas, along with some fancier dishes such as c*amarones a la diabla* (prawns and mushrooms in a spicy red sauce). American hamburgers, steaks, and chicken please the more pedestrian palate. Lunch and dinner daily. & (West Cleveland)

PARKER'S
2801 Bridge Ave.

Ohio City
216/771-7130
$$$

This Ohio City restaurant is the pride and joy of chef Parker Bosley. The continental menu features meat, poultry, seafood, pasta, and vegetable entrées that change by the week. The chef's signature dessert is lemon soufflé, and he also offers a chef's menu of special delights prepared for the entire table. Or try the chef's tasting menu, a seven-course dinner of tasting portions that include soup, two appetizers, a seafood and two meat or poultry courses, salad, and dessert samplers. Jackets are no longer required for men but dress is upscale casual in the two small dining rooms. Dinner Mon–Sun, brunch Sun. Reservations recommended. & (West Cleveland)

PIER W
12700 Lake Ave.
Lakewood
216/228-2250
$$$

Pier W is one of those restaurants that friends recommend, and for good reason: the combination of great seafood and a picture-postcard view of the Cleveland skyline make it a sensory treat. The bouillabaisse is a house specialty that lives up to its reputation. Another specialty worth trying is the coconut shrimp. This stretch of western suburban shoreline is called the Gold Coast, which is also the name of the house salad topped with blue cheese and bacon. Children have their own menu, and those with a big appetite can try the Pegleg pie, a baked Alaska–style dessert. Reservations recommended. Lunch weekdays, dinner daily, brunch Sun. & (West Cleveland)

SALMON DAVE'S PACIFIC GRILLE
19015 Old Lake Rd.
Rocky River
440/331-2739
$$$

Seafood lovers have discovered this westside restaurant decorated in a style best described as Pacific northwestern. The restaurant is known for its salmon and pan-seared tuna. Bay of Fundy salmon is prepared three different ways: baked, blackened, or chargrilled. Word of mouth has made this restaurant extremely popular, and reservations are suggested on weekends. Lunch, dinner Mon–Sat; dinner Sun. & (West Cleveland)

SFORZO'S FAMILY RESTAURANT
5517 Memphis Ave.
Brooklyn
216/351-3703
$$

Locals from all over greater Cleveland love Sforzo's for its unpretentious menu of northern Italian cuisine, featuring pizza, pasta, chicken, veal, and seafood dishes. Diners also appreciate the old-school, attentive Italian service. Daily specials are always worth a try. Some American sandwiches and entrées are available. Lunch and dinner Mon–Sat. Reservations recommended on weekends. & (West Cleveland)

SOUTH CLEVELAND

PARMA PIEROGIES
Parmatown Plaza,
7707 W. Ridgewood Dr.
Cleveland
440/888-1200
$–$$

This is Eastern European cooking in a fast-food setting. Although Eastern European cuisine has never been touted as vegetarian health food, the folks at Parma Pierogies are interested in taking their menu to new heights. The pierogies are made fresh daily and are cooked to order. Fillings include potato, potato and cheddar, sweet cottage cheese, sauerkraut, broccoli and cheddar, spinach and mozzarella, cheeseburger, Joey's pizza, mushroom and Swiss and prune. They also make four dessert pierogie fillings: chocolate, apple, apricot, and raspberry. The stuffed cabbage, potato pancakes, and kielbasa are the real thing, too. (Kielbasa is the only meat remnant on the menu.) Plenty of booster seats and high chairs. Clevelanders can also buy Parma Pierogies frozen in local grocery stores in six flavors: potato, potato and cheddar, sauerkraut, sweet cottage cheese, Joey's pizza, and spinach & mozzarella. & (South Cleveland)

PUFFERBELLY LTD.
30 Depot St.
Berea
440/234-1144
$$–$$$

This restaurant on Depot Street was once a working railroad depot. Now it is the charmingly restored home of Pufferbelly Ltd., serving an eclectic menu that includes a breaded chicken pufferbelly on fettucini primavera and the open-faced San Francisco beef sandwich on dark rye with mushroom sauce and Colby cheese. Appetizers include soups such as the turkey florentine with dill, homemade chili, or Indonesian-style chicken kebabs served with a spicy peanut sauce. A variety of salads feature chicken over greens or pasta. The Triad salad is hummus, falafel, and brown rice salad served over lettuce with pita bread. Entrées include ribs, steaks, fish, and chicken. Guests can enjoy all the old-time railroad memorabilia and seasonal outdoor dining. Kids have their own menu. Lunch and dinner Mon–Sat, brunch Sun. Reservations accepted, especially for parties of six or more. ♿ (South Cleveland)

5

SIGHTS AND ATTRACTIONS

As you might expect from a city with 200 years under its belt, Cleveland has more sights to see and explore than are possible to squeeze into a single visit. Downtown skyscrapers provide a view of Cleveland that once only the sea gulls could enjoy. The architectural restoration of the massive Playhouse Square theaters has brought an entire neighborhood back to life while providing top-notch performance spaces for opera, ballet, live theater, and music. From the colorfully lighted bridges that span the Cuyahoga River to the enormous Free Stamp next to City Hall, this is a city with many visual surprises.

DOWNTOWN CLEVELAND

CLEVELAND PUBLIC LIBRARY
325 Superior Ave.
Cleveland
216/623-2822 (tour info)
One of Cleveland's finest legacies is the Cleveland Public Library system. From 1884 to 1938, Cleveland's library went from being one of the worst metropolitan libraries to the outstanding facility it is today. In 1890, William Howard Brett was the first librarian of a major metropolitan library to open the shelves to the public. Until that time, patrons had to fill out a request for a book, and a librarian would bring it to them for inspection. Critics of the open-shelves system predicted the patrons would either wreck the books or steal them outright. Instead, circulation increased 44 percent, fewer books were lost, and the salary budget dropped 13 percent because fewer librarians were needed.

Brett also took the daring position of encouraging children to use the library. The Children's Library League was organized in 1897, and

DOWNTOWN CLEVELAND

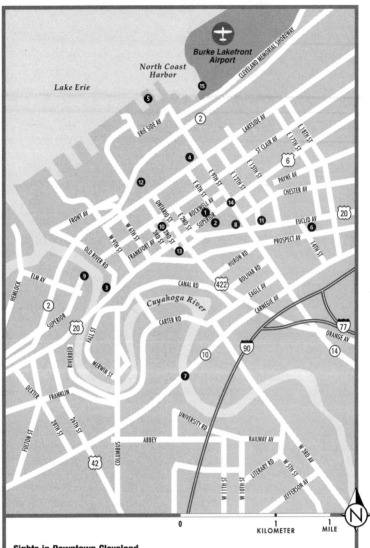

Sights in Downtown Cleveland

1 Cleveland Public Library
2 Federal Reserve Bank of Cleveland
3 The Flats
4 Free Stamp
5 Goodtime III
6 Hanna Cabaret
7 Hope Memorial Bridge Pylons
8 Huntington Bank Building

9 Nautica Queen
10 Old Stone Church
11 Playhouse Square Center
12 Portal Sculpture
13 Tower City Observation Deck
14 Triple-L Eccentric Gyratory III
15 USS *Cod*

USS Cod

During World War II, the Cod *made history by performing the only international submarine-to-submarine rescue. In 1945, the* Cod *came to the aid of a Dutch submarine that had accidentally grounded on a reef deep in the enemy-controlled waters of the South China Sea. After two days of attempting to pull the Allied sub off the reef, the* Cod *took the 56 Dutch submariners aboard. The* Cod *had no other choice but to destroy the Dutch sub with torpedoes and gunfire to prevent the Japanese from obtaining military secrets. Although space was tight and fresh air was in short supply, the sub sailed for three days to the nearest Allied port with 153 men aboard. The Dutch sailors, accustomed to eating canned food, were amazed when their evening meal aboard the* Cod *consisted of a fresh chicken dinner and ice cream for dessert.*

Brett proudly opened his first children's room in 1898. The main library building, which opened in 1925, is an architectural jewel. The sculpted white marble staircases are so beautiful that you'll want to skip taking the elevator. Spending an afternoon here, surrounded by carved wood, painted murals, and decorated ceilings, you'll feel like a true scholar. A new $65 million Louis Stokes wing opened in April 1997. This futuristic 257,000-square-foot building is a 10-story glass and marble oval. It houses half of the library's collection. (Downtown Cleveland)

FEDERAL RESERVE BANK OF CLEVELAND
E. Sixth and Superior
Cleveland
216/579-2847

The Federal Reserve Bank of Cleveland is one of only 12 reserve banks in the country, and its magnificent headquarters combines historic architecture with 21st-century technology. The bank features a golden marble lobby and a display of U.S. money dating from the Civil War. The bank's original two-story vault is said to be the largest vault door installation in the world. The 100-ton steel door is so perfectly balanced that one person can swing it closed. This vault is maintained for visitor viewing. Today the bank uses a state-of-the-art cash handling system and machines that read and process 90,000 checks an hour. Free seasonal 90-minute tours on Fri at 1. Group tours by special arrangement. Reservations required for all tours. For more information call 800/543-3489. (Downtown Cleveland)

THE FLATS
Cleveland
216/566-1046
(Flats Oxbow Association)

Named for the flat land on both sides of the Cuyahoga River, the Flats is where Cleveland truly began. Founder Moses Cleaveland landed with a surveying party in 1796 at a spot now commemorated as Settlers Landing Park. An easy way to get there is to take the RTA's Waterfront Line from the Tower City terminal. For $1.50 round-trip, you can climb aboard the RTA's newest rail line and disembark at the Settler's Landing station. You can lounge on the large stone steps and watch the international ships churn by. It is especially fun to watch gigantic freighters make the hairpin turn in the Cuyahoga River, known to locals as Collision Bend. Although this is still a working neighborhood of industrial and shipping companies, the banks of the Flats have been transformed into a fun-filled entertainment neighborhood of seafood restaurants, dance clubs,

Free Stamp, p. 86

© 1996 Jonathan Wayne

music clubs, and bars. Families can find kid-friendly restaurants for lunch or dinner on both banks. At night the Flats offers a dazzling display of lights coming from the boats, restaurants and the bridges. In 1976, to commemorate the city's 200th birthday, the "City of Bridges" project illuminated the massive overhead bridges with covered lights,

Old Stone Church

Although the building you see today was constructed in 1855, the Old Stone Church has had many incarnations. Just 19 months after the church was built, a fire swept from the roof to the 250-foot steeple, which toppled and crashed across Ontario Street. The church was rebuilt in 1858, only to be hit by fire again in 1884. At the end of the Civil War, a service of thanksgiving was held and a new "Peace Bell" was added to the belfry. That same bell rang for the memorial service of Abraham Lincoln, whose funeral cortege stopped at Public Square on its way back to Springfield, Illinois.

Top Ten (Plus Three) Historic Cleveland Sites

by Carol Poh Miller, historical consultant and coauthor of *Cleveland: A Concise History, 1796–1996*

1. First Presbyterian (Old Stone) Church (1855), 91 Public Square
2. Lake View Cemetery (1869), 12316 Euclid Ave.
3. Rockefeller Park bridges (1896–1907), spanning Martin Luther King Jr. Blvd. in Rockefeller Park, University Circle
4. Center Street Swing Bridge (1901), spanning the Cuyahoga River at Center St.
5. Hulett ore unloaders (1912), C&P Ore Dock, Whiskey Island.
6. West Side Market (1912), corner of W. 25th St. and Lorain Ave.
7. Historic Warehouse District, St. Clair Ave. and W. Sixth St.
8. Tremont Historic District, east of I-71 and north of Starkweather Ave.
9. Little Italy Historic District, Mayfield and Murray Hill Rds., University Circle
10. Huntington Bank (formerly Union Trust) Building (1924), corner of Euclid Ave. and E. Ninth St.
11. Federal Reserve Bank of Cleveland (1923), corner of Superior Ave. and E. Sixth St.
12. Playhouse Square theaters: State, Ohio, Allen, Hanna (all 1921), and Palace (1922), Euclid Ave. and E. 14th St.
13. Severance Hall (1931), Euclid Ave. at East Blvd., University Circle

turning them into nighttime sculpture. ♿ (Downtown Cleveland)

FREE STAMP
Willard Park next to City Hall
Cleveland

It looks like this sculpture fell from some giant clerk's hand while he was climbing down the beanstalk. The *Free Stamp* sculpture is a 48-foot office stamp that prints the word "Free." Designed by Claes Oldenburg and Cosje van Bruggen, the work was originally commissioned by BP Oil for its new office tower. But the political and social commentary that the sculpture invited was apparently too much for the owners. They offered the piece to the city of Cleveland (for free!), and city officials were more than happy to accept. & (Downtown Cleveland)

GOODTIME III
E. Ninth Street Pier
North Coast Harbor
Cleveland
216/861-5110
This is a thousand-passenger ship that offers sightseeing tours and entertainment cruises on the Cuyahoga River and Lake Erie. The two-hour, narrated cruises begin at noon and 3 daily from mid-June to September. The *Goodtime III* also offers a 6 p.m. cruise on Sunday. Dinner/dance cruises are also available. $10 adults, $9.50 seniors, $6 ages 2 to 11. Parking available at nearby Burke Lakefront Airport, the Port Authority, or North Point parking garage. Call for group rates, private charters, and the schedule for dinner/dance cruises. & (Downtown Cleveland)

HANNA CABARET
2067 E. 14th St.
Cleveland
216/771-1664
When the Euclid Avenue Opera House was destroyed in a fire in 1892, U.S. Senator Marcus Alonzo Hanna restored the building and owned it until he died in 1904. His son, Daniel Rhodes Hanna, built the Hanna Building and created the Hanna Theater in tribute to his father. The theater opened in 1921 on Playhouse Square and became a stopping point for legendary names on the American stage: Henry Fonda, Helen Hayes, Ethel Barrymore, Al Jolson, Katherine Hepburn, Carol Channing, Buddy Ebsen, Ginger Rodgers, Mary Martin, and Anthony Quinn. For decades the Hanna Theater staged national touring shows. Rodgers and Hammerstein opened their national road tours at the Hanna. Today the theater is a cabaret that stages

---

Federal Reserve Bank: A Mighty Fortress

Cleveland was named the Fourth Federal Reserve District when the nation's central banking system was created in 1913. In 1921, construction began on a 12-story, $8.25 million building modeled after those of the great bankers of the early Renaissance, the Medici family. Like the Medici family's palace in Florence, Italy, this building is a fortress. The security system has armed guard stations. The main entrance is protected by two larger-than-life marble figures: on the right is Security, *on the left is* Integrity. *A third bronze figure on the Superior Avenue side of the building,* Energy In Repose, *weighs nearly three tons and is about four times life size.*

---

musical productions. (Downtown Cleveland)

HOPE MEMORIAL BRIDGE PYLONS
Between Lorain and Carnegie Aves.

Cleveland
When it comes to art deco, these pylons are a feast for the eyes. Drive west on Carnegie Avenue past Jacobs Field and view these Depression-era sculptures. A pair of 43-foot pylons are located at

Cleveland's Eiffel Towers

by Carol Poh Miller, historical consultant and coauthor of *Cleveland: A Concise History, 1796–1996*

The four massive Hulett ore unloaders, located on Lake Erie at Whiskey Island, were built between 1910 and 1912 for the Pennsylvania Railroad as part of the largest ore-unloading dock in the world. Resembling dinosaurs, these 12-story giants reached into the hulls of lake freighters and pulled out millions of tons of iron ore at a time when America's steels mills were going full tilt.

Invented by Clevelander George H. Hulett (1846–1923), the Hulett ore unloader revolutionized the handling of iron ore by replacing gangs of hand shovelers with 17-ton grab buckets. By 1913, Hulett unloaders were at work at almost every port on Lake Erie. Gradually eclipsed by self-unloading boats, which carried their own boom and conveyor system, the machines unloaded their last cargo of iron ore in 1992. Since then, they have become the object of a grassroots preservation campaign.

Smithsonian maritime history curator Paul F. Johnson writes, "Nothing I know can provide such a powerful sense of the scale of Cleveland's maritime heritage."

The Hulett unloaders can be seen from the fishing pier at the eastern end of Edgewater Park or by taking the unmarked and unpaved road immediately east of the Westerly Wastewater Treatment Plant (5800 W. Memorial Shoreway) directly to the dock. The latter approach will require permission from the dock security guard.

Check out the two pairs of 43-foot-high sandstone figures that adorn the Hope Memorial Bridge. The art deco figures from the 1930s are supposed to represent the "Guardians of Traffic." They depict the Greek god of commerce, Hermes, holding a hayrack, covered wagon, stagecoach, passenger car, and four types of trucks. The bridge spans the industrial valley of the Flats and connects Lorain Avenue on the city's west side to Carnegie Avenue on the east side. The bridge was named in honor of comedian Bob Hope's family, who were Cleveland stonemasons.

each end of the bridge that connects Carnegie Avenue downtown with Lorain Avenue on the west side. Made of local sandstone from the nearby town of Berea, these sculptures were done in the 1930s as part of a federal work project. Each one represents the figure of Hermes holding a progression of vehicles, from a horse-drawn coach to a tank truck, symbolizing the evolution of transportation. One of the stone carvers was the father of comedian Bob Hope, and the bridge was recently renamed in his honor. & (Downtown Cleveland)

HUNTINGTON BANK BUILDING
917 Euclid Ave.
Cleveland

When you walk past the doors of the Huntington Bank Building on the corner of East Ninth Street and Euclid Avenue, the building's classic but unassuming exterior gives no warning as to the scale and majesty of its interior. Modeled after the great basilicas of Rome, the L-shaped banking hall was the largest in the United States when it was built in 1924 and the second

largest office building in the world. The floor is 30-acres large with a three-story ceiling. The barrel-vaulted, skylit ceilings are supported by massive marble columns. The grand lobby is part of a 22-story office building, now housing major corporations and professional offices. (Downtown Cleveland)

NAUTICA QUEEN
Nautica Entertainment Center
West Bank of the Flats
Cleveland
216/696-8888 or 800/837-0604

A dining cruise ship, the *Nautica Queen* sails daily and serves both lunch and dinner buffets, plus a Sunday brunch buffet. The ship can serve as many as 400 passengers and runs from Easter Sunday through New Year's Eve. The two enclosed, climate-controlled decks allow you to dine in rain or shine. Lunches are $20.95 for adults and $10.95 for children 12 and under. Dinners are about twice the price of lunch. Senior citizen get 10 percent discounts Sunday through Thursday. Call for seating times. The ship has limited manual wheel-

Outdoor Reading Retreat

The Eastman Reading Garden, located between the original library and the new Louis Stokes wing, is named for Linda Eastman, Cleveland Library director from 1918 to 1938. The landscaped garden has moveable chairs so that library patrons can find just the right spot for reading. The centerpiece of this leafy retreat is a water sculpture created by Maya Lin, designer of the Vietnam War Memorial in Washington, D.C. The garden is open from April to October.

chair accessibility, but electric wheelchairs cannot be accommodated. (Downtown Cleveland)

OLD STONE CHURCH
91 Public Square
Cleveland
216/241-6145
Located on the north side of Public Square and the west side of Ontario Street, the Old Stone Church has had a congregation ever since 1820. Rebecca Carter (wife of Lorenzo, the first permanent settler of Cleveland) was a charter member of the first stone church on the site.

Built in 1855 at a cost of $60,000, the Old Stone Church is the oldest building in downtown Cleveland. The foundation and walls are sandstone lined with brick. The Victorian Romanesque interior has a trussed, wood-beamed vaulted ceiling, and four of the windows were created by Louis Tiffany (two are signed by the famous glass artist). Whatever your faith, you can be married in this Presbyterian church. The church has a professional choir, the Old Stone Singers, who perform heavenly music. To find out when the choir will be singing, call the church. Services are held at 10 a.m.

T i P

Free tours of the Allen, Ohio, State, and Palace Theatres in Playhouse Square are offered from 10 to 11:30 on designated Saturdays. Tours depart every 15 minutes from the State Theatre box office. Visitors see a 20-minute slide presentation before taking the guided tour through the auditoriums and lobbies of the four restored theaters. Backstage areas of "dark" (not in use) theaters are included in the tour.

Garfield's Tomb

President James Garfield's tomb is a 180-foot, High Victorian Gothic gray-stone mausoleum in Lakeview Cemetery. A marble statue of Garfield stands in the memorial chapel. In a crypt below are the caskets of the slain president and his wife, Lucretia, who lived 37 years after her husband's assassination. An urn holds the ashes of their daughter, Mary Garfield Stanley-Brown. (She was married to her father's secretary, Joseph Stanley-Brown.) Two winding staircases lead up to a balcony with a panoramic view of the city and 40 miles of Lake Erie shoreline.

Sunday. Don't miss the magnificent annual Christmas concert. All performances are free. ♿ (Downtown Cleveland)

PLAYHOUSE SQUARE CENTER
1519 Euclid Ave.
Cleveland
216/771-4444
This theater district, at Euclid Avenue and East 14th Street, consists of four magnificently restored theaters: The Ohio, Allen, State, and Palace. These four theaters—once separate entities and now linked by lobbies—seat more than 7,000 people in total and provide entertainment for more than one million people every year. Playhouse Square ranks second only in size to New York's Lincoln Center, with nearly 10,000 seats in four theaters. (Downtown Cleveland)

PORTAL SCULPTURE
Cleveland Justice Center,
Ontario St. at Lakeside Ave.
Cleveland
The George Gund Foundation do-
nated this 36-foot-high sculpture by Isamu Noguchi to the city. Some people find this painted black steel piece at the entrance to the Justice Center a little too offbeat. Others think it is Noguchi's best work. He created the piece in 1976. ♿ (Downtown Cleveland)

TOWER CITY
OBSERVATION DECK
Tower City
Cleveland
216/621-7981 or 216/621-4110
ext. 237
For 60 years, Cleveland's Terminal Tower was the city's tallest building and most recognized landmark (See Chapter 1, "Welcome to Cleveland"). The 52-story tower is 708 feet tall—the tallest building between New York and Chicago until 1992, when the 888-foot Key Center Tower was built across Public Square. On Saturday and Sunday, you can ride the elevator up 42 floors to the observation deck for a great view of the city. On a clear day you can see about 32 miles. May–Sept 11–4:30, Oct–April 11–3:30.

Call for holiday hours. $2 adults, $1 ages 6–16. & (Downtown Cleveland)

TRIPLE-L ECCENTRIC GYRATORY III
In front of National City Center
E. Ninth St. and Euclid Ave.
Cleveland

George Rickey built this brushed stainless steel, wind-activated mobile so that the sculpture is always changing shape. The L-shaped arms turn around a 27-foot radius at probably the busiest intersection in downtown Cleveland. Neither motorists nor pedestrians are ever bored while waiting for the stoplight to change. The sculpture is 38 feet tall and weighs 1,400 pound, yet the piece moves with the grace and poise of a ballerina. & (Downtown Cleveland)

TROLLEY TOURS OF CLEVELAND
P.O. Box 91658
Cleveland 44101-3658
216/771-4484 or 800/848-0173
One of the easiest, most fun-filled

ways to see Cleveland is on Lolly the Trolley. Lolly is a bright red trolley that takes passengers on one- or two-hour narrated tours of the city's most interesting sights.

Lolly's one-hour tour takes you to North Coast Harbor, home of the Rock and Roll Hall of Fame and Museum, the Great Lakes Science Center and Museum, the USS *Cod* submarine, the steamship *William Mather* ore freighter, the Gateway sports complex, and Burke Lakefront Airport. You'll visit downtown sights, the Flats riverfront restaurants, the Warehouse District, and Ohio City.

The two-hour tour adds a drive along Lake Erie's coastline and a visit to Playhouse Square and University Circle. Lolly's owner, Cheryl Paul, says that good kids get to ring Lolly's clang-clang-clang bell at the end of the tour. & (Downtown Cleveland)

USS COD
1089 E. Ninth St.
Cleveland
216/566-8770

The lagoon in University Circle

Margaret Bourke-White

Margaret Bourke-White was fresh out of Cornell University when she moved to Cleveland to live with her mother in 1927. Bourke-White's degree was in biology, but it was photography that flipped her switch. She fell in love with the Flats (long before the rest of us) and began taking photos of the factories, smokestacks, and steel mills. During the late 1920s she shot photos of the Terminal Tower looming above Cleveland. Her big break came when Henry Luce hired her as one of the original photographers for Life magazine. Bourke-White later became the first woman war correspondent of World War II.

Permanently moored between the William Mather Museum and Burke Lakefront Airport, the USS *Cod* was one of 200 submarines in the U.S. fleet serving in the South Pacific during World War II. The 312-foot sub had a crew of 105. After the war, the Navy used her for training NATO anti-submarine forces in the Atlantic Ocean. The sub came to Cleveland in 1959 to serve as a Navy Reserve training vessel and was saved from the scrap yard by her civilian guardians in 1976. Today the Cod is the only sub of the fleet that is still in original condition and in the water. The volunteers who sell tickets and answer questions all served on submarines during World War II. They are crusty but likable old salts who know this sub backwards and forwards.

Climb aboard and enter the forward torpedo room. Work your way through the officers' quarters, the engine and electrical rooms, and the after torpedo room. To tour the *Cod*, you must be able to climb ladders and fit through the hatchways. In order to preserve the ship's his-torical authenticity, no portals have been enlarged or made accessible for the disabled. May 1–Sept 30 daily 10–5. $4 adults, $2 students. (Downtown Cleveland)

UNIVERSITY CIRCLE

This 488-acre cultural enclave is the only arrangement of its kind in the world. University Circle began to take shape in the 1880s when Western Reserve University and the Case School of Applied Science relocated to the area. Cleveland philanthropist Jeptha H. Wade donated a large piece of land to the city on the agreement that it be used for an art gallery and public park.

University Circle became the pet project of Cleveland's wealthiest families, who moved into the surrounding mansions, donated millions, and served on the boards of trustees. By the mid-1930s, University Circle had an orchestra hall, a natural history museum, a garden center, an historical society, and a major hospital complex.

GREATER CLEVELAND

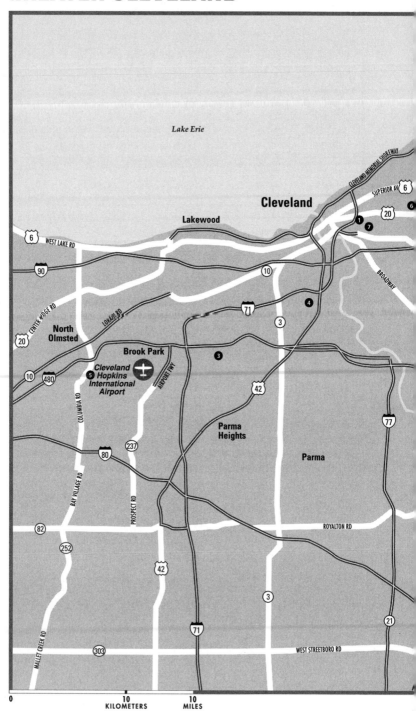

Lake Erie

Cleveland

Lakewood

Cleveland Memorial Shoreway

SUPERIOR AV

6

20

6

1

7

6 US WEST LAKE RD

90

10

BROADWAY

CENTER RIDGE RD

LORAIN RD

North
Olmsted

20

71

4

3

Brook Park

3

480

10

*Cleveland
5 Hopkins
International
Airport*

AIRPORT PWY

42

77

COLUMBIA RD

Parma
Heights

Parma

80

237

BAY VILLAGE RD

82

PROSPECT RD

ROYALTON RD

252

42

3

21

71

MALLET CREEK RD

303

WEST STREETBORO RD

0   10   10
KILOMETERS MILES

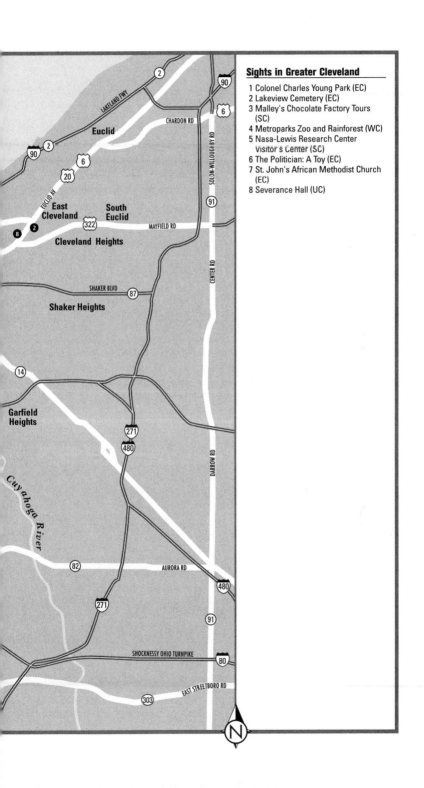

Sights in Greater Cleveland

1 Colonel Charles Young Park (EC)
2 Lakeview Cemetery (EC)
3 Malley's Chocolate Factory Tours (SC)
4 Metroparks Zoo and Rainforest (WC)
5 Nasa-Lewis Research Center Visitor's Center (SC)
6 The Politician: A Toy (EC)
7 St. John's African Methodist Church (EC)
8 Severance Hall (UC)

Over the past 14 years, Lolly the Trolley has carried passengers nearly 3 million miles around the city. The trolley is sometimes hired for weddings and has carried more than 3,000 bridal couples on their special day.

From downtown, take Chester, Euclid, or Carnegie Avenues east five miles. Or go to Tower City and catch the RTA Rapid Red Line going east to Windmere. The Red Line has a stop at University Circle, and you can catch a free shuttle bus to most attractions. The museums of University Circle are listed in Chapter 6.

SEVERANCE HALL
11001 Euclid Ave.
Cleveland
216/231-7300
The home of the Cleveland Orchestra is one of University Circle's most familiar and magnificent landmarks. Driving east on Euclid Avenue, Severance Hall sits just past Wade Lagoon, where East Boulevard angles off Euclid Avenue. Prominent businessman John L. Severance donated $2.5 million to build the hall in 1929, as a memorial to his wife, Elizabeth DeWitt Severance. The concert hall seats 1,844, and a chamber-music hall on the ground floor seats 400. Box office hours are Mon–Fri 9–5. Call 216/231-1111 or 800/686-1141 for performance information. (University Circle)

EAST CLEVELAND

COLONEL CHARLES YOUNG PARK
E. 46th St., Carnegie and
Prospect Aves.
Cleveland

This park—a large triangle where three streets meet—is dedicated to Colonel Charles Young, World War II's highest ranking black soldier. Relax on one of the benches and bring along a carry-out snack or meal from Ruthie & Moe's diner, located one block west on Prospect Avenue. (East Cleveland)

LAKEVIEW CEMETERY
12316 Euclid Ave.
Cleveland
This 200-acre cemetery is the final resting place for some of the most famous and wealthy citizens in Cleveland's history. The most prominent is President James A. Garfield.

Garfield Memorial in Lakeview Cemetery

© 1996 Jonathan Wayne

Playhouse Square

After World War I, Cleveland's theater district was created by local realtor Joseph Laronge and New York theater manager Marcus Loew of the Loew theater syndicate. Local newspapers coined the term "Playhouse Square" to describe the district of 12 working playhouses. The State, designed for "legitimate theater," and the Ohio, designed for movies and vaudeville, were the first two to open in 1921. Architect Thomas W. Lamb designed the State's Italian Renaissance lobby to be 45 by 180 feet, the longest of any theater in the world. The State's huge auditorium seats 3,400. The Allen Theatre, which opened two months later, was designed to show movies, with an auditorium that seats 1,400. This was followed by the Palace Theatre, a lavish 3,580-seat auditorium built for vaudeville shows, with two curving marble staircases and a three-story lobby. Cleveland was a major stop on the American vaudeville circuit. The Marx Brothers, Fanny Brice, Burns and Allen, Jack Benny, Sophie Tucker, and magician Harry Houdini all performed here. As vaudeville faded and television grew in popularity, the theater district began to crumble. By the late 1960s, the Allen, Ohio, State, and Palace theaters were all slated for demolition.

In 1970, a Cleveland Schools employee named Ray Shepardson was looking for a space to hold a meeting and saw the interiors of the closed theaters. Awed by their magnificence, Shepardson organized the Playhouse Square Associates to save the buildings. To show that Cleveland would support downtown entertainment, Playhouse Square Associates opened a cabaret in the lobby of the State Theatre. Originally scheduled to run for three weeks, the show ran for two years.

Thanks to the combined efforts of Cleveland foundations, government, corporations, and volunteers, the theaters have been restored to their original elegance and updated. This restoration and the creation of Playhouse Square is the largest project of its kind ever completed in the United States.

Nautica Queen, p. 89

(See sidebar on page 91.) The cemetery was formed in 1869 with telegraph pioneer Jethpa Wade as president. The rolling hills and beautiful views made it a favorite place for Sunday outings. Impressive monuments mark the graves of streetlight inventor Charles F. Brush, John D. Rockefeller, Terminal Tower creators O. P. and M. J. Van Swearingen, and writer Charles Chestnutt. The Wade Memorial Chapel, named in honor of Jeptha Wade, has stained glass windows designed by glass artist Louis C. Tiffany. (East Cleveland)

THE POLITICIAN: A TOY
Chester Ave. at E. 66th St.
Cleveland
This sculpture, created by Billie Lawless of painted steel, is sure to wake up anyone driving or walking past on Chester Avenue. The modern sculpture depicts the politician as a giant pull-toy with spinning wheels, moving jaw, the tail of a rocking horse, and eyes made out of television monitors. Even the iron fence around the sculpture has political buzz words around the base. (East Cleveland)

ST. JOHN'S AFRICAN METHODIST CHURCH
2261 E. 40th St.
Cleveland
216/431-2560
The oldest African American church in Cleveland was organized in 1830 by circuit rider William Paul Quinn. The church began with six members and was originally located on Bolivar Street. (Cleveland baseball fans know Bolivar because it became the northern gateway to Jacobs Field.) In 1905, the church moved to its present location on East 40th Street. Services begin Sunday at 10:45. The current pastor is the Reverend Lyman W. Liggins. (East Cleveland)

WEST CLEVELAND

CLEVELAND METROPARKS ZOO AND RAINFOREST
3900 Wildlife Way

Cleveland
216/661-6500

Visiting the zoo is like a whirlwind tour of the world. The African Plains area has the largest herd of Masai giraffes in the country, as well as antelopes, zebras, lions, and birds. Rhinoceroses and cheetahs live peacefully in the same habitat. Monkey Island is home to graceful black Colobus monkeys with their flowing manes of white hair.

The Northern Trek area is home to polar bears, brown bears, sea lions, harbor seals, Bactrian camels, and other cold-weather animals. The newest exhibit in the Northern Trek area is Wolf Wilderness. The wolf pack shares this northern forest habitat with bald eagles, beavers, turtles, and fish.

Before you visit, put on comfortable shoes: the zoo covers 165 acres of woods and plains, and the 3,300 animals live in roomy habitats. Free Zootrams carry you from one area to another, but if you want to see all the animals, you will still do a lot of walking. Take a break in one of the rest, picnic, or play areas.

The RainForest, a steamy, indoor tropical jungle, is home to 600 animals and 10,000 plants. Your tour begins at a 25-foot waterfall and winds through dense foliage, a scientist's hut, and a walk-through aviary of South American tapirs, capybara, giant anteaters, porcupines, and sloths. On down the path are ocelots, clouded leopards, and a fishing cat. Tree shrews and Francois' langurs live in a two-story tree habitat. Orangutans live in a domed habitat bathed in sunshine. On the lower level, fruit bats munch in the treetops. Every 12 minutes, a tropical rainstorm blows through a large ex-

hibit, complete with simulated thunder, lightning, wind, and rain.

Hundreds of rain-forest insects are shown, including leaf-cutting ants, hissing cockroaches, and walking sticks. Steps lead down to an eye-to-eye view of two mammoth crocodiles. But the scariest exhibits in the RainForest are those that explain just how quickly the rain forests are being destroyed. Zoo open year-round daily 9–5. RainForest open year-round daily 10–5 and Wed until 9. Extended hours in summer. $7 adults, $4 ages 2 to 11. Ticket sales end one hour prior to closing. Parking is free. (West Cleveland)

SOUTH CLEVELAND

MALLEY'S CHOCOLATE FACTORY TOURS
13400 Brookpark Rd.
Cleveland
800/835-5684

On this delicious tour, hear the history of how chocolate came to be the world's favorite flavor. A trip through Malley's chocolate works allows visitors to see the various filling centers being dipped in chocolate, chocolate molds being filled, and chefs cooking candy in copper kettles over open flames. The nut shop tour shows how the nuts are roasted, salted, and then dipped in chocolate. Malley's generous samples make this tour a fun trip for chocoholics of all ages. (South Cleveland)

NASA-LEWIS RESEARCH CENTER VISITOR'S CENTER
21000 Brookpark Rd.
Cleveland
216/433-2201

Next door to Cleveland Hopkins

Airport (look for the big white NASA letters on the base's air hangar when you fly in or out of Cleveland), Lewis Research Center's Visitor's Center is open every day. The *Apollo Skylab 3* command module (the actual scorched spacecraft) is on display, and a working ham radio station monitors whatever space project is currently in orbit. You can enjoy this museum several different ways, depending on your space acumen. Science buffs will breeze through the exhibits on spacecraft propulsion or materials and structures research. But space fledglings (especially kids) might not be able to follow the technical displays. The hourly audiovisual programs in the auditorium are more helpful. During the week, tours can be arranged in advance. Mon–Fri 9–5, Sat 10–3, Sun 1–5. Free. (South Cleveland)

Great Lakes Science Center

6

MUSEUMS AND GALLERIES

The museums of Greater Cleveland cover every facet of culture, from punk rock to period art. Many museums are located in University Circle on the city's east side. Created in the 1880s by the wealthiest families in town, University Circle is a 488-acre campus of cultural, educational, religious, and social service organizations. The anchor of University Circle is the Cleveland Museum of Art, built in 1916 and recognized today as one of the finest art museums in the United States. University Circle is also home to the Cleveland Museum of Natural History, the Western Reserve Historical Society, and the Rainbow Children's Museum. Nearby is the African American Museum, which celebrates Cleveland's African American community. The Dunham Tavern Museum on Euclid Avenue is a restored Western Reserve tavern built in 1824.

With the redevelopment of downtown, new museums have sprouted along Lake Erie's shoreline. The Rock and Roll Hall of Fame and Museum opened in 1995 in Northcoast Harbor. Next door is the Great Lakes Science Center and the 320-seat Omnimax Theater, which opened in 1996. Northcoast Harbor is also home to the USS Cod, a World War II submarine unchanged from its days as a working sub. Another floating museum is the Steamship William G. Mather, a restored ore freighter. Public and privately owned art galleries can be found throughout the city.

ART MUSEUMS

AFRICAN AMERICAN MUSEUM
1765 Crawford Rd.
Cleveland
216/791-1700
One of the oldest African American museums in the country, this institution documents the history of Africans and African Americans in Cleveland, the United States, and the world. The museum has 11 permanent exhibits. Starting with ancient Egypt and the rise and fall of Timbuktu, it explores the eras of the great kings and queens of Africa, the Atlantic slave trade, the Underground Railroad, and the Tuskegee Institute. Visitors will even see the original stoplight invented by Cleveland genius inventor Garrett Morgan. The Science Corner has hands-on exhibits that were inspired by famous scientists from George Washington Carver to astronaut Guyenne Blueford. Other attractions include the African Room and the Cleveland Corner. Tue–Fri 10–3. (University Circle)

CLEVELAND CENTER FOR CONTEMPORARY ART
8501 Carnegie Ave.
Cleveland
216/421-8671
Located in a renovated building within the Cleveland Play House complex, the Center strives to bring the latest and most important contempo-

---

Cleveland Crimefighter

Eliot Ness came to Cleveland in 1934. Even though Prohibition had been repealed the year before, bootleggers were still making and selling their own whiskey to avoid taxes. Ness, part of the Treasury Department's Alcohol Tax Unit, was brought to Cleveland to curb the flow of local stills and rumrunners coming across Lake Erie from Canada. Ness closed stills at a rate of one per day. When a new mayor came into office, Ness was chosen to clean up the corruption that Prohibition had brought to the city's police department. He formed his own group of Cleveland "Untouchables"—undercover men who rooted out corruption without falling prey to it.

Under Ness's leadership, a three-month police academy was created. Ness went after labor racketeers who were extorting local businessmen. His career as a crimefighter was successful, but his 1947 campaign for mayor was not. He collaborated with a journalist to write The Untouchables, *a best-selling book about his career in Chicago. Ness died of a heart attack at age 55, before the book was published.*

Cleveland Museum of Art

rary artwork to Cleveland. Thanks to the Center, Cleveland art lovers have enjoyed the works of more than 400 emerging and established artists. Founded in 1968, the Center has shown the work of Andy Warhol, Jasper Johns, Roy Lichtenstein, and Claes Oldenburg (whose work *Free Stamp* rests in Willard Park next to City Hall). Group tours are available upon request. Call for hours. Free. (University Circle)

CLEVELAND INSTITUTE OF ART
11141 East Blvd.
Cleveland
216/421-7400
The institute is a five-year college of fine art and design. The public is welcome to enjoy its gallery exhibitions, continuing education, children's classes, and Cleveland Cinematheque film program (see Chapter 10, "Performing Arts"). Sun 1–4, Mon 9:30–4, Tue–Sat 9:30–9. Call for summer hours. (University Circle)

CLEVELAND MUSEUM OF ART
11150 East Blvd.

Cleveland
216/421-7340
One of the world's great art museums sits on a 15-acre park called the Fine Arts Garden. The white Georgian marble building opened in 1916. The museum now houses 30,000 works of art in 70 galleries, an auditorium, lecture halls, classrooms, a museum store, and a café.

One of the most pleasant ways to spend a day is by browsing through the museum's incredible collections of ancient, Asian, Mayan, African, European, American, and contemporary masters. The kids always enjoy exploring Armor Court, a gallery devoted to suits of armor, swords, daggers, and other way-cool medieval weapons.

You can park for a small fee in the museum parking lot off Wade Oval near the north entrance. Or take the free shuttle bus from the University Circle stop on the RTA Red Line. Tue, Thu, Fri 10–5:45; Wed 10–9:45; Sat 9–4:45.; Sun 1–5:45. Free. (University Circle)

SCIENCE AND HISTORY MUSEUMS

CLEVELAND MUSEUM OF NATURAL HISTORY
1 Wade Oval Dr.
Cleveland
216/231-04600
In 1835, a group of young men began meeting in a building near Public Square. They called their meeting place the Ark because they kept their mounted animal specimens there. Although this group of "Arkites" was gone by the end of the 1800s, the idea for a natural history museum surfaced again in 1920. The current museum was built in 1958.

Today the museum has much to offer. The four-story facility houses Happy, a 70-foot-long, 150-million-year-old *Haplocanthosaurus delfsi* dinosaur skeleton; a planetarium and observatory; an outdoor environmental courtyard with live waterfowl in a running brook; and the Hall of Man, which features Lucy, one of the world's oldest fossil skeletons of a human ancestor. The museum's shop, Ark in the Park, has a nice selection of books, educational toys, rocks, minerals, tools, and pottery.

The Sears Hall of Human Ecology is a collection of mounted animals from 11 geographical areas through-out the world. Kids marvel at the bears, lions, jaguars, and other predators in the exhibit. The museum's mounted hunting trophies from an earlier age serve as a reminder of how yesterday's trophy is today's endangered species. Open Mon–Sat 10–5, Sun 12–5, Sept–May Wed 10–10 for stargazing in the observatory. $6 adults, $4 seniors and ages 5 to 17, free age 4 and under. Free Tue and Thu 3–5. (University Circle)

GREAT LAKES SCIENCE CENTER
North Coast Harbor
Cleveland

Garrett Morgan

Sometimes called Cleveland's Black Edison, Garrett Morgan was the inventor of many devices, including the gas mask, the automatic traffic signal, a woman's hat fastener, a round belt fastener, a friction drive clutch, and a safety helmet that protected the wearer from inhaling smoke and ammonia. Morgan's gas mask received the ultimate test when he was called out of bed in 1916 to help rescue miners trapped in a gas-filled tunnel they were digging for the city's water system under Lake Erie. Although he risked his own safety to save the lives of the miners, he was mentioned in only one of all the newspaper stories as a "negro" who had led one of the search parties. Morgan went on to found a clothing manufacturing shop, invented and sold a hair-straightening product, manufactured the gas masks, and sold his patent on the stoplight to General Electric for $40,000 in 1923. He founded the Cleveland Call *newspaper, today's* Call & Post. *He died in May 1949. In 1991, 75 years after his heroic rescue, the Division Avenue Filtration Plant was renamed the Garrett Morgan Waterworks.*

TRIVIA

The Health Museum, opened November 13, 1940, was the first permanent health museum in America.

216/694-2000

The $59 million state-of-the-art museum, which opened in July 1996, is the ninth largest hands-on science center in the United States. With more than 300 interactive exhibits on three floors, guests can experience the wonders of science, the environment, and technology. Pilot a blimp, test your science knowledge at the Quiz Show in the Great Lakes Situation Room, or see an indoor tornado. Daily science demonstrations explore the mysteries of Wild Weather, Cryogenics, Bubblemania, Fire in the Sky, and much more. The six-story-high domed Omnimax Theater uses the most advanced sound and film projection system in the world to take viewers on the film experience of a lifetime. A new 500-car parking garage has solved the parking shortage in the North Coast Harbor area. Omnimax shows tend to sell out quickly on weekends and holidays, so arrive early or order tickets through Ticketmaster at 216/241-5555. Daily 9:30–5:30. Admission to either the museum or the Omnimax: $7.75 adults, $5.25 ages 3 to 17. Admission to both attractions: $10.95 adults, $7.75 ages 3 to 17. &. (Downtown Cleveland)

HEALTH MUSEUM
8911 Euclid Ave.
Cleveland
216/231-5010

Juno, the talking transparent woman, is one of the favorite exhibits at this museum. So is the giant tooth. Stuffee, the nine-foot-tall stuffed doll, can unzip his skin and take out his organs to to teach kids how the body functions. Stuffee's seven-foot twin tours schools and health fairs. The museum is currently in the midst of a giant overhaul of interactive exhibits that will explain health through the entire human life cycle. Mon–Fri 9–5, Sat 10–5, Sun 12–5. $4.50 adults, $3 senior citizens and ages 4 to 17. &. (University Circle)

WESTERN RESERVE
HISTORICAL SOCIETY

T I P

After exploring several galleries at the Cleveland Museum of Art take a break and enjoy a snack or a meal at the cut-above Museum Café. In good weather you can eat in the sublime atmosphere of the outdoor sculpture court.

The Great Lakes Science Center is home to the world's largest hands-on exhibit on the Great Lakes environment. An entire floor of exhibits and computer stations cover this unique natural environment that supplies 20 percent of the world's freshwater.

10825 East Blvd.
Cleveland
216/721-5722
www.wrhs.org

In 1867, the Western Reserve Historical Society was formed to preserve the records and artifacts of Cleveland and the Western Reserve. Today it is the largest privately supported regional historical society in the nation.

The society houses two museums and a library with more than 5 million books, rolls of microfilm, photographs, and manuscripts. The collection archives the urban, African American, ethnic, Jewish, and labor histories of this area and has one of the largest family history research centers in the country.

The History Museum features the 1911 Hay-McKinney Mansion, which shows the lifestyle differences between the wealthy and their servants. The son of President James A. Garfield built the home. The museum's Crossroads exhibit includes stories of Cleveland's development from settlement to a booming industrial force. If fashion is your thing, check out the Chisolm Halle Costume Wing. Rotating exhibits display the collection's 30,000 garments dating from the mid-1700s. All the garments belonged to, or were worn by, people in the Western Reserve region.

The Crawford Auto-Aviation Museum is a collection of nearly 200 antique, vintage, and classic automobiles and airplanes ranging from the oldest horseless carriage to modern-day race cars. Special focus is given to automobiles produced in the late 1800s and early 1900s, when Cleveland was the automotive center of the nation. Rotating mini-exhibits include bizarre cars and model trains. Mon–Sat 10–5, Sun 12–5. WRHS Library open Tue–Sat 9–5, Wed 9–9. Admission to History Museum, Crawford Auto-Aviation Museum, and library: $6.50 adults, $5.50 seniors, $4.50 ages 6 to 12. ⛹ (University Circle)

Museum of Natural History, p. 103

© 1996 Jonathan Wayne

OTHER MUSEUMS

CLEVELAND POLICE MUSEUM
Justice Center
1300 Ontario St.
Cleveland
216/623-5055

Located in police headquarters, the Cleveland Police Museum is a collection of artifacts and photos from Cleveland's crimefighting days of yore. Among the items on display: an assortment of confiscated weapons, the 1887 book of mug shots, the 1926 fingerprinting table, and the Harley Davidson police motorcycles. The museum even has an old-style jail cell, complete with iron bars, which tour groups may enter.

Although most people associate "Untouchables" crimefighter Eliot Ness with the city of Chicago, Ness sealed his reputation in Cleveland while serving as the city's safety director. The museum exhibits the Smith & Wesson revolver signed out to Ness during his tenure with the force. Weekdays 10–4. Tours arranged in advance. Free. (Downtown Cleveland)

DUNHAM TAVERN MUSEUM
6709 Euclid Ave.
Cleveland
216/431-1060

Massachusetts pioneers Rufus and Jane Pratt Dunham came to the Western Reserve in 1819 to farm. In 1824, they built the northern portion of what became known as Dunham Tavern. In addition to farming his 13.5 acres, Rufus became a tavernkeeper and his home became the place to go for turkey shoots and Whig Party meetings. The tavern was a stop on the old Buffalo–Cleveland–Detroit post road. During the Depression, the tavern was used as studio space for a group of artists and printmakers employed by the WPA.

Today Dunham Tavern is the oldest building in Cuyahoga County still standing on its original site. The structure has been completely

Old Bones, New Clues

The Cleveland Museum of Natural History's fossil named Lucy is actually a cast replica. Lucy's real 3 million-year-old bones were discovered in 1974 in northeastern Ethiopia by Cleveland Museum of Natural History curator Donald Johansen. Johansen brought Lucy back to Cleveland, where researchers studied her bones for five years. Her skeleton provided evidence of an entire new species of human being. After the researchers were finished, the bones were returned to their Ethiopian homeland. Casts of Lucy's bones can be found in museums all over the world. All of them were made by the professionals at this museum.

Rock and Roll Hall of Fame and Museum

James Blank/Nu-Vista Prints

restored to its original look, and several of the rooms are furnished with 19th-century Ohio antiques. Wed and Sun 1–4. Group tours offered by appointment. $2 adults, $1 children. (University Circle)

POLKA HALL OF FAME
Shore Cultural Center
291 E. 222nd St.
Euclid
216/261-3263
When thousands of Eastern European immigrants came to Cleveland, they brought their love of polka with them. To honor Cleveland's polka legacy, the Polka Hall of Fame was created at the Shore Cultural Center in Euclid. The former school building now houses memorabilia and exhibits about U.S. Polka King (and Cleveland native) Frankie Yankovic. Yankovic's accordians, autographed records, and the shirt he wore on the Cleveland TV show *Polka Varieties* are on display. The Hall of Fame has free admission, but you'll have plenty of opportunities to spend your money in the gift shop. Polka music of different nationalities is for sale on cassettes, CDs, LPs, 45s, and even eight-track tapes. Souvenirs include flags, patches, coffee mugs, hats, and bibs printed with the phrase "Born to Polka." Mon, Thur, Fri noon–5, Tue 3–7, Sat 10–2. (East Cleveland)

ROCK AND ROLL HALL OF FAME
AND MUSEUM
1 Key Plaza, North Coast Harbor
Cleveland
216/781-7625
After an extensive search for the right location, Cleveland was picked in 1986 as the home of the $92 million Rock and Roll Hall of Fame and Museum. Although some rock fans in other cities grumbled, most Clevelanders saw that choice as a no-brainer.

Cleveland has always been an important music town, and it was Cleveland disc jockey Alan Freed who coined the term *rock 'n' roll*. The collection of artifacts on display include John Lennon's Sgt. Pepper uniform and his Rickenbacker guitar, Elvis Presley's black leather stage outfit, Chuck Berry's handwritten lyrics to the songs *Carol* and *School Days*, Jim Morrison's cub scout uniform, the Supremes' "butterfly gowns," and a gazillion other off-the-wall rock memorabilia. But before you get to the displays, take time to watch the two short introductory films that chronicle the evolution of rock music. And be warned that this museum may be too mature for some youngsters. The second film includes segments showing Madonna's sexually explicit stage antics, and an Alice Cooper exhibit includes a decapitated head that looks just like Alice. Daily 10–5:30, Wed 10–9. $14.95 adults, $11.50 seniors 55 and older and children ages 4 to 11. Museum members free. ♿ (Downtown Cleveland)

STEAMSHIP WILLIAM G. MATHER MUSEUM
1001 E. Ninth St. Pier
Cleveland
216/574-6262
Open May through October, the *Mather* is the former flagship of the Cleveland Cliffs Steamship Company's line of ore freighters. Now docked northeast of the Rock and Roll Hall of Fame and Museum, the 618-foot-long ship was built in 1925 and hauled millions of tons of iron ore, grain, stone, and coal for 55 years. Tours take you through the huge cargo holds, the crew's quarters, officers' quarters, pilot house, and engine room. You can see the elegant dining room and staterooms where the owners and wealthy passengers stayed. $5 adults, $4 seniors, $3 students 5 to 18. ♿ (Downtown Cleveland)

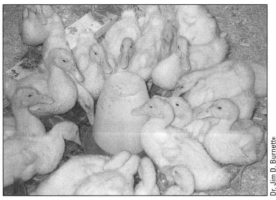

Dr. Jim D. Burnette

7

KIDS' STUFF

Cleveland is a family-oriented city with activities for all age groups. Because of the changes in seasons, the city has as many indoor activities as outdoor, and many facilities combine both. Bring comfy clothes and leave the dressy duds at home. Especially with youngsters, sightseeing is more fun in shorts, jeans, and sweats.

ANIMALS AND THE GREAT OUTDOORS

BURNETTE'S FARM AND EDUCATIONAL CENTER
6940 Columbia Rd.
Olmsted Township
216/235-4050

Former teacher Jim Burnette created this one-of-a-kind, nonprofit farm where kids can feed, pet, and learn about the one thousand farm animals who live here. Burnette is a modern-day Dr. Doolittle who takes in orphaned or injured animals from the wild and raises everything from Barbary apes to armadillos. His two-hour tours are a combination petting zoo and open-air science class. You can

bring fresh fruit, vegetables, or bread to feed the animals or buy food at the farm to help pay for the animals' up-keep. Burnette is always looking for volunteers to help tend the animals and gardens. Reservations recommended. $5 adults, $4 kids, infants free. Tue–Sat 10–11 and 2–3, Sun 2–3. (West Cleveland)

CLEVELAND METROPARKS ZOO AND RAINFOREST
3900 Wildlife Way
Cleveland
216/661-6500

Visiting the zoo is like a whirlwind tour of the world. The African Plains area has the largest herd of Masai giraffes in the country, as well as

Chilly Thrills

You can have fun sledding in Cleveland even if there is no snow on the ground. Cleveland Metroparks has two refrigerated toboggan chutes at the Chalet Recreation Area in Mill Stream Run Reservation. From November through February, you can bundle up in warm clothes and zoom down the 1,000-foot hill. Afterward, warm up by the huge stone fireplaces in the lodge and sip hot cocoa. For more inforamtion, call 440/572-9990.

antelopes, zebras, lions, and birds. The rhinoceroses and cheetahs live peacefully in the same habitat. Monkey Island is home to the graceful black Colobus monkeys with their flowing manes of white hair.

Cold-weather animals live in the Northern Trek area: polar bears, brown bears, sea lions, harbor seals, and Bactrian camels. The newest exhibit in the Northern Trek area is Wolf Wilderness. The wolf pack shares this northern forest habitat with bald eagles, beavers, turtles, and fish.

Before you visit, put on comfortable shoes: the Zoo covers 165 acres of woods and plains, and the 3,300 animals live in roomy habitats. Free

Zootrams carry you from one area to another, but if you want to see all the animals, you will still do a lot of walking. Take a break in one of the rest, picnic, or play areas.

Three major rainforests from Africa, Asia, and the Americas are represented at the RainForest at Cleveland Metroparks Zoo. This steamy, indoor tropical jungle is home to 600 animals and 10,000 plants. Your tour begins at a 25-foot waterfall and winds through dense foliage, a scientist's hut, and a walk-through aviary of South American tapirs, capybara, giant anteaters, porcupines, and sloths. On down the path are natural displays where ocelots, clouded leopards, and a fishing cat live.

T i P

At the zoo, be sure to spend time with the gorillas in the Primate, Cat, and Aquatics building. Watch the three "bachelor" adults: Brooks, Bebac, and Mokolo. "It's like a fraternity house up there," says the zoo's Sue Allen.

Tree shrews and Francois' langurs live in the two-story tree habitat. The orangutans live in a domed habitat bathed in sunshine. On the lower level, fruit bats munch in the treetops. Every 12 minutes, a tropical rainstorm blows through a large exhibit, complete with simulated thunder, lightning, wind, and rain.

Hundreds of rain-forest insects are shown, including leaf-cutting ants, hissing cockroaches, and walking sticks. Steps lead down to an eye-to-eye view of two mammoth crocodiles. But the scariest exhibits in the RainForest are those that explain just how quickly the rain forests are being destroyed. Zoo open daily 9–5; extended hours in summer. Rain-Forest open daily 10–5, Wed 10–9; extended hours in summer. $7 adults, $4 ages 2 to 11. Free parking. ♿ (West Cleveland)

Lake Farmpark

Sanford Gross/Lake Farmpark

EDGEWATER PARK
6700 Memorial Shoreway
Cleveland

A great place to run, play, and enjoy the Lake Erie shoreline is Edgewater Park, just west of downtown. Families love to play on the sandy, 900-foot-long beach and go swimming in the lake. A lifeguard is on duty from noon to dusk in the summer. Be sure to bring a picnic lunch and enjoy your stay in this 100-acre park. (West Cleveland)

LAKE FARMPARK
8800 Chardon Rd.
Kirtland
440/256-2122 or
800/366-3276

About 25 miles southeast of Cleveland in Kirtland, this 235-acre former Arabian horse farm is owned and operated by Lake Metroparks of Lake County. It is now a working farm with a mission: to help people of all ages become more aware of how our food supply is created. To make the learning fun and entertaining, the farm uses hands-on, interactive exhibits and programs. The Farmpark's Visitor's Center, shaped like a barn, has four exhibit areas, a theater, gift shop, restaurant, and offices. One of the most popular attractions in the Visitors Center is the Milking Parlor, where guests are invited to hand-milk the cows. Skeggs Arena shelters many of the farm's horses and houses an indoor facility for special events. More than 50 breeds of farm animals, including endangered breeds, live here. There is a plant science center, an orchard, and fields where crops are planted and harvested. The farm also has a year-round schedule of festivals and shows. Daily 9–5. Closed Mon in Jan, Feb, and Mar. $6 ages 12 to 64, $5 seniors 65 and older, $4 ages 2 to 11. ♿ (East Cleveland)

MUSEUMS

CRAWFORD AUTO-AVIATION MUSEUM
Western Reserve Historical Society
10825 East Blvd.
Cleveland
216/721-5722

From 1896 to 1932, Cleveland was a center of the automobile industry, home to some 80 different automakers. Cleveland pilot Frederick Crawford collected many rare cars, as well as early aircraft. He donated his collection of 150 cars, airplanes, and bikes to the Western Reserve Historical Society, and today the collection is displayed in a huge underground showroom. You can even see the specially equipped limousine used by Presidents Johnson, Nixon, Ford, and Carter. The windows have half-inch-thick bulletproof glass. Mon–Sat 10–5, Sun 12–5. $6.50 adults, $5.50 seniors, $4.50 ages 6 to 12. (University Circle)

GREAT LAKES SCIENCE CENTER
North Coast Harbor
Cleveland
216/694-2000

This museum was created for kids who love science experiments. Hands-on demonstration stations teach them about everything from tornadoes to electrical storms. There are 300 interactive exhibits on three floors. The Omnimax Theater is housed in a dome six stories high. Its screen extends around the audience to create a wraparound film experience. Shows sell out quickly on weekends and holidays, so arrive early or order tickets through Ticketmaster at 216/241-5555 Daily 9:30–5:30. Admission to either the museum or the Omnimax: $7.75 adults, $5.25 ages 3 to 17. Combination admission: $10.95 adults, $7.75 ages 3 to 17. (Downtown Cleveland)

NASA-LEWIS RESEARCH CENTER VISITOR'S CENTER
21000 Brookpark Rd.
Cleveland
216/433-2001

Ohio is home to more astronauts than any other state—21. You can see their pictures at the Lewis Research Center Visitor's Center. You can also see *Sojourner*, a life-size model of the Mars *Pathfinder*'s roving robot. Three of the experiments on the robot were developed at Lewis Research Center. The *Apollo Skylab 3* command module (the actual scorched spacecraft) is also on display. You can learn about space by wandering through the museum exhibits, then watching audiovisual programs in the auditorium. Weekday tours can be arranged in advance. Mon–Fri 9–4, Sat 10–3, Sun 1–5, holidays 10–3. Free. ♿ (South Cleveland)

RAINBOW CHILDREN'S MUSEUM & TRW'S EARLY LEARNING CENTER
10730 Euclid Ave.
Cleveland
216/791-KIDS (5437)

Rainbow Children's Museum & TRW's Early Learning Center invite your family to discover the world through play. The museum's attractions are designed to engage and provide a fun and rewarding hands-on adventure that will capture imaginations time and time again. Daily programs and intriguing activites are provided for children of all ages. Daily 10–5. $6 adults, $4.50 seniors 65 and up, $4 ages 18 months to 15 years, members free. ♿ (University Circle)

TRIVIA

Check out the largest tomato plant on earth, or at least a replica of one. At Lake Farmpark, there is an enormous exhibit of a tomato plant with 12-foot leaves, 6-foot tomatoes, and vines as thick as your waist. The interactive exhibit explores the life processes of plants and food production. To make it more realistic, the creators of the exhibit threw in a giant tomato hornworm.

STEAMSHIP WILLIAM G. MATHER MUSEUM
1001 E. Ninth St. Pier
Cleveland
216/574-6262
For 55 years, the *William G. Mather* was a working steamship that hauled iron ore, grain, stone, and coal on the Great Lakes. Today the ship is a floating museum. This is one big ship: 618 feet, longer than two football fields from end to end. Tours take you through the enormous cargo holds, the engine room, and the crew's quarters. You can also see the elegant dining room and staterooms where the wealthy stayed when they traveled on the ship. The museum deck is wheelchair accessible but the rest of the tour is not. Memorial Day–Labor Day daily 10–5, Sun noon–5. May, Sept, Oct weekends only. (Downtown Cleveland)

USS COD
1089 E. Ninth St.
Cleveland
216/566-8770
During World War II, the USS *Cod* was one of 200 submarines in the United States Navy. In 1959 the *Cod* came to the Naval Reserve station in Cleveland to provide submarine training. In 1976 locals saved the *Cod* from the scrap heap and started giving tours of the sub. Unlike other submarines, the *Cod* looks just the way it did during the Second World War. You can climb through the same hatchways and up the same ladders that the sailors used. The tour guides are all sailors who served on submarines during the war and can answer all of your questions. May 1–Sep 30 daily 10-5. $4 adults, $2 students grades K–12. (Downtown Cleveland)

THEME PARKS

BROOKPARK FUN AND GAMES EMPORIUM
6770 Brookpark Rd.
Cleveland
216/351-1910
Brookpark offers indoor and outdoor activities for year-round fun. The outside fun consists of two 18-hole miniature golf courses, go-karts, and a batting cage. The indoor fun comes from a video arcade, skeeball machines, and a climbing room for kids under 4.5 feet tall. A small collection of indoor kiddie rides includes a horse, motorcycle, and boat. (South Cleveland)

DISCOVERY ZONE
**Golden Gate Shopping Center
6420 Mayfield Rd.
Cleveland
440/461-8887**

Discovery Zone is a year-round activity center that is especially wonderful in foul weather. The kids climb through a giant, padded, multistoried maze, complete with slides and netting. Mon–Thur 10–8, Fri and Sat 10–9, Sun 11–7. $7.99 for kids 38 inches and taller, $4.99 under 38 inches tall, adults free. Also at Great Lakes Mall, 7601 W. Ridgewood Dr., Parma, 440/842-3866. ♿ (East Cleveland)

GOODTIMES
**33777 Chester Rd.
Cleveland
216/236-6600 or 216/236-6601**

From May through September, this family fun center has bumper boats, bumper cars, race cars (designed for parent and tot), mini-golf, a video arcade, and batting cages. Free admission. Packages start at $6.50 for

I-X Center Indoor Amusement Park

© 1996 Jonathan Wayne

individual ride tickets. Hours vary throughout the season—call ahead. (West Cleveland)

I-X CENTER INDOOR AMUSEMENT PARK
**6200 Riverside Dr. (west of Hopkins Airport)
216/676-6000**

This former 20-acre tank factory is now a huge convention center. But for six weeks a year in April and May, the I-X Center becomes a huge indoor amusement park with more than 150 rides, games, shows, and special events. A permanent fixture is a 10-story Ferris wheel, the world's tallest. The top of the wheel is covered by a glass-enclosed atrium that allows riders at the top to see the airport and the city beyond. The mini-golf, video arcade, and roller coaster are popular attractions. The younger set can stay busy with kiddie rides and a petting zoo. ♿ (South Cleveland)

MEMPHIS KIDDIE PARK
**10340 Memphis Ave.
Brooklyn
216/941-5995**

In operation since 1952, Memphis Kiddie Park is a charming place to take young ones for a fun day at a reasonable price. The park has 11 rides, most of them for youngsters ages one to eight. Older kids and adults can enjoy the Little Dipper roller coaster (which moves at a good clip), the train, and the carousel. The best part: Admission is free, so you pay only for the rides. There is a reasonably priced refreshment stand and an 18-hole mini-golf course. Tickets: 85 cents each, 10 for $7.50, 25 for $14. Miniature golf course: $3.75 adults, $3.25 ages 6 to 11, 5

Tower City

and under free with an adult. ♿ (South Cleveland)

SWINGS 'N' THINGS FAMILY FUN PARK
8501 Stearns Rd.
Olmsted Township
440/235-4420

The largest family fun center in Ohio has a giant game room, go-carts, bumper boats, and batting cages. Two 18-hole miniature golf courses have clubs sized just right for kids. Mid-Mar–mid-Oct Sun–Thur 11–11, Fri and Sat 11–midnight. Prices vary. ♿ (West Cleveland)

TROLLEYVILLE U.S.A.
7100 Columbia Rd.
Olmsted Township
440/235-4725

Trolley lovers can see trolleys from all over the world here. You can ride a restored trolley on the park's railroad tracks and enjoy a picnic lunch or snack. May–Nov Wed and Fri 10–3, Sat, Sun, and holidays noon–5. $4 adults, $2 ages 3 to 11. ♿ (West Cleveland)

STORES KIDS LOVE

THE GALLERIA AT ERIEVIEW
E. Ninth St. and St. Clair Ave.
Cleveland
216/621-9999

This is a great place to let the older kids browse through the music store, bookstore, and smaller boutiques filled with gadgets and Cleveland souvenirs. Hometown shops include the Cleveland Indians Team Shop and Malley's Chocolates. The food court has offerings for all ages, outdoor patio seating, and plenty of indoor seating. ♿ (Downtown Cleveland)

TOWER CITY
50 Public Square
Cleveland
216/771-0033

Kids love this downtown indoor shopping plaza because it has some recognizable favorites: a Disney store and a Warner Brothers store. Other attractions include sports memorabilia shops, music stores, several kids' clothes stores, movie theaters, a Nature Company store with ecologically oriented games and puzzles, and a gigantic food court of bottom-feeder junk food and higher-up-the-food-chain eateries. On warm days, take your food tray to one of the balconies that overlooks the Cuyahoga River and watch the boats maneuver around Collision Bend while you dine. You can ride the Rapid to Tower City (or park in the Tower City lot on West Huron Road). The Avenue is located one level above the rapid terminal. ♿ (Downtown Cleveland)

(ETHNIC) RESTAURANTS KIDS LOVE

by Laura Taxel, author of *Cleveland Ethnic Eats*

BALATON RESTAURANT
13133 Shaker Square
Cleveland
216/921-9691
This is Cleveland's oldest Hungarian restaurant. Everything is home-made, from the *Becsi-Szelet* (thin, boneless breaded veal cutlet), goulash, and stuffed cabbage, to the strudel, *palacsinta* (crepe), and *dobos* torte (an eight-layer cake). (East Cleveland)

FANNY'S
3539 E. 156th St.
Cleveland
216/531-1231
Slovenian specialties such as *imuk* (a stew), beef goulash served over spaetzles, and *ajmont* soup (chicken soup made Slovenian style with a dash of vinegar), as well as home-

cooked basics for the less adventur-ous. (East Cleveland)

FRANKIE'S ITALIAN CUISINE
4641 Great Northern Blvd.
Cleveland
216/734-8646
The casual atmosphere and irre-sistible Italian food in generous quan-tities will appeal to kids. The garlic bread is wonderful, as are the sauce, meatballs, lasagna, and pizza. Also at 25930 Detroit Rd., Westlake, 216/892-0064. (West Cleveland)

HOFBRAU HAUS
1400 E. 55th St.
Cleveland
216/881-7773
All-you-can-eat, self-serve buffet of schnitzel, potato pancakes, *rouladen* (thin slices of beef rolled around a stuffing), sauerbraten, Koenigsburger *klops* (meatballs), and strudel, plus standard American dishes. Kids love it. (East Cleveland)

MAMA SANTA'S
12305 Mayfield Rd.
Cleveland
216/231-9567
Mama Santa's serves Sicilian-style pizza baked to order and homemade pasta for families. It is located near University Circle museums and attractions and offers an extremely kid-friendly environment with comfy booths. (East Cleveland)

MAX'S DELI
19337 Detroit Rd.
Rocky River
216/356-2226
Max is a New York–style deli with such favorites as corned beef on rye, blintzes, potato pancakes, chopped liver, salads, vegetarian sandwiches,

and chicken soup with matzo balls. (West Cleveland)

NUEVO ACAPULCO
24409 Lorain Rd.
North Olmsted
216/734-3100
Near the Great Northern Mall, this place sells American hamburgers, steaks, and chicken for those who would rather not come face to face with *camarones a la diabla* (prawns and mushrooms in a spicy red sauce). (West Cleveland)

PARMA PIEROGIES
Parmatown Plaza, 7707 W.
Ridgewood Dr.
Cleveland
216/888-1200
If you want your kids to eat more pierogies and fewer hamburgers, take them to Parma Pierogies when the restaurant's mascot, Pingo the Flamingo, makes an appearance. Kids get to say hello to Pingo and shake his pink wing. This is Polish cooking in a fast-food setting.

Plenty of booster seats and high-chairs. (South Cleveland)

SEOUL HOT POT & DE ANGELO'S PIZZA
3709 Payne Ave.
Cleveland
216/881-1221
This Korean/pizza restaurant seats only 40, but it's the only place you can get a meatball sub with *jaey-ook bokum* (marinated pork) and *twikim mandu* (fried dumpling). The exterior is rough, but the interior is simple but pleasant. (East Cleveland)

SFORZO'S ITALIAN FAMILY RESTAURANT
5517 Memphis Ave.
Cleveland
216/351-3703
Locals come from all over Cleveland for Sforzo's pasta, veal, and chicken dinners. Daily specials are sublime. Some American-style entrées and sandwiches. Half-orders are available for many dishes. (West Cleveland)

James Blank/Nu-Vista Prints

8

PARKS AND GARDENS

The people of Greater Cleveland picnic, fish, hike, bike, boat, and just plain relax more than 40 million times a year in Cleveland Metroparks. If that sounds a bit crowded, don't worry—the Park District has more than 19,000 acres.

In 1902, a visionary named William Stinchcomb was appointed chief engineer for the city's parks department. He mapped out a plan to buy the ravines, gullies, and other land considered worthless for farming or building. Those purchases today comprise the most pristine and beautiful valleys, gorges, and riverways in northeast Ohio.

During the Depression, Stinchcomb hired thousands of people through the Civilian Conservation Corps and the Public Works Administration. These workers made the park accessible to its citizens by building trails, roads, picnic shelters, bridges, and ballfields.

"The Emerald Necklace," as it is known today, encircles the Cleveland area like a precious string of jewels. Beginning in the west on Lake Erie, Cleveland Metroparks follows the Rocky River south to Strongsville, turns east to the Cuyahoga River in Brecksville, follows Tinkers Creek to Bedford, and then heads north along the Chagrin River valley to Lake Erie.

The parks contain 60 miles of paved all-purpose trails for cycling, walking, running, and in-line skating. There are nearly 82 miles of unpaved bridle trails. There are eight physical fitness trails with 18 exercise stations over a 1.5-mile path. Each of the 15 reservations in Cleveland Metroparks has trails designated exclusively for hiking.

During his four decades of public service, Stinchcomb was also responsible for preventing the city from selling $30 million of Lake Erie coastline to the railroads. Today some of that coastline has become the Cleveland Lakefront State Park, a series of beaches, boat launches, and fishing and picnic areas. Both city and state park admission are free.

Holden Arboretum

Harvard University was mining magnate Albert Fairchild Holden's first choice when he decided to give some of his money away. Luckily for Cleveland, Holden's sister Roberta convinced him that his city needed an arboretum. In fact, Roberta and her husband donated the first 100 acres of the project in Kirtland Township. In typical Cleveland noblesse fashion, wealthy donors, corporations, and foundations pitched in to create a 3,100-acre expanse of gardens, woods, fields, ravines, and hiking trails.

CLEVELAND METROPARKS

Cleveland Metroparks are open from 6 to 11 every day of the year. The four nature centers are open from 9:30 to 5 every day except Thanksgiving, Christmas, and New Year's Day. For more information, call Cleveland Metroparks at 216/351-6300, or visit the Cleveland Metroparks Web site at www.clemetparks.com.

BEDFORD RESERVATION
**Gorge Pkwy. between
Ebgert and Broadway
Cleveland
216/351-6300**
Over the last few thousand years, Tinkers Creek has cut a dramatic gorge through this valley. The vista, designated as a National Natural Landmark, is best enjoyed from the Tinkers Creek Gorge Scenic Overlook. This reservation is also home to the 18-hole and short nine par 3 Shawnee Hills Golf Courses, Bridal Veil Falls, and six picnic areas. The all-purpose trail running through this reservation serves as a middle link between Brecksville and South Chagrin reservations. (South Cleveland)

BIG CREEK RESERVATION
**Big Creek Pkwy.
Middleburgh Heights
216/351-6300**
A wildlife corridor that runs parallel to Pearl Road, this park has an all-purpose trail, three picnic areas with grills, and Lake Isaac Waterfowl Sanctuary, a "glacial pothole" created thousands of years ago and now a popular rest area for migratory waterfowl. During winter evenings, there is illuminated sledding at the Memphis Picnic Area. (South Cleveland)

BRADLEY WOODS RESERVATION
**Bradley Rd. south of
Center Ridge Rd.
North Olmsted and Westlake
216/351-6300**
More than 50 years ago, this Berea sandstone quarry provided fine-grade sandstone for grindstones and building stones. The remaining big hole is now Bunns Lake. In summer, visitors enjoy fishing, hiking trails, a picnic

shelter, and a small playground. In winter, people go cross-country skiing and ice fishing. The reservation also has a wildlife habitat that is home to a large population of deer. (West Cleveland)

BRECKSVILLE RESERVATION
Chippewa Creek Dr. and Valley Pkwy.
Brecksville
216/351-6300
This reservation has everything from horse stables and the Sleepy Hollow Golf Course to a nature center and the Squire Rich Home and Museum, managed by the Brecksville Historical Society. This park has eight picnic areas and an extensive system of trails including the Buckeye Trail, which crosses the state. (South Cleveland)

EUCLID CREEK RESERVATION
Euclid Creek Pkwy. south of Euclid Ave.
Cleveland
216/351-6300
The southern part of the reservation is Bluestone, site of a town that flourished in the late 1800s and early 1900s. The area's blue-gray siltstone was once quarried for sidewalks, and visitors can still see examples in the Quarry Picnic Area. The reservation has an all-purpose trail, cross-country ski trails, six picnic areas, ballfields, and sledding at the Kelly Picnic Area. (East Cleveland)

GARFIELD PARK RESERVATION
Garfield Park Dr. between Broadway and Turney
Garfield Heights
216/351-6300
Officially created as Newburg Park by the City of Cleveland in 1895, this is one of the smaller parks in the Emerald Necklace. But it has much to offer, from four picnic areas to the songbird woodlands of the Iron Spring Wildlife Preserve. Garfield Park Nature Center is home to live turtles, fish, toads, frogs, snakes, and even a working beehive. Naturalists lead children's programs of hikes, crafts, and stories for three groups spanning ages 3 to 10. (East Cleveland)

A Castle in Cleveland

Squire's Castle in the North Chagrin Reservation is the brick and stone remains of a lodge built in the 1890s by Cleveland oil pioneer Fergus B. Squire (1850–1932), vice president and general manager of Standard Oil. The castle was built as a gatekeeper's lodge on 525 acres that Squire planned to use for his estate. He never built the large country house that was to go behind the lodge, but he used the lodge itself as a weekend retreat. Today it is a shelter house and picnic area.

HINCKLEY RESERVATION
off Bellus and State Rds.
Cleveland
216/351-6300

Swimming is permitted in Hinckley Reservation's 90-acre lake spillway pool. There is also a concession stand and a boathouse that rents canoes, electric motor boats, and kayaks from April to November. A scenic hiking path circles the lake. But the reason crowds of people visit Hinckley Lake in the middle of March is to witness the return of the Hinckley buzzards. On those crisp, early-spring Buzzard Sunday mornings, humans visitors bearing binoculars turn out for the annual pancake breakfast and a glimpse of the turkey buzzards returning to Buzzard Roost. A splendid time is had by all the scavengers, with or without feathers. (South Cleveland)

HUNTINGTON RESERVATION
Porter Creek Dr. off Lake Rd.
Bay Village
216/351-6300

Euclid Beach, p. 123

James Blank/Nu-Vista Prints

Named for Cleveland industrialist and previous owner John Huntington, the reservation still includes the Huntington Water Tower, which he built to pump water from Lake Erie for his vineyards. The reservation offers a sandy beach for swimming in Lake Erie, picnic tables and grills, a small playground, a bathhouse, and rest-rooms. Huntington is also home to three Cleveland Metroparks affiliates: BayCrafters, Lake Erie Nature and Science Center, and Huntington Playhouse. (West Cleveland)

MILL STREAM RUN RESERVATION
Valley Pkwy. between Bagley and
Drake Rds.
Cleveland
216/351-6300

This reservation has nine picnic areas and an all-purpose trail running through it. The nearby Chalet Recreation Area is available for group rental. Hayrides for groups are available year-round and for individuals on Saturday nights and Sunday afternoons in October. Twin ice toboggan chutes add winter excitement.

Former sandstone quarries are now the Baldwin and Wallace Lakes, which offer non-motorized boating, fishing, and swimming. Paddleboats are for rent at Wallace Lake concession area from Memorial Day through Labor Day. On winter evenings, visitors can enjoy lighted ice skating on frozen Wallace Lake and lighted sledding at the Pawpaw Picnic Area. (South Cleveland)

NORTH CHAGRIN RESERVATION
Buttermilk Falls Pkwy.
Cleveland
216/351-6300

Euclid Beach

Located eight miles from Public Square, Euclid Beach was, in its heyday, one of the nation's best-known amusement parks. Built by a group of investors in 1894, the park was patterned after New York City's famous Coney Island. In those days the "amusements" consisted of beer gardens, freak shows, and gambling. In 1901, the Humphrey family took over the park with a five-year lease and a new perspective on amusement, expressed by their slogan: "Nothing to depress or demoralize."

The Humphreys expanded the swimming and beach area, added more wholesome entertainment, and cut out the beer concessions. Families responded in droves, and the park remained popular through the first half of this century. But racial discrimination against blacks, dating back to the late 1800s, eventually fomented the Euclid Beach Park Riot in 1946. This prompted city legislation revoking an amusement park's license if it practiced racial discrimination. By the mid-1960s, other negative forces had taken their toll. A polluted lake, changing lifestyles, and rising operational costs also contributed to a decline in attendance. The park closed on September 28, 1969. All that remains is the carved archway entrance to the park, declared a historic Cleveland landmark in 1973.

This reservation is an interesting mix of natural and artificial wonders. The natural wonders have such picturesque names as Buttermilk Falls, Oxbow Lagoon, and Strawberry Pond.

Manakiki Golf Course, originally the estate of Cleveland industrialist Howard Hanna, uses the Hanna mansion as its clubhouse. North Chagrin Nature Center has an indoor play area with environmental games and puzzles. The kids will enjoy the live snake and turtle exhibits. You can rent Rollerblades during summer. (East Cleveland)

OHIO & ERIE CANAL RESERVATION
E. 49th St.
Cuyahoga Heights
216/351-6300
This new, 315-acre reservation offers many trails, including a 4.5-mile

Ten Unusual Places to Get Married in Cleveland

by Cleveland writer Melanie Payne

1. Cleveland Metroparks Zoo and RainForest, 216/661-6500. Fees range from $500 (ceremony only) to $3,000 and up (including roooption).

2. Wade Hall, Cleveland Metroparks Zoo, 216/661-6500. Built in 1884 and restored as a Victorian-style ice cream shop, Wade Hall provides a unique setting for a wedding.

3. Crawford Auto-Aviation Museum, 216/721-5722. Get married among the museum's collection of vintage automobiles or in the Reinberger Gallery.

4. Soldiers and Sailors Monument, Public Square, 216/932-6300. Because this is a memorial, only dignified ceremonies, without alcohol, are allowed. Throwing rice, confetti, or birdseed is prohibited.

5. Hale Farm & Village, 800/589-9703. For a wedding with an historical theme, choose the Meeting House (circa 1850). The idyllic chapel is perfect for a Victorian country wedding. The modern gatehouse is available for receptions.

6. Cultural Gardens, Rockefeller Park, 216/664-2484. Of the 21 cultural gardens, most popular for weddings is the Italian Cultural Gardens. All gardens are available for a $5 permit fee. City crews spruce up the site the day before the ceremony.

7. Wildwood Cultural Center, 216/942-8796. Wedding parties can use the 1908 Wildwood Mansion (the earliest example of English Tudor Revival style in northeast Ohio) and 34 acres of grounds for a seven-hour period.

8. Music Mound, Mill Stream Run Reservation, 216/351-6300. Bridal parties can decorate the area to their liking or just enjoy its natural beauty.

9. Bridal Veil Falls, Bedford Reservation, 216/351-6300. Features a deck overlooking cascading water.

10. Squire's Castle, North Chagrin Reservation, 216/351-6300. Medieval romance in the restored ruins of a millionaire's home.

Hold on Tight!

The most thrill-packed moments in Cleveland occur from November through February (no snow necessary) when brave souls ride the two 1,000-foot twin refrigerated toboggan chutes at the Chalet Recreation Area in Mill Stream Run Reservation. After the ride, tobogganers may warm up in front of the two huge stone fireplaces in the nearby lodge. Call 440/572-9990 for more information.

stretch of the 160-year-old Ohio & Erie Canal. The reservation features picnic shelters, observation platforms, interactive exhibits, fishing opportunities, and wildlife management areas. A 9,000-square-foot visitor center tells the history of the canal. The reservation is connected to the 20-mile Towpath Trail in the Cuyahoga Valley National Recreation Area and Cleveland Metroparks' five-mile Brookside Trail. The park is part of the Ohio & Erie Canal Corridor, which runs along the 87-mile route of the original canal, from Cleveland to the tiny town of Zoar. (Downtown)

ROCKY RIVER RESERVATION
2400 Valley Pkwy.
North Olmsted
216/351-6300
This reservation follows the meandering Rocky River through Berea, Brook Park, Cleveland, Fairview Park, Lakewood, North Olmsted, Olmsted Township, and (where else?) Rocky River. A hiking trail runs the length of the reservation and there's much to see along the way. Cleveland Metroparks founder

William Stinchcomb's 30-foot memorial tower sits atop a scenic overlook, befitting the man who created the Emerald Necklace. There are nine picnic areas and three golf courses in Rocky River Reservation: Little Met, Big Met, and Mastick Woods. The Emerald Necklace Marina at 1500 Scenic Park Drive features a boat launch and a bait-and-tackle refreshments/catering facility. Frostville Museum, located on Cedar Point Road west of Valley Parkway, is a small settlement circa 1819 that includes a one-room cabin and a general store. Throughout the year, the museum hosts Civil War reenactments, Friday night square dances, and a pioneer Christmas celebration. (West Cleveland, South Cleveland)

SOUTH CHAGRIN RESERVATION
Sulpher Springs Dr.
Cleveland
216/351-6300
Artist Henry Church Jr. was a Cleveland blacksmith in the late 1800s. But he never let his day job get in the way of his creative interests: playing

bass viola and horn in a local orchestra and sculpting in metal and stone. His bas-relief sandstone carvings are this reservation's centerpiece. They include a Native American woman surrounded by a snake, a panther, and a quiver of arrows. The South Chagrin Reservation also features an arboretum, polo fields, and the Look About Lodge, a special outdoor education facility with programs and activities. (East Cleveland, South Cleveland)

OTHER PARKS AND GARDENS

CLEVELAND BOTANIC GARDEN
11030 East Blvd.
Cleveland
216/721-1600
Founded in 1930, this is the oldest civic garden in the country. Its 7.5 acres are filled with 3,000 plant and shrub specimens. A large garden library has a special section for youngsters and story times for preschoolers. Craft and garden classes are available for children

ages three and older. School-age children can participate in a spring gardening program. Register for the annual kids' holiday events on Valentine's Day, Easter, and during the Christmas holiday. Outdoor hours: Dawn–dusk. Indoor hours: Mon–Fri 9–5, Sat 12–5, Sun 1–5. Free. (University Circle)

CLEVELAND LAKEFRONT STATE PARK
8701 Lakeshore Blvd. NE
(park office)
Cleveland
This state park is actually a total of 476 acres that originally hosted a Catholic girls' school and one of the nation's best-known amusement parks. (Downtown Cleveland)

EAST 55TH STREET MARINA
Cleveland Memorial Shoreway
Cleveland
Traveling east on the East Shoreway, the first park in the Lakefront State Park group is the 55th Street Marina, where 335 seasonal docks have fresh water and electric hookups. A concession stand serves the marina and

Solar System Walk

The Rocky River Reservation is home to the three-quarter-mile Solar System Walk. To give people a sense of how big the universe is, this educational trail was developed by Cleveland Metroparks with NASA Lewis Research Center and support from TRW. Signs posted along the trail mark the sun and each of the planets' average distance from the sun. One foot equals one million miles! Another solar system walk is located at Trolley Turn Picnic Area in the Garfield Park Reservation.

Hang gliding at Edgewater Park

the 1,200-foot fishing platform. (East Cleveland)

EDGEWATER PARK
6700 Memorial Shoreway
Cleveland

This 100-acre park has a 900-foot-long sandy beach for swimming, with a lifeguard on duty from noon to dusk. You will also find a fishing pier, a fitness trail, a boat ramp, and a picnic area. One of the best spots from which to view the downtown skyline is in the circle parking lot next to Edgewater Park. This is the only Lakefront State Park situated west of downtown. (West Cleveland)

EUCLID BEACH,
VILLA ANGELA,
AND WILDWOOD PARKS
Lakeshore Blvd.
Cleveland

These three parks are connected by a one-mile all-purpose path for cyclists, walkers, joggers, and Rollerbladers. This ground was once the site of Euclid Beach Park, an amusement park built in 1894. Now Euclid Beach sports old-fashioned light posts and park benches reflecting those days of old. The picnic area above the beach can accommodate 300 to 400 people and is reservable. The park has 650 feet of swimming beach and a scenic observation pier.

Villa Angela Park's name comes from the Catholic girls' school built on this site in 1878. Now the park offers 1,000 feet of beach, a scenic boardwalk, a fitness trail, a bathhouse, and a wheelchair-accessible fishing pier. A bridge connects this park to adjacent Wildwood Park.

Fishing and boating enthusiasts will find much to love about Wildwood Park. Two rock breakwalls jut into the lake, giving shore-fishing enthusiasts access to the summer walleye that populate the central basin of Lake Erie. In the spring, coho salmon anglers try their luck in Euclid Creek, which runs through the park. There is also a six-ramp boat launch. (East Cleveland)

GORDON PARK
Cleveland Memorial Shoreway
Cleveland

Next to the East 55th Street Marina is Gordon Park, with six free public boat launch ramps and a large parking lot to accommodate boat trailers. There is also a picnic area and the state park office. Fishing enthusiasts use the onshore fishing platforms to pull out winter catches of steelhead and salmon, thanks to the warm water discharge from the Cleveland Electric and Illuminating Company. (East Cleveland)

HEADLANDS BEACH
9601 Headlands Rd.
Painesville

Although this park is 28 miles east of downtown, it has no problem attracting visitors. Its mile-long natural sand beach is the largest in the state, and the shallow water is appealing for family swimming. There are changing booths, concession areas, and rest rooms for sunbathers and swimmers. Windsurfers

Holden Arboretum

(and lessons) are available for rent, as are volleyballs, lawn chairs, and umbrellas. Those fishing off the federal breakwall at the east end of the park may be rewarded with smallmouth, largemouth, and rock bass, yellow perch, bluegill, walleye, coho salmon, or carp.

For those less beach-minded, there are three miles of hiking trails and the northern end of the trans-Ohio Buckeye Trail. For naturalists, there is the Headlands Dunes State Nature Preserve, one of the last and best examples of Lake Erie beach and dune ecosystems in Ohio. When the winter chill arrives, fun can still be had at areas designated for sledding, ice skating, and cross-country skiing. (East Cleveland)

HOLDEN ARBORETUM
9500 Sperry Rd.
Cleveland
216/256-1110

The largest arboretum in the United States, this year-round facility east of Cleveland contains a series of paths with signs explaining local plants, animals, and ecosystems. Kids can use a loaner backpack with an audiotape and activity kit to accompany the tour. Tues–Sun 10–5 (open holiday Mon). $2.50 adults, $1.75 seniors with Golden Buckeye Card and children 6 to 12. (East Cleveland)

ROCKEFELLER PARK
GREENHOUSE
750 E. 88th St.
Cleveland
216/66-3103

These greenhouses were built in 1905 on land donated by John D. Rockefeller, who was, at that time, the richest man in the world. The outdoor and indoor collections are beautifully designed and maintained. Outdoors, the Talking Garden for the Blind has recorded explanations of the displays. The Japanese garden is a delightful place, complete with a quaint footbridge. Inside, it is steamy and lush with plants from all over the world. You can see everything from cacti to orchids. Daily 10–4. Free. (University Circle)

© 1996 Jonathan W⹀ne

9

SHOPPING

During the 1970s, shopping downtown was limited to a couple of aging depart-ment stores and some well-hidden specialty shops. Most of the retail business had followed the money to the suburbs. But that was before the rebirth of downtown. Now the difficulty is in finding enough time to browse through all that the area has to offer, from upscale retail enclaves to tiny, family-owned shops. Downtown alone offers three major indoor shopping complexes, one of which was the first enclosed shopping mall built in the United States (in 1890). From antique shops to roasted nut stores, one-of-a-kind shopping odysseys fill the greater Cleveland area.

DOWNTOWN SHOPPING AREAS

THE ARCADE
401 Euclid Ave.
Cleveland
216/621-8500
The Arcade was America's first en-closed shopping mall. Opening on Memorial Day of 1890, it was hailed as an architectural marvel. The five-story arcade has a glass ceil-ing, and the railed balconies are or-nate brass. These days The Arcade is a National Historic Landmark

filled with 35 specialty shops and 20 eateries. You can enter the block-long building from Superior or Euclid Avenues. (Downtown Cleveland)

THE AVENUE AT TOWER CITY
50 Public Square
Cleveland
216/771-0033
Situated in the heart of downtown Cleveland on Public Square, Tower City Center is a visually dazzling retail, dining, and entertainment complex built around Cleveland's

Novelist Toni Morrison earned the Pulitzer Prize in 1987 for her Ohio-based novel *Beloved* and the Nobel Prize for Literature in 1993. Her early years were spent working as a copy editor before she wrote her first novel, *The Bluest Eye*, set in northeast Ohio.

landmark Terminal Tower. A city within a city, The Avenue at Tower City has under one roof both the Ritz-Carlton and Renaissance Cleveland hotels, over 100 shops and services, 16 cafés and eateries, five full-service restaurants, 11 movie theaters, and three parking garages. The stores are covered by an enormous glass dome and graced by a 60-foot fountain. Connected to Gund Arena and Jacobs Field with an indoor walkway, Tower City is the hub of many downtown activities. The Avenue is located one level above the Rapid terminal. (Downtown Cleveland)

THE GALLERIA AT ERIEVIEW
E. Ninth St. and St. Clair Ave.
Cleveland
216/861-4343 or
216/621-9999
This two-story atrium mall shelters a variety of catalog stores, from Eddie Bauer clothes and Brookstone gadgets to Williams-Sonoma kitchenware. Hometown shops include the Cleveland Indians Team Shop and Malley's Chocolates. In addition to an atrium food court with outdoor patio seating, the Galleria has Café Sausalito, which welcomes the lunch and dinner crowd as well as theater patrons from nearby Playhouse Square. (Downtown Cleveland)

THE HALLE BUILDING
1228 Euclid Ave.
Cleveland
216/696-7701
Clevelanders remember Halle's, a downtown department store from 1891 to 1982, as the place where Mr. Jinga-ling (an elf friend of Santa Claus) would listen to children's Christmas requests. Today the Halle Building houses offices, an upscale Chinese restaurant called Lu Cuisine, 10 specialty stores, and eight fast-food eateries. If the outside of the building looks strangely familiar, it should. The white terra cotta facade is often shown on the *Drew Carey*

The Galleria

© 1996 Jonathan Wayne

Show as the Winfred Louder Department Store where Drew works. (Downtown Cleveland)

WEST SIDE MARKET
1995 W. 25th St.
Cleveland
216/664-3386

An open air market makes grocery shopping an adventure. This is the place where everyone from restaurant chefs to ordinary shoppers buys fruits, vegetables, baked goods, meats, and cheeses. It's easy to find; look for the 137-foot copper-domed clock tower on the corner. Take your time wandering through the 180 stands. Smell the wonderful breads. Hear the shouts of the vendors. Then pick out fruits, rolls, deli salads, meats, and cheeses for an impromptu picnic. Weekends can get crowded, but that's just part of the hustle-bustle and charm of the place. The market was built in 1912 and is now a National Historic Landmark. (West Cleveland)

SPECIALTY STORES

Antiques and Art

ANTIQUES ON LORAIN AVENUE
7806 Lorain Ave.
Cleveland
216/281-4432

This antique district includes Lorain Avenue from West 41st Street to West 100th Street. More than 30 shops comprise one of Cleveland's best antique districts. Styles include French, Victorian, Mission, art nouveau, deco, and '50s Modern. You'll find lighting, architectural, glassware, china, silver, pottery, hardware, and collectibles. The association shops also provide picture framing, upholstery, fine fabrics, vintage yard goods, furniture stripping, refinishing, wood carving, antique jewelry repairs, and antique importing from Europe. For more information, call president Kathleen Benco at the association's number above. (West Cleveland)

West Side Market

Jim Baron/The Image Finders

My Favorite Art and Antique Galleries
by Cleveland artist Tom Balbo

In the Murray Hill area:
- *Avante Gallery, 2062 Murray Hill Rd., 216/791-1622*
- *Folkarte Gallery, 2026 Murray Hill Rd., 216/791-8833*
- *Riley Hawk Glass Art Galleries, 2026 Murray Hill Rd., 216/421-1445*
- *Verne Collection of Japanese Art, 2207 Murray Hill Rd., 216/231-8866*

In Larchmere:
- *Shaker Square Antiques, 12733 Larchmere Blvd., 216/231-8804*
- *Sylvia Ullman American Crafts Gallery, 13010 Larchmere Blvd., 216/231-2008*
- *Yoder Conservation, Inc., 12702 Larchmere Blvd., 216/231-7880*

In the Tremont area:
- *Eddie Moved Gallery, 2379 Professor St., 216/621-0262*
- *Safran Studio, 1009 Kenilworth Ave., 216/241-1889*

In various locations:
- *Art at the Powerhouse Gallery, 2000 Sycamore (in the Flats), 216/696-1942*
- *Art Source, 23533 Mercantile Rd., Beachwood, 216/464-0898*
- *The Bonfoey Company, 1710 Euclid Ave., 216/621-0178*
- *Brenda Kroos Gallery, 1360 W. Ninth St., Warehouse District, 216/621-1164*
- *The Brett Mitchell Collection, 28500 Chagrin Blvd., 216/831-8666*
- *Chelsea Galleries, 23225 Mercantile Rd., Beachwood, 216/591-1066*

LARCHMERE BOULEVARD
Cleveland
216/751-9204 (Larchmere Merchants Association)
The Larchmere Boulevard shopping district was founded in the late 1920s. One block north of Shaker Square on the city's east side, the district includes a wealth of antique shops, art galleries, eateries, bookstores, jewelry shops, and craft galleries. The annual Larchmere Boulevard Outdoor Antique show is in June. Special events include an annual two-day auction in March and a Holiday Stroll on Thanksgiving weekend. (East Cleveland)

TOM BALBO GALLERY
Shaker Square, 12801 Buckeye Rd.
Cleveland
216/752-5577
The gallery features ceramics, handmade paperwork, sculpture, and painting. Ask Tom to show you his studio and its claymaking, papermaking, and printmaking facilities. Open by appointment only. (East Cleveland)

WOLF'S
1239 W. Sixth St.
Cleveland
216/575-9653
This auction house and gallery specializes in high-quality fine art, decorations, furnishings, and jewelry. (Downtown Cleveland)

BOOKS, MAGAZINES, AND NEWSSTANDS

CLEVELAND ANTIQUARIAN BOOKS
Shaker Square
13127 Shaker Blvd.
Cleveland
216/561-2665
Quality new, used, and rare books antique bookcases and other library furnishings, historic autographs, and antique maps and artworks are featured here. The store hosts recitals from area choral and music groups. The ambiance is a book-lover's paradise. "It looks like an old English library," says owner William Chrisant. (East Cleveland)

DOUBLEDAY BOOK SHOP
The Avenue at Tower City, 230 Huron Rd. NW
Cleveland
216/621-6880
Located on the Public Square level

T I P

The Galleria Customer Service Center at the East Ninth Street entrance offers free gift wrap and delivery to anywhere in Cuyahoga County. It also sells mall gift certificates and offers a cash-only Ticketmaster outlet. In addition to its parking lots and garages, the Galleria offers valet parking service at its Ninth and 12th Street entrances.

Charles Chestnutt

Cleveland author Charles Chestnutt was a slave prior to the Civil War. After the war, in 1884, he came to Cleveland, studied law, and passed the bar in 1887. But instead of going into practice, Chestnutt founded a legal stenography company. Income from his business allowed him to write, and he was the first African American to gain fame as a professional writer in the United States. He published his first book in 1899.

of The Avenue at Tower City Center, Doubleday Book Shop is a gem of a store. The shop sells an impressive array of Cleveland-related books as well as current fiction and nonfiction. "We carry a broad range of things, even though we're a small store," says manager John Pritchard. His staff is friendy and knowledgeable, and the store offers corporate discounts, will special order books, and handles shipping. (Downtown Cleveland)

NORTH COAST NOSTALGIA
2169 Lee Rd.
Cleveland Heights
216/932-1111
Nostalgia has comic books, sports cards, videos, models, and figures from *Star Wars* to *Star Trek*. Two other suburban locations. (East Cleveland)

CHOCOLATES AND NUTS

CHOCOLATE EMPORIUM
14439 Cedar Rd.
South Euclid
216/382-0140

This specialty confectioner features kosher hand-dipped chocolate and gift baskets. (East Cleveland)

FAROH'S CANDIES
6890 Pearl Rd.
Middleburgh Heights
216/842-4070
After 50 years of candy-making in Cleveland, Faroh's is especially known for its nut mallow (marshmallow and nuts covered in chocolate) and caramel corn. Look for the big candy cane in front of the Middleburgh Heights store. The candy plant is in back. Faroh's has three other suburban locations. (South Cleveland)

LONDON CHOCOLATIER
Hopkins International Airport
5300 Riverside Dr.
Cleveland
216/676-5050
This full-service gourmet candy store in the airport is a great place to pick up an edible souvenir of Cleveland. To find out where to watch the candy being made, see Chapter 13: "Day Trips from Cleveland." (South Cleveland)

Our Favorite Used and Rare Bookstores

By Eric and Eileen Kindig, owners of Garrison House Books, an on-line bookstore (www.abebooks.com) offering out-of-print American history books, children's literature, and general nonfiction.

Bookhounds of any breed, take note! The Cleveland area used- and rare-book scene is alive and well and not to be missed. We especially love the following:

John T. Zubal, Inc., *2969 West 25th Street., 216/241-7640*

When it comes to out-of-print publications, John Zubal is THE MAN. His store may not be in the best neighborhood, but his million-plus titles are so dazzling, who cares? Expect to be a bit taken aback when you walk in the front door. Instead of the usual bookshop backdrop, you'll be greeted by desks, computers, and a phalanx of people busily processing titles. If you're lucky, you'll be greeted by Zubal himself, a friendly, outgoing guy who sits at a desk to your left. He'll ask what you're interested in, then guide you through a maze of hallways to the huge factory space lit by bare bulbs with pull-chains. Be sure to check out the ends of the aisles. If you appreciate great old advertising art, you'll be delighted by the stacked pear crates used to contain the overflow. Zubal's books run the gamut, but he has an especially impressive collection of scholarly topics. In business since 1959, he really knows his stuff—and it shows.

Discount Books, *1127 Euclid Avenue, 216/781-1666*

This store is so great you won't be surprised to find out that it, too, is owned by John Zubal. Here you'll find everything from hypermodern first editions in mint condition to golden oldies—and all for only $3.97 each. Paperbacks are one dollar, and there are specials all the time, such as hardcover business books for a mere two bucks. Manager Bill Kubat says he has 100 categories to choose from. It's no wonder the place thrums and hums with activity. Stay long enough and you're guaranteed to eavesdrop on some truly great book talk! In business since 1993.

Old Erie Street Bookstore, *2128 East Ninth Street, 216/575-0743*

We fell in love with this place, located just one block north of Jacobs Field, the second we saw the garlanded and beribboned moosehead on the wall. So what if it happened to be May! At this charming two-room shop, every day is Christmas. The tone is eclectic—you'll see everything from first-edition Hemingways and Steinbecks in glass cases to shelf after shelf of old and modern titles in a wide variety of areas, especially pop culture, sci-fi, and fantasy. For a visual treat, be sure to to drink in the color and splendor of the leather-bound special editions to the right of the main showroom. Prices on general stock aren't cheap, but they won't knock your socks off either. Climb an old wooden ladder to book heaven and you're practically guaranteed to find a "must have" (or two, or three). In the event that you don't find what you want in stock, the shop offers a search service. As your purchases are being rung up, check out the glass showcases to see a great display of Cleveland Browns and Indians memorabilia. In business since 1976.

Out-of-Print Books, *1873 Prospect Avenue, 216/696-7045*

The store is located across from Cleveland State University's Convocation Center, and owner Donald Kapela really knows Cleveland. He also really knows books. Though he says that a great deal of his business is done by mail, his cozy two-room shop is a browser's delight. Prices are reasonable—on our first visit we found a fat nineteenth-century history title sporting bright blue boards, crisp lettering, and square corners for a mere $5. Of course, many titles have steeper prices, but we were far from scared off.

MALLEY'S CHOCOLATES
Galleria at Erieview,
E. Ninth St. and St. Clair Ave.
Cleveland
216/781-3747

Mike Malley began making chocolates in 1935. Now the company is run by his son William. Malley's is a chocolate lover's paradise. Try the nut mallow (marshmallow and walnuts covered in chocolate), the Bordeaux (Mike Malley's favorite recipe of English toffee dipped in chocolate and rolled in crushed almonds), Billybobs (caramel and pecans covered in chocolate, also known as turtles), and chocolate-covered pretzels. Malley's has 10 other locations in Cleveland. Take the company tour (See Chapter 5: "Sights") and sample a bit of heaven. (Downtown Cleveland)

MORROW NUT HOUSE
144 Public Square
Cleveland
216/621-1069

After a hard day of sightseeing or shopping downtown, stop in for a bag of Morrow's Energy mix: raw nuts, raisins, pepitas, and sunflower seeds. Or try the Stars and Stripes milk chocolate balls, wrapped in patriotic foil. Morrow will put together a $2 bag of your favorite goodies, and there's lots to choose from. (Downtown Cleveland)

PETERSON NUT COMPANY
E. Ninth St. and Carnegie Ave.
Cleveland
216/642-3388

On your way to Jacobs Field for an Indians baseball game, stop at this Cleveland landmark for nuts and candy. (Peterson's supplies the stadium with salted peanuts in the shell.) Do yourself a favor and try the Crunchy Delight, a popular snack mix of nuts, sesame seeds, toasted corn, and honey sesame sticks. Peterson's is open for every Indians home game. (Downtown Cleveland)

SOUVENIRS

CLEVELAND REFLECTIONS
The Avenue at Tower City

It's on the Wall

The long wall of the Peterson Nut Company is decorated with a mural entitled The Birth of Gateway. *This colorful mural depicts nine stages of a peanut shell gradually opening to reveal a baseball and basketball—a reference to the Gateway sports complex across the street, where the Cleveland Indians and Cavaliers play their home games. Cleveland Art Institute student Sarah Hayes won a contest in 1994 to paint her award-winning design. Peterson's then presented the mural to the city of Cleveland.*

TRIVIA

In the 1870s, Cleveland clothing manufacturer Herman Black revolutionized the clothing industry by making the first ready-to-wear clothes in standard sizes.

50 Public Square
Cleveland
216/566-1556
An all-Cleveland and souvenir shop, including Indians and Cavaliers merchandise. (Downtown Cleveland)

DAFFY DAN'S
2102 Superior Ave.
Cleveland
216/621-0030
Back in the early 1970s, Cleveland hippie Daffy Dan began printing T-shirts for rock groups. Today Dan is the undisputed T-shirt king of Cleveland, making and selling T-shirts, mugs, magnets, and even Cleveland snow domes printed with about 200 designs of Cleveland teams and landmarks. He has a store at 148 Euclid Avenue on Public Square, a gift shop in the Holiday Inn Lakeside, and seven suburban locations. (Downtown Cleveland)

THE FLAVOR OF OHIO
28879 Lorain Rd.
North Olmsted
216/779-2400 or 800/755-6466
This all-Ohio food, craft, and gift basket store features many wonderfully offbeat reminders of the North Coast. Edible souvenirs include pasta in the shape of Ohio and a chocolate map of Cleveland. The store is located in a strip shopping center with lots of free parking and easy access to I-480. (West Cleveland)

WHAT A CARD
Galleria at Erieview, E. Ninth St.
and St. Clair Ave.
Cleveland
216/241-5333
A great place to browse through the Cleveland postcards, T-shirts, games, collector spoons, shot glasses, friendship bands, and magnets. (Downtown Cleveland)

SHOPPING MALLS AND CENTERS

BEACHCLIFF MARKET SQUARE
19300 Detroit Rd.
Cleveland
440/333-5074
Honored by the state of Ohio for "innovative readaptation," the vintage 1930s movie theater is now home to more than 20 specialty shops and three restaurants. The square is located just west of the Lakewood border, near the mouth of the Rocky River and the Cleveland Yacht Club. (West Cleveland)

BEACHWOOD PLACE MALL
26300 Cedar
Beachwood
216/464-9460
All the name brands can be found here: Saks Fifth Avenue, Nordstrom, Dillard's, Nine West, Ann Taylor, Speedo, The Gap, Coach, Pottery Barn, and more than 100 other

Five years after The Arcade opened, the glass-ceilinged building was converted into an enormous banquet hall for 2,000 delegates to the national convention of Republican clubs. Among the guests was William McKinley, then Ohio's governor and soon to be the 25th president of the United States.

stores and shops. The mall is located less than one mile west of I-271 in Beachwood. (East Cleveland)

COVENTRY ROAD SHOPS
1600–1800 Coventry Rd.
Cleveland
If you've got an itch to see Cleveland's counterculture shopping district, this is it. Described as "a little Greenwich Village," the Coventry Road shops include one-of-a-kind restaurants, toy stores, and gift, pet, clothing, and crafts shops. (East Cleveland)

ETON COLLECTION
28601 Chagrin Blvd.
Woodmere
216/591-0544
A specialty shopping center with 19 upscale clothing, jewelry, accessory, and home furnishing stores. The center also has hair salons and three restaurants. Eton Collection prides itself on exceptionally personal customer service. It's located one mile east of I-271 on Chagrin Boulevard. (East Cleveland)

GREAT NORTHERN MALL
4954 Great Northern Mall
Cleveland
440/734-6300
This ever-expanding shopping district on Cleveland's west side includes a large enclosed mall and a host of smaller plazas and restaurants. Many of the national and regional chain stores have an outpost here, as do a variety of local specialty shops. (West Cleveland)

LA PLACE FASHION CENTRE
2101 Richmond Rd.
Beachwood
216/831-3198
This upscale retail center offers women's fashions, cookware, bath and body supplies, restaurants, bookstores, and the top two hair salons in the Cleveland area. La Place is located on the southeast corner of the Cedar-Richmonds intersection, one quarter mile west of the Cedar Road exit on I-271. (East Cleveland)

LANDERWOOD PLAZA SHOPPING CENTER
30559 Pinetree Rd.
(Lander Circle)
Pepper Pike
216/831-1455
This is an interesting collection of specialty stores, selling everything from toys and gifts to children's and men's clothing. The emphasis is on high-quality, unusual merchandise. Landerwood is two miles east of I-271 on Chagrin Boulevard at Lander Circle. (East Cleveland)

PARMATOWN MALL
7899 W. Ridgewood Dr.
Cleveland
216/885-2090

Parmatown Mall is home to more than 150 specialty stores and restaurants, including a food court. Department stores are JCPenney, Dillards, and Kaufmann's. The mall is conveniently located three miles south of the I-480 Ridge Road exit. (South Cleveland)

PAVILION MALL
24055 Chagrin Blvd.
Cleveland
216/292-7765

About one mile west of I-271 in Beachwood, Pavilion Mall has a collection of shops including home decorating and clothing stores. Eating spots include Szechwan House Chinese Cuisine, Steve's Ice Cream, and two full-service restaurants, Ruby Tuesday and Houlihan's. (East Cleveland)

RANDALL PARK MALL
Emery and Northfield Rds.
Cleveland
216/663-1250

The largest mall in Ohio, Randall Park boasts 2 million square feet of shopping area. Stores include Burlington Coat Factory, Dillard's, Kaufmann's, JCPenney, and Sears. Randall Park Mall is located minutes from I-271 and I-480 at Miles (Ohio Route 43) and Northfield Roads. (East Cleveland)

SHAKER SQUARE
13221 Shaker Square
Cleveland
216/991-8700

The nation's second oldest shopping center is built in a circle around green lawns. The Georgian architec-

tural style is reminiscent of a New England village. Shaker Square is located about 15 minutes southeast of downtown. Take the RTA Rapid Train from Tower City east to the square for a pleasant day of shopping and dining. (East Cleveland)

SOUTHLAND SHOPPING CENTER
W. 130th St. and Pearl Rd.
Cleveland
216/464-5550

This newly renovated, plaza-style shopping center has expanded over the years to include row upon row of retail stores and restaurants. Burlington Coat Factory, a discount clothing and linens store, is only one of the destination stops in this retail expanse. There is something for everyone here. (South Cleveland)

SOUTHPARK CENTER MALL
I-71 at Rte. 82 W.
Strongsville
440/238-9000

The newest mall in northeast Ohio has more than 130 shops and

Aurora Premium Outlets, p. 142

Larry Falke

restaurants. It features Dillard's, JCPenney, Kaufmann's, Sears, and Kohl's department stores. (South Cleveland)

WESTGATE SHOPPING MALL
3211 Westgate Mall
Cleveland
440/333-8334
Built in 1954 as a shopping plaza, Westgate was enclosed as a mall in 1969. The mall has continued to grow and prosper with the addition of a food court in 1989. Westgate features both Dillard's and Kohl's department stores and more than 90 specialty shops and eateries. To get there from downtown, take I-90 west to the Hilliard Road exit, then go left on Wagar Road to Center Ridge Road. (West Cleveland)

FACTORY OUTLET STORES

AURORA PREMIUM OUTLETS
549 South Chillicothe Rd.
Aurora
330/562-2000
Originally established in 1929 as an auction house and flea market, Aurora Premium Outlets was Ohio's first factory outlet center when it opened in 1987. Today the outlet center attracts more than one million shoppers a year. In place of a standard shopping center design, this outlet reflects the layout of an early American village. Seventy upscale outlet stores, a full-service restaurant, and various eateries can be found here. The stores include Off 5th (Saks Fifth Avenue Outlet), Liz Claiborne, Brooks Brothers, Jones New York, Bose, The Gap, Lenox, Reebok, Levi's, Oshkosh B'Gosh, Mikasa, Royal Doulton, Oneida, and Pfaltzgraff. (East Cleveland)

HUGO BOSS FACTORY OUTLET
2149 W. 53rd St
Cleveland
216/961-3907
Men's tailored and casual fashions by Hugo Boss. (West Cleveland)

© 1996 Jonathan Wayne

10

Historically, sports and recreation have always been an important part of the Cleveland landscape. During his 1900–1914 term, social reformist Mayor Tom Johnson began a massive campaign to bring playgrounds and athletic fields to the city's poorest neighborhoods. Cleveland has been called "the cradle of amateur baseball." It was the first city to sponsor teams for youth ages 8 to 14 and to equip youngsters with complete outfits.

Professional sports are well represented by Cleveland's baseball, basketball, soccer, and hockey teams. A new football stadium is under construction to house Cleveland's next National Football League team. The Cleveland Indians are one of the oldest baseball franchises, organized in 1901. The Heisman Memorial Trophy—awarded every year to the top college football player—is named for Clevelander John W. Heisman. If horse racing is your thing, Cleveland has both harness racing and a thoroughbred racing track for year-round excitement. Golf is also part of the green, rolling landscape of northeast Ohio. It is no accident that the NEC World Series of Golf is played at Firestone Country Club in nearby Akron.

For those who want to play instead of just watch, Cleveland Metroparks' "Emerald Necklace" provides more than 19,000 acres of recreational space and facilities for almost every conceivable sport. Cleveland Metroparks are open 6 a.m. to 11 p.m. every day of the year.

PROFESSIONAL SPORTS

Baseball

CLEVELAND INDIANS
Jacobs Field, 2401 Ontario
Cleveland
216/420-4200
Founded in 1901, the Indians baseball team is a part of the Cleveland sports scene in a way that no other team can claim. The Indians have a proud legacy of "firsts": Larry Doby was the first African American player in the American League, and Frank Robinson was the first African American manager of a major league baseball team. Although the "Chief Wahoo" Native American logo has come under attack for cultural insensitivity in recent years, the team and its fans have a mutual, ongoing love affair.

The Indians have enjoyed a great deal of success since moving to Jacobs Field in 1994, winning four strainght American League Central Division titles from 1995 to 1998. The team has also enjoyed a major-league record 292 straight sellouts since June 1995 in the state-of-the-art, baseball-only facility, which has a capacity of 43,368. Tickets are hard to get. Tours of the ballpark are available during spring and summer. Call 216/241-8888 or 216/420-4385 for tour information.

Basketball

CLEVELAND CAVALIERS
Gund Arena, 1 Center Court
Cleveland
216/420-2000
Cleveland's NBA team plays regular- season games from November through April. The Cav's head coach, Mike Fratello, has become a welcome fixture in Cleveland, thanks to a long-term contract. Stars includes Shawn Kemp, six-time NBA all-star player, and Zydurunas Ilgauskas, a 7' 3" star on the rise. Fans are predicting a new basketball dynasty and an NBA championship for the city. To check out the latest on the Cav's activities,

Cleveland Cavaliers basketball team

Fernando Medina

Whammer is the name of the Cavaliers' polar bear mascot, an agile bear who helps out with halftime entertainment—dunking the basketball and dancing with the Cavaliers' dance team.

check out the team's Web page at: www.cavs.com. & (Downtown Cleveland)

Football

CLEVELAND BROWNS
Cleveland Stadium
1085 W. Third St.
Cleveland
888/891-1999
In November 1995 a collective piercing scream went up from the disbelieving fans of the Cleveland Browns. Owner Art Modell announced that he was relocating the Browns to Baltimore and renaming the team the Baltimore Ravens. Ever since Arthur (Mickey) McBride started the Browns in 1946, Cleveland fans had rabidly supported the team. In more recent years, the end zone at Cleveland Municipal Stadium was known as the Dawg Pound, and fans wearing dog ears and snouts cheered and barked for their team. But Browns fans were rescued from their misery in 1996 when the city of Cleveland and the National Football League made a deal to return the name, colors, and team heritage to Cleveland. Old Municipal Stadium, built in 1932, was demolished, and a new Cleveland Stadium has risen in the same location on the Lake Erie shoreline west of the Great Lakes Science Museum. The first Browns game with

the new team and new stadium will be played in fall 1999. And the stadium's new Dawg Pound will once again be filled with happy, barking fans. For the latest Browns happenings, visit the Browns Web site at www.clevelandbrowns.com.

Hockey

CLEVELAND LUMBERJACKS
1 Center Ice, 200 Huron Rd.
Cleveland
216/420-0000
Cleveland has been a professional hockey town since the Cleveland Barons played in the late 1930s. The Cleveland Lumberjacks brought professional hockey back to the city with the 1992–93 season after a 14-year absence. Hockey fans have come back in droves, with attendance records of 372,345 in the 1995–96 season. The Jacks' mascot is Buzz, who makes spectacular entrances onto the ice, either on skates, in a four-wheel-drive vehicle, or by rappelling down ropes from the center of the ice. Fans of all ages are invited to bring their skates to Friday night home games and skate after games with selected players. The Jacks play at Gund Arena; home games run from October through May. Adult tickets cost $10 to $20; kids age 17 and under receive a $2 discount. Individual game tickets are available at Gund Arena box office,

Heisman Memorial Trophy

John W. Heisman's name will forever be linked to the college football award that bears his name. Heisman is also known as "the Father of the Forward Pass" and is credited with many of the game's innovations; he changed the game from halves to quarters and created the hidden-ball play, the double pass, the center snap, interference on end runs, the scoreboard listing downs and yards gained, even the quarterback's vocal signal to start plays. After retiring from an illustrious college coaching career that included Oberlin, Auburn, Clemson, Rice, Pennsylvania, and Georgia Tech, Heisman moved to New York City, organized the New York Touchdown Club, and directed the Downtown Athletic Club. In 1935, the club began to award a trophy for the best college football player. After Heisman died in 1936, the trophy was named in his honor. Heisman's birthplace on Bridge Street at West 29th Street still stands in the near-westside Cleveland neighborhood of Ohio City.

Ticketmaster outlets, and Ticketmaster charge-by-phone: 216/241-5555. (Downtown Cleveland)

Horse Racing

NORTHFIELD PARK
10705 Northfield Rd.
Cleveland
330/467-4101
Northfield has year-round night harness racing and full-card simulcasting—wagering on horse races from all over the world. As the Northfield jingle goes, "With full-card simulcasting, every 19 seconds the place goes crazy." The horse races are shown on large-screen TV monitors. Open daily. (East Cleveland)

THISTLEDOWN RACE TRACK
Emery and Northfield Rds.
Cleveland
216/662-8600
Here you can enjoy thoroughbred racing in a climate-controlled, enclosed grandstand with dining terraces. Banquet facilities are available. The year's biggest race is the $300,000 Grade II Ohio Derby, one of the Midwest's premier races for three-year-olds. Open seven days a week, year-round, with simulcast racing from across the United States. (East Cleveland)

Soccer

CLEVELAND CRUNCH
Cleveland State University
Convocation Center
2000 Prospect Ave.
Cleveland
Box office 216/687-5082
Ticketmaster 216/241-5555

The Cleveland Crunch, 1994 and 1996 Champion of the National Professional Soccer League, plays in the Convocation Center at Cleveland State University. During breaks between quarters, team members throw Crunch mini-soccer balls to their fans. At home games, announcers tell which two players will be signing autographs after the game; bring your program or something else to be autographed. Call for game schedule and times. Tickets range from $11 to $18, available at the Convocation Center box office. For more information, call the Crunch office at 440/349-2090. Crunch team offices are located at 34200 Solon Road in Solon. ♿ (Downtown Cleveland)

RECREATION

Alpine Skiing

BOSTON MILLS/BRANDYWINE
SKI RESORTS
7100 Riverview Rd.
Peninsula
330/467-2242

The resort has 19 slopes with 17 chairlifts and six surface tows. Expanded beginner and first-aid facilities. (South Cleveland)

Boating

EMERALD NECKLACE MARINA
Scenic Park off Valley Pkwy.
Rocky River Reservation
Lakewood
216/226-3030

The lease-operated marina, with boat docks and year-round storage facilities, supplies bait, tackle, boating accessories, and refreshments. A boat launch, with car and trailer parking, provides access to Lake Erie via the Rocky River. (West Cleveland)

Polo in Cleveland

The Cleveland Polo Club draws as many as 300 people on a typical Sunday afternoon. Some spectators love to dress up, others lounge in jeans. Some bring tailgate picnics and make a party of it. Spectators can even get into the game between matches. When the announcer calls out, "It's time to stomp the divots!" interested parties can go out on the field and press the divots back into place with their feet. (Be very careful what you stomp on, though.)

Follow the White Ball

Cleveland is the birthplace of the modern golf ball. It was Cleve-lander Coburn Haskell who thought of winding a fine rubber thread around a rubber core, then patented his idea in 1899. Haskell's friend was Bertram Work, an executive at the B. F. Goodrich rubber company in nearby Akron. Goodrich employee John R. Gammeter invented the machinery to make the ball, and the results were impressive: the ball could be hit longer dis-tances, which led to lower scores, redesigned courses, and in-creased enthusiasm for the game. In 1904, American Walter Travis used the new ball to become the first American to win the British championship.

HINCKLEY LAKE BOATHOUSE
West Dr. between Bellus and State Rds.
Hinckley Reservation
Hinckley Township
216/278-2122
Here you can rent rowboats, electric motorboats, canoes, paddleboats, kayaks, in-line skates, and bicycles. The *Hinckley Queen* pontoon boat can accommodate up to a dozen vis-itors for one-hour tours. The facility, which is open April to November, also offers refreshments, fishing tackle, and live bait. You can launch private boats and canoes at the east end of the lake at State Road. (South Cleveland)

WALLACE LAKE
Valley Pkwy. south of Bagley Rd.
Mill Stream Run Reservation
Berea
Wallace Lake is for non-motorized boats. The Quarry Rock Café oper-ates from Memorial Day to Labor Day,

selling refreshments and renting pad-dle boats. (South Cleveland)

Golf
by John H. Tidyman, author of The Cleveland Golfer's Bible

AVALON LAKES GOLF INC.
1 American Way
Warren
330/856-8898
Avalon Lakes is the second of two Pete Dye courses open for daily-fee play, and it calls for a big game to play it well. This course, built in 1967, doesn't have Dye's trademark railroad ties, but he used standing timber to shape holes and create narrow landing areas. The greens here are big and subtle, the sand bunkers are big figure 8s. There is plenty of water. Great care was taken in making this course one of the prettiest around. Flowers of all sorts are cultivated here, including geraniums, impatiens, foxglove, and

red and blue salvia. The head pro here is John Diana, who shot the record score when he was a mere 17 years old: 67 from the blues, which measure 6,825, par 71. He says, "The strong points are the finishing holes, the size of the greens, and the length; it can be stretched out to 7,000 yards." From the whites, it's 6,453. (East Cleveland)

FOWLER'S MILL
13095 Rockhaven Rd.
Chesterland
216/729-7569

Fowler's Mill is a Pete Dye–designed course that delights the eye and challenges the player. Take every club you can fit; they will all be used. No. 4 is the hole of legend around here; it's a par 4 that wraps around a lake en route to the green. Many have tried, but none have succeeded in driving over the water, including Big Cat Williams, the long-drive champ. Among many signature holes are No. 9, which features a fairway split down the

middle by a wide creek and No. 18, a great, rolling, dog-legged, sand-trapped par 5. After playing the course a few times, it occurs to golfers that the more one thinks, the better one scores. Dye's talent for fashioning great golf holes from rolling terrain is clear at this course, where every hole is different from the last. Few courses are better maintained than Fowler's Mill, which last year had a "rough renovation" program and this year opened (finally!) a new clubhouse. Mr. Dye flew in for the party. (East Cleveland)

GLENEAGLES GOLF CLUB
2615 Glenwood Dr.
Twinsburg
330/425-3334

The patron saint of this course is Lazarus. The course was opened prematurely in 1990 and didn't recover until a couple years ago, when it was purchased by the city. Now that conditioning is a priority, the innate beauty of the track is

Cleveland Indians baseball, p. 144

Jim Baron/The Image Finders

Skating Around Town

When the ice is thick enough, skating is allowed in Public Square and in Cleveland Metroparks at Hinckley Lake, Wallace Lake, Rocky River Lagoon, and Shadow Lake. For ice skating after sundown, try the lighted Strawberry Pond at North Chagrin Reservation, Mayfield Village. Indoor ice skating is available at many locations throughout Cleveland. Most of the rinks listed below offer skate and locker rentals and blade sharpening. Many can be rented for private parties. Times vary to accommodate lessons, hockey games, and private parties, so phone ahead for current times.

Brooklyn Ice Rink, *7600 Memphis Ave., Brooklyn, 216/351-5334*

Cleveland Heights Pavilion, *1 Monticello Blvd., Cleveland Heights, 216/691-7373*

Euclid Orr Ice Rink, *22550 Milton Dr., Euclid, 216/289-8649 or 216/289-8630*

Kostel Recreation Center, *5411 Turney Rd., Garfield Heights, 216/475-7272*

North Olmsted Recreation Center, *26000 Lorain Rd., North Olmsted, 440/734-8200*

Parma Heights Recreation Center, *6200 Pearl Rd., Parma Heights, 216/842-5005*

Rocky River Recreation Center, *21018 Hilliard Blvd., Rocky River, 440/356-5657 or 440/356-5666 (evenings and weekends)*

Thornton Park, *20701 Farnsleigh Rd., Shaker Heights, 216/491-1290*

Winterhurst Municipal Ice Rink, *14750 Lakewood Heights Blvd., Lakewood, 216/529-4236*

TRIVIA

There are 400,000 registered boaters on Lake Erie. The annual sailing season's high point is Cleveland Race Week in July, when sailors from all over the country compete in a weeklong regatta.

blooming. It goes over hill and dale, many of the holes defined by mature hardwoods. What used to be one of the great finishing holes, a 389-yard par 4, is uphill, and water comes into play after the drive. The fairway suddenly narrows, and the green appears to shrink. But the city, for reasons never made clear, switched nines, so the great finishing hole is just No. 9. Still, this track is a very good one. (South Cleveland)

HAWKS NEST GOLF CLUB
2800 E. Pleasant Home Rd.
Creston
330/435-4611
Hawks Nest was created by Betty Hawkins, who ran a cafeteria and loves golf. Designer Steve Burns had 200 acres to work with and, except for one par 5 where the first two shots are blind, no course is more fun to play. After the opening hole, a par 4 that runs along the two-lane blacktop next to the course, players encounter a wonderful roller coaster of holes, each so different from the last that you doubt they're related. It's a rare course that is both challenging and fun to play. (South Cleveland)

PAINESVILLE COUNTRY CLUB
84 Golf Dr.
Painesville Township
216/354-3469

It's not really a country club, it's a golf club. The stone clubhouse was built in the twenties and has the most handsome clubhouse bar in the country. Little has changed this century, except for the price of beer and green fees. The front side here begins with a rolling par 5, then swoops and runs along level and sometimes hilly ground. Hilly and tight, the back side is far different. The maintenance includes creative mowing that delights the eye. It's fair, but demanding. (East Cleveland)

SKYLAND GOLF COURSE
2085 Center Rd.
Hinckley
330/225-5698
This course (thought to be the oldest in Medina County) is somewhat open and rolling on the front side. It gets tighter and the hills get steeper on the back side. It's not a resort course and it's not a championship course. It is a very pretty, very playable 18 holes with a 113 slope. Handsome trees line most of the fairways, and the course is surrounded by farmland. It's perfect for autumn golf. (South Cleveland)

SLEEPY HOLLOW GOLF CLUB
9305 Brecksville Rd.
Brecksville
440/526-4285
This one-time private club is the most powerful of the five courses owned and operated by Cleveland

Metroparks. Senior PGA Tour pro Charley Sifford was the longtime pro here. The front nine begins with a downhill par 5, then it's the "Par 3 From Hell," a 210-yard hole with a two-tiered green, a ravine running down the right side, and an old oak that hangs over part of the green. Good advice: mid iron off the tee, pitch on, putt, and get away. The back nine is the greatest back nine in town: every hole is different, and each is challenging. The course has a new clubhouse. (South Cleveland)

STONE WATER GOLF CLUB
1 Club Dr.
Highland Heights
216/461-4653
The course was honored by *Golf Magazine* and *Golf Digest* last year after its first full season. It is the course for players who want the amenities of a private club but don't have 20 grand for the initiation. Your cart (included in the green fees of $72) is freshly washed and stocked with towels; the driving range (also included in the green fees) features the best range, public or private, in the area; caddies are available at $30 per bag; lessons are given by a former touring pro; and bag boys clean your sticks after the round. The course is powerful—filled with risk-and-reward opportunities—and features stonework unlike any you've seen. The front side is open, and trouble is easy to avoid; the back side is carved out of the forest. Sand has never been such a gorgeous and dangerous feature since *Lawrence of Arabia*. Stone Water is the number-one course in the area. (East Cleveland)

THUNDER HILL GOLF COURSE
7050 Griswold Rd.
Madison

Cruising Cleveland Metroparks

Thanks to Cleveland Metroparks, it is possible to ride a bicycle through some of the most breathtaking scenery in northeast Ohio. With 60 miles of paved all-purpose trails, there is more than enough room for cyclists, as well as in-line skaters, walkers, and joggers. Most of the 14 reservations that make up Cleveland Metroparks are connected, so cyclists can ride as far as their sinewy legs can pedal.

Cross-country skiers can also use the unpaved hiking trails and the paved all-purpose trails of Cleveland Metroparks (bridle trails are off limits). In addition, cross-country skiing is allowed when a four-inch snow base covers the fairway and rough areas of Cleveland Metroparks golf courses Big Met, Little Met, and Sleepy Hollow.

Jacobs Field sports the largest freestanding scoreboard in the United States. The scoreboard stands directly over the bleacher section in left field and includes a Sony Jumbotron instant replay board; a game-in-progress board for team lineups, statistics, and line scores; and a starburst color board that displays colorful animated messages.

216/298-3474
Thunder Hill is an unusual name for a golf course, but this is an unusual course. The renovation has just been finished, and players who have passed up the course after reviewing its 150 slope rating might want to reconsider. Long referred to as a novelty (with nearly 100 lakes and ponds and so many blind shots that it didn't make a difference whether you were playing at midnight or high noon), the course remains somewhat intimidating but is now a great golf challenge. The front side meanders around stocked ponds, bumps over a few hills, and finishes at a long and handsome par 3—190 yards over water to a big, flat green. The back nine climbs into hills that were once apple orchards and slips between stands of tall pine. Some of the vistas are worthy of postcards. At least for your first round or two, take your best shag balls to play. (East Cleveland)

WINDMILL LAKES GOLF CLUB
6544 Ohio Rte. 14
Ravenna
330/297-0440
Maryland architect Edward Ault designed this course in 1970. It reflects the design trends of the day: huge greens (7,000 to 8,000 square feet), big tee boxes, lots of green-side bunkers. It is the home course of Kent State University, the only northern school in the nation to consistently rank in the top 20. The rough here reminds players to stay in the short grass, kept at one-half inch by the superintendent. The terrain here rolls gently, providing a good cardiovascular workout for those so inclined. In addition to a great pro shop, the course is home to Cipriano's Restaurant. Change your shoes before being seated, please. (East Cleveland)

Boston Mills/Brandywine
Ski Resort, p. 147

Boston Mills/Brandywine Ski Resort

Horseback Riding

Cleveland Metroparks has 82 miles of trails for equestrian use. You'll find a complete map of the trails in *Pathfinder: A Guide to Cleveland Metroparks*. For a free copy, call 216/351-6300 or get a map from one of the four Cleveland Metroparks Nature Centers listed in Chapter 8. The Chagrin Valley Trails and Riding Club (216/351-6300) is a Cleveland Metroparks affiliate.

BRECKSVILLE STABLES
11921 Parkview Dr.
Brecksville Reservation
Brecksville
440/526-6767
Call for information on riding programs, pony rides, and boarding. (South Cleveland)

ROCKY RIVER STABLES
19901 Puritas Rd.
Rocky River Reservation
Lakewood
216/267-2525
Call for information on riding programs, pony rides, and boarding. (West Cleveland)

11

PERFORMING ARTS

The performing arts have always been a thriving part of Cleveland's entertainment scene. The grand show palaces on Playhouse Square that were once a major stop on the vaudeville circuits now feature the works of touring theater, resident theater, and dance companies. A broad spectrum of community, alternative, and children's theater; the Cleveland International Film Festival; art film series; and the world-renowned Cleveland Orchestra fill the calendar with a never-ending bounty of quality performances.

THEATER

BECK CENTER FOR THE ARTS
17801 Detroit Rd.
Lakewood
216/521-2540
Beck Center is well known and respected for many reasons: the quality Main Stage Theater season of musicals, drama, and comedies directed by a professional staff; the Children and Teen Theater Program; the Children's Theatre on Wheels program that brings live theater to schools and community centers; drawing, painting, cartooning, calligraphy, and pottery classes for adults and children; a superb dance depart-

ment led by professional dancers; an outreach program for at-risk youth and minority students; and the the Beck Center Gallery, managed by the Cleveland Artists Foundation, where northeastern Ohio artists exhibit and sell their work. ⅜ (West Cleveland)

CAIN PARK
Lee and Superior Rds.
Cleveland Heights
216/371-3000
Cain Park is an unexplainable wonder. In 1938, the Cleveland Heights city recreation department created a 22-acre park that includes an amphitheater. The auditorium seats 1,200, with additional lawn seating,

and has an 80-foot-wide stage. The WPA hired a group of Italian stonemasons to build the theater. Every summer, the city hosts a full concert series of the top names in jazz, folk, zydeco, classic soul, and those performers without category. Cain Park also has a summer theater guest series of cabaret, light opera, dance, and classical music. It also produces two musicals each summer. And to top it off, the mid-summer three-day Cain Park Arts Festival is rated the fifth-best fine-arts show in the country. The free festival includes 160 artists, gourmet foods, live music, and children's programs. The stated purpose of Cain Park: to bring people of different races, religions, and ethnic backgrounds together in a universal human experience. ♿ (East Cleveland)

CLEVELAND PLAY HOUSE
8500 Euclid Ave.
Cleveland
216/795-7000

The Play House is nationally recognized as one of America's leading professional theaters. Founded in 1915, it is also the longest running regional theater in the country. The mission of the Cleveland Play House is to present an artistically exciting, and balanced repetoire of new, contemporary, and classic plays, comedies, and musicals. The Play House is also one of the largest theater complexes

---

Cultural Visionaries

Of all the noble causes launched in Cleveland, Karamu House, Inc., is perhaps the noblest. In 1915, a young Oberlin College couple named Russell and Rowena Jelliffe took on the enormous task of "building a better society" in the "Roaring Third" neighborhood of East 38th and Central Avenue.

Nationally, it was an era of racial strife. The neighborhood included almost all of the city's 15,000 African Americans and many Austrian, Italian, Russian, Jewish, Syrian, Chinese, and other immigrants. The Jelliffes bought two clapboard cottages and opened a community center that would promote the arts as a means to interracial cooperation.

The center spawned a variety of programs, including the Karamu Performing Arts Theatre, the Early Childhood Development Center, and the Center of Arts and Education. After 80 years, Karamu continues to be recognized nationally as a proving ground and springboard for talented playwrights, actors, and artists.

Los Lobos at Cain Park, p. 155

in the country, housing four theaters. All provide intimate seating. The Bolton Theatre has 612 seats, the Drury Theatre has 508, The Brooks Theatre has 136, and Studio One has 120. Education and outreach programs are an integral part of the Play House's service to the community. More than 38,000 students from the region attend productions annually. The Play House's acting classes began in 1933 and now serve as a national model for training youngsters. Notables trained here include Paul Newman, Jack Weston, Joel Grey, Margaret Hamilton, and Ray Walston. & (University Circle)

CLEVELAND PUBLIC THEATRE
6415 Detroit Ave.
Cleveland
216/631-2727
An off-Broadway–style arts organization, the Cleveland Public Theatre develops, produces, and presents experimental and progressive performances for those who enjoy cutting-edge theater, music, performance art,

dance, and sound. The multicultural programming includes the voices of African Americans, Native Americans, Hispanics, women, and gays and lesbians. Cleveland Act Now (CAN!) is a yearlong theater education program in which students design and build sets, write scripts, and perform. (West Cleveland)

CLEVELAND SIGNSTAGE THEATRE
8500 Euclid Ave.
Cleveland
216/229-2838 (voice)
216/229-0431 (TTY)
signstage@aol.com
Formerly known to many Clevelanders as Fairmount Theatre of the Deaf, SIGNSTAGE was founded in 1975 by one hearing actor and one deaf actor. The productions blend speaking text with American Sign Language and mime. The results are award-winning productions that bring hearing-impaired and hearing audiences together. The professional company's regular season includes a three-show mainstage season at the Cleveland Play House, a national touring schedule, and a regional tour of 100 schools. You haven't seen *Children of a Lesser God* until you've seen this company's interpretation. (University Circle)

DOBAMA THEATRE
1846 Coventry Rd.
Cleveland Heights
216/932-6838 or 216/932-3259
Dobama is Cleveland's first "off-Broadway" theater, offering area premieres of the latest works by emerging and pivotal playwrights of our day. Lanford Wilson, Caryl Churchill, Jon Robin Baitz, John Guare, A. R. Gurney, George Walker—some of the biggest names in contemporary theater had

Private Lives *at the Cleveland Play House, p. 156*

their first Cleveland productions at Dobama.

In addition to the regular season of six plays, Dobama offers a variety of alternative projects, like the Owen Kelly Adopt-a-Playwright Program (in which new playwrights become part of the production process) and Dobama's Night Kitchen (a late-night improvisational theater for teenage to thirty-something audiences).

The Marilyn Bianchi Kids' Playwriting Festival is an annual contest for Cuyahoga County students in the first through twelfth grades. Dobama sponsors workshops on playwriting for teachers and families. Thirteen to 20 winning scripts are chosen, some of them written by first and second graders, and about 10 of those scripts are then produced. During the first weekend in June the plays are staged free to the public. & (East Cleveland)

GREAT LAKES THEATER FESTIVAL
Ohio Theatre, Playhouse Square
Cleveland
216/241-5490
From Shakespeare to Arthur Miller, this company offers venerable theatrical productions geared toward adults and students alike. Student matinees and a participatory residency program have created a strong relationship with area schools. Pre-performance discussion programs, symposium weekends, and a touring outreach program make this theater a cultural asset to Clevelanders. GLTF productions have gone on to other stages throughout the country. Subscription plans start as low as $48. Call the Subscriber Hotline at 216/771-3999 for information. Or write to the company at 1501 Euclid Ave. Suite 423, Cleveland 44115. For individual tickets call Advantix at 216/241-6000 or 800/766-6048. & (Downtown Cleveland)

KARAMU PERFORMING ARTS
THEATRE CENTER
2355 E. 89th St.
Cleveland
216/795-7077 (box office)

TRIVIA

Beck Center has two stages: the Main Stage, which seats 488 people, and the Studio Theater, which seats 83. The two theaters stage about a dozen productions each year.

Movement as Medicine

DanceCleveland sponsors young people's concerts, workshops, master classes, lectures, and open rehearsals with visiting artists and companies. The group brings international physicians and therapists to Cleveland to train the local medical community, educators, and the public in dance/movement therapy, which uses movement to treat physical disabilities, neurological damage, and emotional problems.

The oldest American theater producing plays by African American playwrights, Karamu (a Swahili word for "a place of joyful gathering") is famous for its takes on the African American experience. Karamu's Theatre Outreach Performance Series (TOPS) is a school touring program featuring plays appropriate for different grade levels. Karamu presents its season in the 100-seat Arena Theatre and the Jelliffe Theatre, a 223-seat proscenium stage. Karamu stages an annual production of Langston Hughes' Black Nativity, a Christmas celebration of gospel, dance, and theater, in the Cleveland Convention Center Music Hall. & (East Cleveland)

NEAR WEST THEATRE
3606 Bridge Ave.
Cleveland
216/732-8324
The Near West Theatre began as a summer youth theater in 1978 in an effort to keep at-risk teenagers off the street. Now the Near West Theatre is a year-round professionally directed theater arts program for children, teens, and adults. In addition to school and community programs, Near West Theatre stages four Broadway musicals annually, in which 40 to 65 children, teens, and adults are cast. The resulting productions are quality performances. Call for the current schedule. & (West Cleveland)

MUSIC AND OPERA

CLEVELAND ORCHESTRA
Severance Hall, 11001 Euclid Ave.
Cleveland
216/231-7300
Considered one of the world's premier orchestras, the Cleveland Orchestra has been under the guidance of six music directors since its inception in 1918: Nikolai Sokolff, 1918–33; Artur Rodzinski, 1933–43; Erich Leinsdorf, 1943–46; George Szell, 1946–70; Lorin Maazel, 1971–82; and Christoph von Dohnanyi, since 1984. The orchestra plays in Severance Hall from September to May and performs at Blossom Music Center on weekends in July and August. It also presents a Christmas concert series, a Sunday afternoon series, and a

Films Shot in Cleveland
by John Ewing, director of the Cleveland Cinematheque

A Christmas Story, *1983. This wonderful Christmas classic was filmed in a house on West 11th Street. The department store scenes were shot in the downtown department store that is now Dillard's. The Christmas parade was shot on Public Square.*

The Deer Hunter, *1978. Filmed at St. Theodosius Church in downtown Cleveland, the Veteran's Administration Hospital, and at LTV steel mills in the industrial area of the Flats, this film won an Academy Award for Best Picture in 1978.*

The Escape Artist, *1982. Francis Ford Coppola produced this movie, featuring Ryan O'Neal's son Griffin, Raul Julia, and Teri Garr.*

The Fortune Cookie, *1966. A Jack Lemmon classic, the movie's early scenes were shot at an actual Cleveland Browns football game.*

The Gathering, *1977. A TV movie classic starring Ed Asner, it was shot in Chagrin Falls.*

It Runs in the Family, *1994. The sequel to* A Christmas Story *starring Charles Grodin, Kiernan Culkin, and Mary Steenburgen. The film was shot in the same house as the first movie. Other scenes were filmed behind the federal courthouse downtown, at Playhouse Square, and at Wilbur Wright Elementary School on Parkhurst Avenue.*

Friday morning series. Severance Hall also hosts a Jazz on the Circle concert series, a weekday Education Concert series for schoolchildren, and Family Concerts for youngsters ages five to nine and their parents. ♿ (University Circle)

LYRIC OPERA CLEVELAND
Cleveland Institute of Music

Kulas Hall
11021 East Blvd.
Cleveland
216/231-2910 (box office)
Begun in 1974 as an outgrowth of the Cleveland Institute of Music, Lyric Opera Cleveland is a fully independent professional opera/musical theater company. The summer Festival Season is performed in

The Kid from Cleveland, *1949. The film stars the 1948 world champion Cleveland Indians baseball team and contains scenes shot throughout Greater Cleveland.*

Light of Day, *1987. Michael J. Fox starred in this rock and roll movie. Concert scenes were shot at the Euclid Tavern.*

One-Trick Pony, *1980. Paul Simon's movie contains scenes shot in Cleveland. The concert scene was filmed at the Agora.*

Stranger Than Paradise, *1984. An important independent film by Jim Jarmusch with a wonderfully funny scene filmed along Lake Erie in winter.*

Telling Lies in America, *1997. Joe Eszterhas's semi-autobiographical coming-of-age film is set in early 1960s Cleveland.*

Those Lips, Those Eyes, *1980. This movie was shot in Cain Park, where the film's writer, David Shaber, had worked in theater as a youth.*

Up Tight, *1968. A Jules Dassin remake of* The Informer.

Kulas Hall. The company's year-round schedule includes community education programs that introduce elementary and secondary students to the intriguing world of opera and musical theater. Call the box office for a summer season schedule or for information on the educational programs. ♿ (University Circle)

OHIO CHAMBER ORCHESTRA
3659 Green Rd., Suite 118
Cleveland
216/464-1755
ohiochamb@aol.com
Founded in 1971, the Ohio Chamber Orchestra is perhaps best known as the official orchestra for the Cleveland Ballet and Cleveland Opera. OCO also offers two concert

A Dramatic Success

Dedicated to presenting classic drama, the Great Lakes Theater Festival is a nonprofit company devoted to cultural preservation. The company was founded as a traveling Shakespeare company in the early 1950s by Antioch College English professor Arthur Lithgow (actor John Lithgow's father). John called his father's company "the Johnny Appleseed of Shakespeare." But the company found a home in 1961, when the members of the Lakewood Board of Education sought to fill the Lakewood Civic Auditorium with culturally enriching entertainment during summer.

In the late 1970s, actor Tom Hanks made his professional debut at GLTF, performing in 11 productions before moving on to stardom. In 1982, the company performed its first season at its current home, the Ohio Theatre on Playhouse Square. James Bundy is the company's artistic director.

series each season. Concerts at Severance feature traditional chamber music with internationally acclaimed soloists. The New American Orchestra series offers multimedia exploration concerts on themes such as "They All Play Ragtime," "What's the Big Deal About Mozart?" and "Calder's Universe." OCO performs at Severance Hall, Playhouse Square Center, and the Cleveland Play House. All seats are $20. Student rush tickets are available at the door for $10. ♿ (University Circle)

DANCE

CLEVELAND BALLET
3615 Euclid Ave.

Suite IA
Cleveland
216/426-2500
It's been a busy quarter century since Cleveland ballet cofounders Dennis Nahat and Ian Horvath left the American Ballet Theatre in New York and came to Cleveland. The city's dance audience embraced this company when it debuted in 1976. Ten years later, the Cleveland Ballet began an innovative co-venture with the city of San Jose, California, establishing San Jose as the ballet's second home.

Today the Cleveland Ballet holds an annual international audition tour and employs dancers from across the United States, Cuba, Mexico, Peru, Brazil, Venezuela,

Vietnam, Hong Kong, France, and the Philippines. Cleveland is understandably proud of this talented, cosmopolitan ballet company, which is still under the direction of Dennis Nahat. Call for a season schedule. & (Downtown Cleveland)

DANCECLEVELAND
Playhouse Square
1148 Euclid Ave.
Cleveland
216/861-2213
The oldest dance organization in the country devoted to modern dance and contemporary movement, the nonprofit company began as a group of volunteers teaching modern dance in the basement of a church. But DanceCleveland's most visible role through the years has been to present an annual concert series. The list of dance companies this group has brought to Cleveland since 1956 reads like a Who's Who of modern dance: from Alvin Ailey and Martha Graham to Pilobolus

Romeo and Juliet
Cleveland Ballet, p. 162

Fran Barkas/Cleveland Ballet

and Bill T. Jones/Arnie Zane. Tickets are available by phone through Advantix, 216/241-6000, or at the Playhouse Square box office. & (Downtown Cleveland)

BUYING TICKETS

ADVANTIX
216/241-6000
800/766-6048
Ticket outlets are located at selected Finast supermarkets and some mall information booths. Call for the closest location. Advantix sells tickets to Playhouse Square Theatres (State, Allen, Ohio, Palace, and Kennedy's), Hanna Cabaret, and the NEC Series of Golf. It also sells tickets to special one-time events throughout the city.

TICKETMASTER
216/241-5555 (Cleveland)
330/945-9400 (Akron)
Ticket purchases are available on the Internet: www.ticketmaster.com. Ticketmaster sells tickets for the Cleveland Indians, Cleveland Cavaliers, Cleveland Lumberjacks, Blossom Music Center, Cleveland Orchestra at Blossom, Cleveland State University Convocation Center, the Cleveland Play House, Cain Park, Agora Theatre, Nautica Stage, Peabody's Down Under, Cleveland Metroparks Zoo, Great Lakes Science Center and Omnimax Theatre, Rock and Roll Hall of Fame and Museum, Cleveland Convention Center, The Odeon, the Grog Shop, Wilbert's, and the University of Akron's E. J. Thomas Hall.

12

NIGHTLIFE

Cleveland is a city that knows how to have a good time. The Flats is proof of that. Once a drab industrial area, the banks of the Cuyahoga River have become the nightclub neighborhood, with dance clubs, bars, music clubs, river taxis, and restaurants. The historic Warehouse District, northwest of Public Square and east of the Flats, is another neighborhood that within the last decade has gone from boarded up to boogie-down. University Circle spans both ends of the spectrum, offering everything from mellow restaurants with jazz music to hard-pounding blues bars. Ohio City is a neighborhood with a growing nightlife scene. West of the Cuyahoga River, it boasts wine bars, brewpubs, and a broad offering of restaurants. Another downtown scene was created in 1994 when the Gateway sports complex was completed. Now Jacobs Field and Gund Arena are surrounded by a new generation of eateries, sports bars, and pubs.

DANCE CLUBS

THE BASEMENT
1078 Old River Rd.
Cleveland
216/344-0001
Year after year, this club in the Flats is voted the favorite place to dance in a local magazine poll. On summer weekend nights, as many as a thousand people in the 20- to 40-year-old crowd boogie to live bands. The Basement has three levels for dancing. To avoid the crush of humanity, come a little earlier than 9 p.m.—or be prepared to wait in line at the door. Thursday is Ladies' Night, when women get their drinks at a discount from 8 to midnight. The club charges no cover and is open every night of the week until 2:30 a.m. (Downtown)

CLEVELAND BEACH CLUB
1064 Old River Rd., the Flats

Cleveland
216/241-1202

The ceiling of the big, boxy room is decorated with day-glo surf boards. Sailboats and lifeguard towers adorn the dance floor. DJs spin a wide variety of music, from top 40 to party music, for the dancing masses, who get an occasional blast of ambiance from the fog machine. This bar caters to the younger crowd, and every Thursday is College ID Night. (Downtown Cleveland)

MIRAGE
2510 Elm St.
Cleveland
216/348-1135

Dance the night away at this club in the Flats. One of the best places in town to spot sports stars and big-name rappers, the Mirage is classy, urban, and contemporary. Casual Thursday only; no sneakers or jeans Friday through Sunday. Free for women on Thur and Sun. (Downtown Cleveland)

SPY BAR
1261 W. Sixth St.
Cleveland
216/621-7907

Have you ever wanted to step into the middle of a James Bond movie? If so, get very dressed up and head to the Spy Bar, an upscale nightclub that is a dead ringer for a London gentleman's club. Lots of overstuffed furniture in which to lounge, with antiques adorning the stately walls. There is a big, cozy fireplace and a bar of darkly polished wood. DJs spin the music, and dancing is the order of the evening. The bar is also a good place to sit and relax. The crowd is mostly thirty-something and up. No kitchen. Cover charge, Mr. Bond. (Downtown Cleveland)

JAZZ CLUBS

CLUB ISABELLA
2025 University Hospitals Dr.
Cleveland
216/229-1177

Great Lakes Brewing Company, p. 169

Great Lakes Brewing Company

You can groove to bebop and mainstream jazz nightly. This 100-year-old carriage house/restaurant is nestled in the middle of the University Hospitals and Case Western Reserve University campus. The club opened in December 1980 and has a loyal following for reasons that become obvious after one visit. Both the cuisine and the scene are serene. Dinner available. Music starts Mon–Thur at 8, Fri and Sat at 9. Closed Sun. (East Cleveland)

NIGHTTOWN
12383 Cedar Rd.
Cleveland Heights
216/795-0550
Named after a James Joyce novel, this restaurant has a classy yet casual ambiance the Irish writer would have appreciated. The menu is a not-to-be-missed selection of American and British appetizers and entrées. Lunch and dinner served seven days a week. Live jazz creates just the right mood Monday through Saturday. On Sunday, the music usually shifts to Irish fare. (East Cleveland)

SIXTH STREET UNDER
1266 W. Sixth St.
Cleveland
216/589-9313
This is a cozy basement nightclub in the Warehouse District. The music is supplied by superb local jazz talent. Several times each month the club features national acts for which the cover charge goes up. The walls are decorated with musical abstract and Afrocentric art. The main room seats 125, and a smaller room holds an additional 75 people. The kitchen serves only a few entrées, but don't miss the Jazz Lovers' Wings in hot, mild, or barbecued varieties. Open-mike poetry readings on Sunday evenings. (Downtown Cleveland)

BLUES CLUBS

EUCLID TAVERN
11629 Euclid Ave.
Cleveland
216/229-7788
For the younger, dressed-down crowd, this old bar has hard-driving music featuring original local bands as well as an eclectic variety of national touring acts in an appropriately shabby atmosphere. One, maybe two, sometimes even three bands perform in one show. Cuisine served is American fare: burgers, wings, steaks, chicken, and sausage sandwiches. (University Circle)

WILBERT'S BAR & GRILLE
1360 W. Ninth St.
Cleveland
216/771-2583
There is no better place to see an endless variety of blues, jazz, zydeco, and combinations thereof.

No one seems to know exactly when Fagan's first opened, but manager Mike Druso estimates that it began in the early 1940s as a small riverside bar. Since then, Fagan's has been remodeled and expanded so often that it has the look of an authentic, rambling party palace in some tropical seaport.

Located in the Warehouse District, Wilbert's Bar and Grille is a destination point for acts billed as "the next big thing," as well as those who have enjoyed a 30-year following, such as Taj Mahal and Koko Taylor. The twenty- to seventy-something crowd dresses any way they want. The menu includes southwestern dishes laced with either hot or mild peppers, so timid tongues need not shy away. Cover varies. (Downtown Cleveland)

OTHER MUSIC CLUBS

AGORA
5000 Euclid Ave.
Cleveland
216/881-6700 (box office)
216/881-6911 (concert line)
Cleveland rock promoter Hank LoConti Sr. opened the Agora in 1966, and many acts that played at the club soon went on to national stardom. Although the original club at 24th and Payne Avenue burned down in 1984, the new location at 55th and Euclid is rich in rock 'n' roll history. Loconti's son Henry Jr. now runs the Agora operations, which include an 1,800-seat theater, a 700-seat ballroom, and a bar. The lobby and lounge area houses an impressive collection of rock memorabilia. The club has a 60-foot-long Bar of Fame, and tabletops are covered

with clippings and other rock music mementos. Agora's marketing director says, "A big difference between us and Hard Rock Cafe is that they buy their memorabilia. We earned ours."

THE ODEON
1295 Old River Rd.
Cleveland
216/732-5331
Once a warehouse, the Odeon now hosts all formats of music. Visiting bands have included Marilyn Manson, the Mighty Mighty Bosstones, and Bela Fleck and the Flecktones. The Odeon handles about 950 people in its big open space. Tickets are all general admission, and prices range from free to $20, depending on the band. The box office accepts cash only. (Downtown Cleveland)

PEABODY'S DOWN UNDER
1059 Old River Rd.
Cleveland
216/241-2451
This club has offered a rich diversity of music for 15 years. You can hear alternative, punk, jazz, reggae, and ska. Music fans of any age are welcome. The bar serves drinks, and on most nights food is available. Peabody's can handle as many as 600 music lovers. "We do get a lot of acts that go on to be big successes," says John Michalak, one of the owners. "Just about everybody

has played here at least once." Tracy Chapman, Tori Amos, and Duran Duran are just a few of Peabody's bands who went on to find fame and fortune. (Downtown Cleveland)

PUBS AND BREWPUBS

DIAMONDBACK BREWERY
724 Prospect Ave.
Cleveland
216/771-1988

Top Ten Cigar-Friendly Restaurants and Bars
By Jim Ponstingle, cigar aficionado and president of Mail Marketing, Inc.

The national cigar trend has not bypassed our city and its burbs. Men and woman from all types of professions and social classes are realizing one of life's great pleasures associated with relaxation and celebration. A little knowledge is very beneficial before entering into the world of cigar smoking. Cigar magazines, videos, and a wealth of information on the Internet can help you get started. A visit to a reputable cigar store is the quickest method for shortening the learning curve. My favorite is Cigars, Cigars, 21802 Center Ridge Road (behind Dunkin Donuts), 440/333-5454. These nightspots will welcome both you and your cigar.

1. **Gamekeepers Lodge**, 19300 Detroit Ave., Rocky River, 440/333-8505
2. **Martini's Restaurant**, 15315 Madison Ave., Lakewood, 216/221-7494
3. **The Humidor**, 1214 W. Sixth St., Cleveland, 216/574-9300
4. **Fulton Bar & Grill** (Ohio City), 1835 Fulton Road, Cleveland, 216/694-2122
5. **Spy Bar**, 1261 W. Sixth St., Cleveland, 216/621-7907
6. **West End Tavern**, 18514 Detroit Ave., Lakewood, 216/521-7684
7. **James Dominic's**, 27200 Detroit, Westlake, 440/835-1661
8. **Hyde Park Grill**, 1823 Coventry, Cleveland Heights, 216/321-6444
9. **Johnny's Downtown**, 1406 W. Sixth St., Cleveland, 216/623-0055
10. **The Rockcliff**, 2589 Wooster Rd., Rocky River, 440/333-2600

The Diamondback Brewery, which opened in 1996, brews eight different types of beers, including an oatmeal stout, a Vienna red beer, a white diamond light, and a wheat beer. Appetizers include Spanish tapas. Artsy murals decorate the walls, and the ceilings are hung with chandeliers. A mezzanine champagne bar overlooks the restaurant. Its full-service menu includes steaks and seafood. (Downtown Cleveland)

GREAT LAKES BREWING COMPANY
2516 Market St.
Cleveland
216/771-4404
The story goes that, after a hard day of crimefighting, Eliot Ness used to visit this bar. The restored mahogany bar sits in a building that dates to 1860. The place was converted to a microbrewery in 1988. Sip one of the company's award-winning lagers or ales, brewed on the premises. The pub-style cuisine features hearty cheese soup and brewmaster pie filled with sausage, cheese, and spinach. An outdoor beer garden opens during warm weather. Business is so good that these folks opened another brewery across the street on West 26th Street in the former Schlather Brewing Company, which operated at the turn of the century. (West Cleveland)

JOHN HARVARD'S BREW HOUSE
1087 Old River Rd.
Cleveland
216/623-2739
The newest brewpub in the Flats is a Massachussetts-based restaurant and microbrew chain. But this Cleveland newcomer is getting rave reviews from local critics, who not only enjoy the fresh brews but also love the food selection and reasonable prices. The grilled meatloaf drenched in homemade gravy is a popular dish, as is the deep-dish chicken pot pie. Upscale dinner specials include venison and catfish. Head brewer Brian O'Reilly says he brews a variety of beers throughout the year, from cherry wheat beer to nut brown ale. (Downtown)

ROCK BOTTOM BREWERY & RESTAURANT
2000 Sycamore
Cleveland
216/623-1555
The handcrafted beers are wonderful here, but don't miss the ribs, chicken, and selection of salads. Appetizers include Asiago cheese dip, tomato basil quesadilla, and stuffed Portobellini mushrooms. Bands play a variety of rock music on the weekend. Upstairs is a billiards room with five pool tables and shuffleboard tables. The riverfront patio serves pizzas and pretzels to

T i P

The Odeon is small and intimate. If you are a serious fan of the band on the bill, you may even get to meet the musicians.

Aussie Brewpubs

Wallaby's

go along with your beer and soft drinks. (Downtown Cleveland)

WALLABY'S GRILLE & BREWPUB
30005 Clemens Rd.
Westlake
440/808-1700
A casual restaurant with an Australian theme, Wallaby's serves up a list of homemade brews with monikers like Great White Wheat, Big Red Roo, Croco-Pale Ale, Raspberry Ice, Kalgoolie Gold, and Maori Milk Stout. Steaks, chicken, and ribs fill out the menu, along with salads and pizza. Down Under desserts include the Mt. Morgan Ice Cream Pie and the Perth Pie, a homemade deep-dish apple pie with brown sugar, pecans, and a scoop of cinnamon ice cream. Wallaby's is highly kid-friendly, with a six-item menu, and the kitchen will attempt other pint-sized specialties, too. High chairs and booster seats abound. The Brewpub lounge is open late. For parties of under 10 people, call ahead one hour to be put on the waiting list. (West Cleveland)

BARS FOR RELAXING

BOHEMIA CLUB CAFE
900 Literary Rd.
Tremont
216/566-0000
Food, people-watching, and art are the three biggest draws here. (West Cleveland)

CAFE D'ORO
2785 Euclid Heights Blvd.
Cleveland Heights
216/932-3001
This downstairs bistro is as cozy-upscale-casual as it gets. Sip a glass of *vino* from the generous wine list. The chef makes a wonderful fresh pasta, gourmet pizza, and seafood. Open at 5 Tue–Sun. (East Cleveland)

D'VINE WINE BAR
836 W. St. Clair Ave.
Cleveland
216/241-8463 (VINE)
Owner Tracy Januska and a group of friends opened this wine bar in the historic Warehouse District in the former George Washington Hard-

ware warehouse. The restored 19th-century building is charmingly decorated with Gothic chandeliers, antique furniture, a mantle, and fireplace. The decor serves as a hip backdrop for the trendy food and drink served here. D'Vine offers its customers 300 wines, 80 by the glass. The wine bar offers a flight—a two-ounce taste of four wines in one category—with a placemat that gives information on the wines. Januska says her mission is to provide a fun, non-snobbish atmosphere for people who want to enjoy wine. D'Vine also sells 24 kinds of bottled beers for those who prefer suds over bubbles. The menu is a broad range of offerings, from tapas and seafood to champagne pan-seared chicken and baked brie topped with honey and almonds. Desserts include a chocolate heart with white chocolate mousse, champagne sorbet, and blueberry cheesecake. Cigar smoking is permitted. Mon–Sat 4 p.m.–1:30 a.m. ♿ (Downtown)

KEKA
2523 Market Ave.
Ohio City
216/241-5352
The tapas menu is a draw here. (West Cleveland)

LIQUID CAFE
1212 W. Sixth St.

Cleveland
216/479-7717
Couches and moving art dominate the scene for this yuppie crowd. The casual atmosphere at this Warehouse District spot is so homey that the place even throws in a few board games. You can play Monopoly, Connect Four, or Operation (to name a few) while you sip your favorite microbrew beer or wine. The full-service kitchen creates lots of tasty appetizers, salads, burgers, sandwiches, and sandwich wraps. Music is provided by the CD jukebox or a live DJ. The patio is open for summertime dining and drinking. Closed Sun. (Downtown Cleveland)

MARKET AVENUE WINE BAR
2524 Market Ave.
Ohio City
216/696-9463
This casual upscale bar has a many-splendored wine list and a few appetizers for those happy-hour hunger pangs. But the real purpose of this place is to let you sip the Sauvignon, or whatever style of grape you fancy. (West Cleveland)

OTTO MOSER'S TAVERN
1425 Euclid Ave.
Cleveland
216/771-3831
Before or after attending the theater at Playhouse Square, stop in for a

TRIVIA

Trent Reznor, of the band Nine Inch Nails, played at Peabody's on a regular basis when he was a member of the Cleveland band Exotic Birds. Richard Patrick, a singer for the now-extinct Exotic Birds, is the drummer for the up-and-coming band Stabbing Westward.

Holy Moses!

Part of the chic in visiting the Flats is to be able to pull up along-side one of the nightclubs in your own boat. If you want to bank-hop from the East Bank to the West Bank and you forgot to bring your powerboat along, don't despair. Holy Moses Water Taxi (216/999-1625) will take you from one side of the river to the other for $3 a person. The Holy Moses *(named for city founder Moses Cleveland) is also available for charter.*

reasonably priced specialty sandwich named for a star of the stage or the screen. Theater, opera, and show biz memorabilia, including a few taxidermied animals not on the menu, adorn the walls and make for great viewing. (Downtown Cleveland)

PETE & DEWEY'S PLANET
812 Huron Rd.
Cleveland
216/522-1500
Across the street from Gateway's Jacobs Field and Gund Arena, this is a restaurant and bar with fresh gourmet pasta, chargrilled pizza, soups, salads, and sandwiches. It's a lively, noisy place when the team is in town, with multi-screen TVs to keep on top of the games in progress or view a selection of rock videos. Hours vary according to Gateway events. Reservations recommended on game nights. (Downtown Cleveland)

PICCOLO MONDO
1352 W. Sixth St.
Cleveland
216/241-1300

Happy hour for a thirtyish-and-over crowd of professionals. A great place in the Warehouse District to sip and people-watch. (Downtown Cleveland)

PARTY-DOWN BARS

FAGAN'S SEAFOOD RESTAURANT
996 Old River Rd.
Cleveland
216/241-6116
One of the earliest Flats landmarks, this East Bank party palace has a theme park feel to it. Landlubbers come by car or taxi, but boaters tie up at the dock. Relax on the riverside patio or by the pool with waterfall and palm trees. The menu, like the decor, offers a little bit of everything—fresh seafood, steaks, chicken, salads, and sandwiches. Live bands perform on weekends year-round. Call ahead for the entertainment update. (Downtown Cleveland)

HOWL AT THE MOON SALOON
2000 Sycamore St.
In the Powerhouse
Cleveland

216/861-4695

Located on the west bank of the Flats, the name of this place gives it away. Even the vocally-challenged join in when the dueling baby grand pianos play. Audience requests are honored and played with gusto. Must be over 21 to enter, much less to sing. (Downtown Cleveland)

SHOOTER'S ON THE WATER
1148 Main Ave.
Cleveland
216/861-6900

One of the true Flats landmarks, Shooter's is many things: the first destination point on the west bank to greet those sailing up the Cuyahoga River; and a year-round, indoor/outdoor, early afternoon to late-night, multi-level expanse of decks and bars. The appetizer menu includes chicken quesadilla, escargot, teriyaki chicken, and spinach dip. New England clam chowder is the featured soup. Grilled Portobello mushroom salad is marinated and served over greens and red peppers. Black

Angus prime rib and steaks satisfy carnivores, while the 12-ounce walleye, served grilled or blackened with fresh vegetables and red-skin potatoes, pleases piscivores. Kids can order chicken fingers, burgers, grilled cheese sandwiches, or spaghetti. (Downtown Cleveland)

SPORTS BARS

GATEWAY SPORTS CLUB AND EATERY
727 Bolivar Rd.
Cleveland
216/621-6644

With 50 TV monitors, two giant screens, and three pool tables, Gateway Sports Club and Eatery is a regular stop for Cleveland's professional athletes. Located near Jacobs Field and Gund Arena, the club allows you to drink and eat and stay on top of the sports action. Gateway serves appetizers, sandwiches, lunch, and dinner. Open weekdays, Saturday and Sunday hours depend

Shooter's on the Water

Mort Tucker/Shooter's

on game times and Gateway events. (Downtown Cleveland)

GRAND SLAM GRILL
The Powerhouse, 2000 Sycamore
Cleveland
216/696-4884
The decor is a mixed metaphor of sports memorabilia and mechanical remnants that once created electricity in this former power plant in the Flats. The indoor and outdoor bars are decoupaged with baseball cards. (Downtown Cleveland)

MEL'S GRILL
2217 E. Ninth St.
Cleveland
216/781-1771
Directly across from Jacobs Field, this bar is one fun place to be when the Tribe is in town. (Downtown Cleveland)

PETE & DEWEY'S PLANET
812 Huron Rd. SE
Cleveland
216/522-1500
Across an asphalt parking lot expanse from Jacobs Field, this is the place to sip pre- or post-game suds in your Indians jersey. (Downtown Cleveland)

COMEDY CLUBS

HILARITIES COMEDY HALL
811 Prospect Ave.
Cleveland
216/781-7733
Hilarities has been a fixture on the Cleveland comedy scene for more than 10 years. When the Regional Transit Authority bought the building that housed Hilarities, owner Nick Kostis moved his club to a new 22,000-square-foot space near the

Gateway sports complex. "We're hoping to build an exciting new daytime and nighttime destination for food, beverage, and live entertainment," says Kostis. The new Hilarities club has a dining area with live magic entertainment. After dinner, the audience moves to a comedy showroom that seats 425. In addition, a 120 seat café will be open from lunchtime to closing every day. Open daily. (Downtown Cleveland)

IMPROVISATION COMEDY CLUB AND RESTAURANT
2000 Sycamore St.
Cleveland
216/696-4677
This 350-seat comedy club has been a regular stop for the likes of comedians such as Cleveland's own Drew Carey. Operating partner Mitch Kutash says the club offers more than a preview of tomorrow's comedy superstars: "It's a nice evening, sitting in the dark for an hour and a half and laughing. It's great therapy." The restaurant serves American nouveau cuisine and is located in the Powerhouse, on the west bank of the Flats. Cover charge. (Downtown Cleveland)

FILM

Cleveland has a very active art movie scene. There are currently a dozen art movie screens showing cutting edge new films from around the world. The east side has two commercial theaters that show art movies. The Cedar-Lee Theatre, 2163 Lee Rd., 216/321-8232, offers six screens. The Centrum Theater, 2781 Euclid Heights Blvd., 216/321-1028, has wheelchair access for two of its three screens.

CLEVELAND CINEMATHEQUE
Cleveland Institute of Art
11141 East Blvd.
Cleveland
216/421-7450

Cleveland's alternative film theater was founded in 1985 by John Ewing. A lifelong film buff and northeast Ohio resident, Ewing felt cheated by the fact that many touring film exhibitions bypassed Cleveland on the way from New York to Chicago. Now the non-profit Cinematheque (pronounced sin-a-ma-TEK) shows art, classic, international, and quality commercial films 50 weekends per year (it shuts down during the weekends of Christmas and New Year). The films are shown in the 616-seat Russell B. Aitken Auditorium in the Gund Building of the Cleveland Institute of Art. Films Thur–Sun eve. $6 one film, $10 two films. ⅊ (University Circle)

CLEVELAND INTERNATIONAL FILM FESTIVAL
Cleveland Film Society
1621 Euclid Ave., Suite 428
Cleveland
216/623-0400

The Cleveland Film Society is a non-profit organization that sponsors the Cleveland International Film Festival. Since it was founded in 1977, the festival has become the premier film event between New York and Chicago, showing 80 feature-length films from 32 countries and more than 100 short films. The 11-day event in mid-March draws 32,000 patrons, including filmmakers and film-associated guests. Panel discussions give audience members a chance to discuss in depth the films they've seen at the festival. Patrons vote on all the films they see and pick the winner of the Roxanne T. Mueller Award, which is the people's choice award, and the $1,000 Best American Independent Film Award. It's a film lover's paradise. Short films compete for many awards and around $2,500 in cash prizes. Eight additional prizes, judged by jury, include Best Ohio Short, Best Documentary Short, Best Student Short, and Best Women's Short. The festival is held in Tower City Cinemas, a multi-screen theater complex in The Avenue at Tower City Center. Advanced seating does go fast, so it is wise to purchase tickets early. ⅊ (Downtown Cleveland)

CLEVELAND MUSEUM OF ART FILM SERIES
Cleveland Museum of Art
11150 East Blvd.
Cleveland
216/421-7340, ext. 465

Cleveland Cinematheque founder John Ewing also runs the art museum's film series. The series shows about 110 films each year on Friday and Wednesday evenings. This is a great place to watch classic and silent films because the museum's 765-seat Gartner Auditorium has a variable-speed projector and an organ for live musical accompaniment. Occasionally the films are shown in the 154-seat Lecture Hall. Phone for scheduled films and times. ⅊ (University Circle)

Paramount Distillers

13

DAY TRIPS

DAY TRIP: Cedar Point

Distance from Cleveland: 60 miles

You don't have to be a coasterhead (people who ride, live, eat, and breathe roller coasters) to enjoy Cedar Point amusement park in Sandusky. But with 12 world-class roller coasters, Cedar Point certainly deserves its nickname as "America's RollerCoast."

From the children's Jr. Gemini roller coaster to the newest $12 million Mantis, thrill-seekers of all ages take more than 17 million rides on Cedar Point coasters every year. Here is Cedar Point's coaster lineup:

- **The Blue Streak**, Cedar Point's oldest existing coaster, is a wooden clickety-clack classic ride. Since it was built in 1964, the Blue Streak has carried more than 45.6 million riders.
- **Cedar Creek Mine Ride**, built in 1969. One of the first coasters to use tubular steel track.
- **Wildcat**, built in 1970. Compact, four-person cars speed through continuous curves and dips.
- **Corkscrew**, built in 1976. Triple-looping coaster entertains spectators below with inverted screaming passengers.
- **Gemini**, built in 1978. Red and blue trains race each other around a wooden figure-8 track. Cedar Point's most popular ride.
- **Jr. Gemini**, built in 1979. This children's roller coaster goes 6 mph, a perfect training ground for future coasterheads.
- **Iron Dragon**, built in 1987. Flight simulator cars hang from a track, swoop over a misty lagoon, and skim above treetops.

CLEVELAND REGION

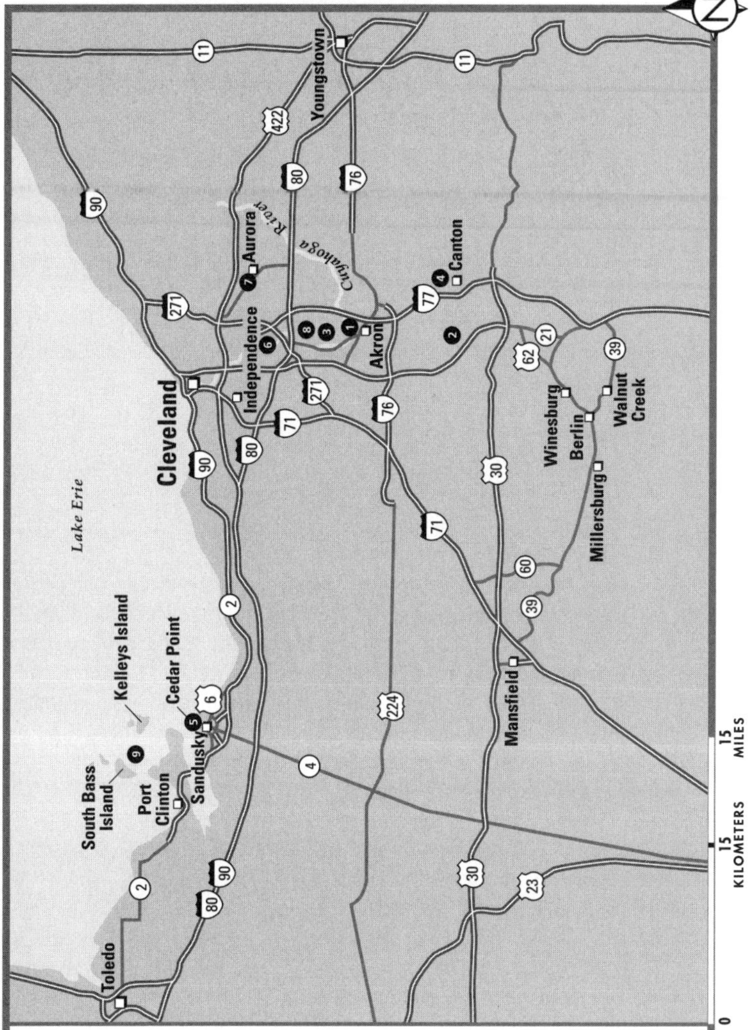

Daytrips from Cleveland

1 Akron
2 Amish Country
3 Blossom Music Center
4 Canton / Pro Football Hall of Fame
5 Cedar Point
6 Cuyahoga Valley Scenic Railroad
7 Geauga Lake and Sea World
8 Hale Farm & Village
9 Lake Erie Islands

TRIVIA

Cedar Point opened its first roller coaster in 1892. The ride wouldn't impress any of today's coasterheads: it was 25 feet tall and traveled no faster than 10 miles per hour.

- **Magnum** XL-200, built in 1989. Voted No. 1 steel roller coaster in the world, Magnum is 205 feet high and goes 72 mph.
- **Disaster Transport**, built in 1990. Space adventure riders encounter attacking space pirates, exploding asteroids, and laser-beaming satellites.
- **Mean Streak**, built in 1991. One of the world's tallest (161 feet) and fastest (65 mph) wooden roller coasters.
- **Raptor**, built in 1994. High-tech inverted roller coaster where riders are suspended below the track in ski lift–style chairs.
- **Mantis**, built in 1996. The tallest, fastest, and steepest stand-up roller coaster in the world.

Don't forget the Power Tower, the park's new four-tower mega-thrill ride. Two of the towers blast you up 24 stories and then you free fall back down. The other two towers carry you to the top and then blast you down 240 feet. Either way, it's a blast. (Riders have to be at least 52 inches tall.)

Aside from these visceral thrills, Cedar Point has its mellow side: classic carousels, paddlewheel boats, antique cars, and a sky ride. There are two kiddie areas with dozens of rides.

In addition to the park's 60 rides, Cedar Point has a sandy beach and boardwalk, the Berenstain Bear Country playland, King Arthur's Court playland, and a petting farm of cuddly farm animals.

Roller Coaster at Cedar Point, p. 176

Dan Fercht

For family entertainment, the park has live stage shows, a frontier trail and town hall museum, and the Cedar Point Cinema's enormous IMAX Theater, with one of the largest indoor movie screens in the world.

Two newly opened attractions next to the park are Challenge Park, a go-kart track, miniature golf, the RipCord bungee-style ride, and the newly expanded 18-acre Soak City waterpark, complete with a wave pool, slides, and a children's area. (Challenge Park and Soak City have separate admission fees.)

Admission depends on how tall you are, with price categories for adults, seniors, and young children. There are special after–5 p.m. prices and bonus weekend prices in the fall. For more information, call 419/627-2350.

Getting There from Cleveland: Go west on the Ohio Turnpike (I-80) to Exit 7. Follow the signs north on U.S. 250.

DAY TRIP: Cuyahoga Valley Scenic Railroad
Distance from Cleveland: 7 miles

Train buffs of all ages will love this trip back through time. The Cuyahoga Valley Scenic Railroad has first-generation 1950s diesel locomotives. The cars are climate-controlled vintage coaches that once carried passengers on the New York Central and Santa Fe Railroads.

Trips come in a variety of lengths and offer several activities. The **Scenic Limited** is a 90-minute round-trip excursion from Independence through the Cuyahoga Valley National Recreation Area to the town of Peninsula. The Peninsula Adventure trip allows passengers to disembark in the historic village of Peninsula. The train depot houses a gift shop and the village is filled with picturesque stores, cafés, art galleries, and antique shops.

The Polar Express

One of the Cuyahoga Valley Scenic Railroad's most popular trips is the Polar Express, named for the popular picture book by Chris Van Allsburg. In the book, a child takes a ride on a magic train and is given a silver sleigh bell by Santa. On this Polar Express ride, the children dress in their pajamas and listen to the story as they ride the train. Then Santa visits each child on the train and hands out silver sleigh bells. Tickets go on sale in October, and trips run weekday evenings through December. Call 800/468-4070 for more information.

All-day round trips go from Independence to downtown Akron. Those 6.5-hour trips include three- to four-hour stops at one of the following: **Hale Farm & Village**, **Stan Hywet Hall & Gardens**, **Quaker Square**, or **Inventure Place**. (For descriptions of these attractions, see Day Trips Hale Farm & Village and Akron.)

The railroad also offers trips that begin in the town of Peninsula and go to the Canal Visitors Center in the national park. The center is a restored house on the Ohio and Erie Canal. On summer weekends, there are demonstrations of how the canal locks operate. The center is staffed with National Park Service rangers who will answer questions about the canal days.

Bike and Hike trips allow you to bring your bike on the train, then get off at one of the stops along the 19 miles of Towpath Trail, a hiking and biking trail that follows the Ohio and Erie Canal. Bike rentals are available in Peninsula.

As the **Cuyahoga Valley Scenic Railroad** carries you through the national park, expect to see lush vegetation and beautiful vistas. The animal life along the way includes hawks, deer, beavers, herons, coyotes, waterfowl, rabbits, and songbirds.

The **Valley Explorer** trip departs from Independence and travels slowly so that you can see the valley's many sites. National Park Service rangers ride along to give a nature presentation and answer your questions. The train makes unscheduled stops wherever wildlife is present. The rangers will even do an escorted hike on established nature trails. Trips are scheduled throughout the year. Special 90-minute **Holiday** excursions run on Memorial Day, Independence Day, Labor Day, and Valentine's Day. Through the month of October, the **Fall Color** tour provides a stunningly beautiful ride through the reds, oranges, and golds of the autumn trees.

Adult ticket prices vary from $7 to $20. Kids' tickets range from $5 to $12. Seniors tickets are in the $6 to $18 range. For information and tickets, call 800/468-4070.

Getting There from Cleveland: Most of the trips begin at Rockside Road in Independence. Take I-77 to the Rockside Road exit (Exit 155). Go east on Rockside 1.2 miles to Canal Road. Go north on Canal Road one short block, then turn west on Old Rockside Road. The boarding site is a tenth of a mile on the left. Signs are posted and parking is free.

DAY TRIP: Hale Farm and Village

Distance from Cleveland: 30 miles

From Memorial Day weekend through October 31, one of the most charming ways to spend a day in northeast Ohio is to visit the Hale Farm

Virgil Wilson

Hale Farm

and Village, located in the Cuyahoga Valley National Recreation Area. The Western Reserve Historical Society created the village next to Hale Farm by collecting century-old buildings from all over northeast Ohio. The buildings were painstakingly dismantled, brought to the fields across Oak Hill Road from Hale Farm, reassembled, and restored to create a Western Reserve township circa 1848.

The **Gatehouse Visitors Center** is a good place to start and finish your tour. The center has a gift shop that sells the craftspeople's wares: hand-blown glass, pottery, baskets, candles, and blacksmith items. Light snacks are also sold in the visitor center.

The brick farmhouse, called Old Brick of Hale Farm, was built by Jonathan Hale in 1827. The farm remained in the Hale family until 1956, when it was given to the Western Reserve Historical Society.

Visitors can meander down country lanes to the 1832-era land office, the pottery shed and kiln, the smokehouse and outbuildings, the sawmill, the glassworks, the log schoolhouse, and the meeting house. Gardens and outbuildings are laid out according to historical documents from that period.

The Carriage Museum, built in 1851, houses the village's 40 carriages and sleighs. The Goldsmith House was constructed by master builder Jonathan Goldsmith in 1832 and is a beautiful example of the architecture of the transition period between Federal and Greek Revival styles. The Jagger House, circa 1844, is a Greek Revival home named after the carriage maker who built it. The Wade Law Office, built in 1852, was owned and occupied by abolitionist leader Senator Benjamin Franklin Wade, president of the Senate during President Andrew Johnson's administration.

Throughout the village and farm, craftspeople in period costumes demonstrate their skills in blacksmithing, music, broom-making, candlemaking, glassblowing, and cheesemaking.

Although this attraction is mostly for warm weather, Hale Farm reopens for the Winter Holiday season and for Maple Sugaring Days in February and March. For seasonal hours or more information, write to Hale Farm & Village, 2686 Oak Hill Road, Bath, OH 44210, or call 800/589-9703 (within Ohio) or 330/666-3711. Year-round admission is $9 for adults, $7.50 for seniors, and $5.50 for children 6 to 12.

Getting There from Cleveland: Take I-77 south for about 30 minutes until you reach Cuyahoga Valley National Recreation Area.

DAY TRIP: Amish Country

Distance from Cleveland: 80 miles

Life in the slow lane takes on new meaning when you travel to Amish country. As soon as you enter Holmes County, you are stepping back in time.

Nowhere in the world can you find a larger, more highly concentrated Amish population. The Mennonite Information Center, 330/893-3192, located off County Road 77 east of Berlin, is a good place to learn about Amish and Mennonite cultures, talk to the friendly guides, and even see the 265-foot cyclorama completed in 1992 by local artist Heinz Gaugel. The painting, entitled *Behalt*, is a visual history of the Amish and Mennonite people from their Anabaptist beginnings in Zurich, Switzerland, all the way to the present time.

The towns in Holmes County are as charming as their names: Walnut Creek, Millersburg, Wilmot, Winesburg, and, of course, Charm. Although the Amish people keep largely to themselves, two farms are open to the public. The **Amish Farm and House**, located just off Ohio 39 between Berlin and Walnut Creek, and **Yoder's Amish Farm**, off Ohio 515 between Walnut Creek and Trail, offer tours of a typical Amish home. Kids can pet the farm animals and even take a ride in a traditional Amish buggy.

To experience Amish life, you have to eat Amish food. That is a pleasurable task, thanks to such down-home restaurants as the **Amish Door** in Wilmot, the **Dutch Country Kitchen** at Ohio 39 and U.S. 62 in Berlin, the **Dutch Harvest** west of Berlin, the **Homestead** in Charm, and **Der Dutchman** in Walnut Creek. Der Dutchman is home of one of the county's largest in-house bakeries. (For people traveling south on I-71 to Columbus, Der Dutchman has opened a second location at the New Lexington exit.)

Shopping is a daylong exercise in itself. The Amish are noted for their solid hand-crafted oak, walnut, and cherry furniture, Amish prints and dolls, Trail bologna, cheese, baked goods, and homemade candies.

The **Holmes County Amish Flea Market** in Walnut Creek is open 9 to 8 on Friday and 9 to 5 on Saturday. The 40,000 square feet of crafts, antiques, food, and collectibles are a browsing bonanza.

Wendell August Forge near Winesburg is a great place to stroll through the handmade metal giftware; don't miss its museum and theater.

Alpine-Alpa on Ohio 62 in Wilmot is one of several cheesemaking operations in Holmes County where visitors can watch the process.

Fourteen varieties of cheese—300,000 pounds per month—are produced in the factory. Alpine-Alpa also has the world's largest cuckoo clock—23.5 feet high, 24 feet long, and 13.5 feet wide.

Holmes County Pottery is located 8500 County Road 373 in the town of Big Prairie. Visitors can see hand-turned pottery being made using traditional techniques. All pottery is fired in Ohio's largest wood-burning kiln. The pottery store is open from 9 to 5 Monday through Saturday.

Getting There from Cleveland: Take I-77 to Ohio 39 west into Holmes County.

DAY TRIP: Lake Erie Islands
Distance from Cleveland: 60 miles

The Islands of Lake Erie are a warm-weather playground with enough activities to last an entire season. But if you have only one day to explore the Bass Islands, *Island Hopper* (800/903-3779) cruises are a great way to go. The *Island Hopper* arrives and departs from each port at two- to three-hour intervals, so you can decide how long to spend at each stop.

The *Island Hopper* is docked at the foot of Jefferson Street in downtown **Port Clinton**. (If you have any extra time, Port Clinton has downtown shopping and restaurants worth exploring.) Buy a round-trip ticket that includes stops on **South Bass** and **Kelleys Island**. (Adults pay $15 to $17 for a round trip, kids 12 and under are only $3, and kids under 3 are free.) The view from the upper sundeck lets you enjoy the lake breezes. Below is an enclosed cabin that serves drinks and snacks. Your first stop is **South Bass**, an hourglass-shaped island. The narrowest part is called Put-In-Bay, site of **Perry's Victory and Peace Memorial**. Check out the view from atop the 352-foot tower (adults $2, seniors and kids 16 and younger are free). The monument

---

The Lonz Winery Tour

The Lonz Winery is located on Middle Bass Island in the heart of the Bass Island chain. Tours of the winery include a wine tasting. For tour information, call 419/285-5411. From South Bass Island, you can get to the Lonz Winery by Sonny S. Water Taxi, open from Memorial Day to Labor Day.

---

commemorates the U.S. victory in the Battle of Lake Erie, when the fledgling U.S. Navy beat the world-dominant British navy during the War of 1812.

South Bass Island has bicycle and golf cart rentals for self-guided tours on a marked bike route. Or you can take a narrated tour of the island on a tram-style train with stop-off privileges at the winery, caves, and memorial. Gift stores and eateries are plentiful. The party-hearty crowd visits **Frosty's**, a pizza tavern landmark.

One mile west of Perry's monument on Catawba Avenue is **Perry's Cave**, a 208-by-165-foot limestone cave with an underground lake. The privately owned cave charges admission for a 20-minute tour. Across the street are **Crystal Cave** and the **Heinman Winery**. Admission provides a tour of the cave and winery, including a glass of wine or grape juice.

For wine enthusiasts, the **Lonz Winery** is located on **Middle Bass Island**, the next island north in the Bass Island chain. A short ride on the *Sonny S* water taxi will get you there.

The second leg of your island-hopping trip is **Kelleys Island**. Once you land on the island's south shore, rent a bike or golf cart. The Village of Kelleys Island has several restaurants, pubs, miniature golf, bed-and-breakfasts, cottages, shops, and marinas. But the rest of Kelleys Island's 2,800 acres is rural and remote. On the northern end are glacial grooves carved out of limestone by the last glacier's visit. Nearby **Kelleys Island State Park** (419/797-4530) offers camping, picnicking, a boat ramp, hiking trails, fishing, a playground, and swimming on a sandy beach.

For shopping enthusiasts on the mainland, the **Lake Erie Factory Outlet Center** is a half-mile north of Ohio Turnpike Exit 7 on U.S. 250, near Sandusky. Call 419/499-2528 for store hours.

Getting There from Cleveland: *To get to the* Island Hopper *cruise, head west on Ohio Route 2 across Sandusky Bay to Exit 163. Go west (left) on Perry Street. The* Island Hopper *is docked at the foot of Jefferson Street in downtown Port Clinton.*

DAY TRIP: Akron

Distance from Cleveland: 35 miles

Akron was once the tire capital of the world. During its heyday from 1900 through the 1950s, the Rubber City was headquarters for Goodyear, Firestone, Goodrich, and other smaller tire companies.

F. A. Seiberling, cofounder of the Goodyear Tire and Rubber Company, left his mark on the Akron landscape when he built a 65-room mansion in 1915. The house, called **Stan Hywet**, which means "stone quarry" in Anglo-Saxon, is considered the finest example of Tudor Revival in this country. For 40 years, Stan Hywet was a family home, but today the home and 70 acres of surrounding gardens and lawns are open to the public seven days a week.

The grounds are open from 9 to 6, and house tours are available from 10 to 4:30. Admission is $7 for adults, $6.50 for seniors, $3.50 for children ages 6 to 12, free to kids under 6. To get there, take I-77 south from Cleveland to the Montrose-Route 18 exit. Go east on Route 18 (West Market Street), left on Twin Oaks, and left again on North Portage Path. To find out about upcoming special events, call 330/836-5533.

In the 1960s and 1970s, when the rubber companies began moving their factories to the Sunbelt and overseas, Akron struggled to find a new identity. **Inventure Place, National Inventors Hall of Fame** is part of Akron's efforts to redefine itself as a high-tech polymer research center. The museum, located at 221 South Broadway Street in downtown Akron, is a combination of many things. The **Inventors Workshop** encourages visitors to experiment with lasers, video animation, magnetism, and other scientific concepts.

The **Hall of Fame** exhibits explain the inventions of the inductees. There is a restaurant, meeting rooms, and a gift store with creative toys, games, and puzzles. Inventure Place is open year-round, with different hours for each season. Call 330/762-6565 for hours. Admission is $7.50 for adults, $6 for seniors and kids ages 3 to 17, free for kids 2 and under. Groups of 25 or more pay $5.50 per person.

Just up the street from Inventure Place, at the corner of Broadway and Mill Street, is **Quaker Square**. If you look north on Broadway, you can't miss it. Those large silos you see were once filled with Quaker Oats. Now they are filled with hotel guests, since their conversion into the Quaker Square Hilton (800/445-8667). It is worth staying here just to be able to say you've spent the night in a grain silo!

Most of Quaker Square is filled with specialty shops selling candy, brass and pewter objects, toys, leather, Christmas decorations, and toy trains; there's a newsstand, too. Quaker Square has several excellent restaurants, including **Schumacher's**, **The Tavern**, and the **Depot Diner**, where diners eat in old railroad cars.

Getting there from Cleveland: Head south on I-77.

DAY TRIP: Geauga Lake and Sea World

Distance from Cleveland: 30 miles

Aurora has two attractions, and both are a full day's worth of fun. Because they are so different from each other and both are within easy driving distance of the city, you really should take two days to visit these family-focused entertainment parks.

Geauga Lake is an amusement park on the shores of its namesake lake. Today it is a combination amusement park and water park with more than 100 rides and attractions.

One of the newest rides is the Mind Eraser, a boomerang-style roller coaster that sends riders through loops and corkscrews, going forward and then backward for a disorienting sense of déjà vu.

Another new ride is the Grizzly Run river raft ride, tossing and turning passengers along 3.5 acres of treelined, rocky, white-water rapids and small waterfalls.

The park's other coaster rides include the wooden Raging Wolf Bobs, the Double Loop, and the classic Big Dipper, built in the 1920s.

Geauga Lake also has rides for those who enjoy a trip to yesteryear. Ride one of the 64 hand-carved horses on the 1926 Marcus Illions Carousel. The Flying Scooters, a ride first introduced at the 1939 World's Fair, is a nostalgic trip any age can enjoy. The attractions include standard kiddie rides and antique cars.

Live entertainment shows are staged at various locations on the midway and at the Stagecoach and the Palace Theaters. While adults relax nearby, youngsters can explore **Butch Hightide's Play Park**, a series of climbing structures and play areas that were created by the Little Tikes toy manufacturer.

If you want to get wet, try the 11 slides, water chutes, and play areas at Turtle Beach (for kids) and Boardwalk Shores (for adults). The Wave is a massive wave pool holding 2 million gallons of water. Geauga Lake admission is $20 for those taller than 48 inches. Children under 48 inches are $6. Children under age 2 are free.

Across the lake is **Sea World**, a 90-acre marine life park that's designed to educate as well as to entertain. More than 25 years ago, Sea World began offering a few shows featuring killer whales, dolphins, and penguins. Today the park has seven live shows and features more than 20 other attractions. Highlights include:

- **The Shamu: World Focus** show includes footage of killer whales from around the world, in addition to Shamu's own fascinating behavior.
- The comic antics of California sea lions **Clyde and Seamore** are featured in a presentation that includes North American river otters, Asian small-clawed otters, and the Pacific walrus.
- In the **Dolphin Cove** interactive habitat, guests can touch and feed bottlenose dolphins. The **Wild Wings** show is a free-flight show featuring macaws, parrots, and a 20-pound condor with a 10-foot wingspan.
- **Patagonia Passage** is a new exhibit of dolphins and penguins from the rocky coastline on the tip of South America.
- **Shark Encounter** is an exhibit in which a moving walkway travels under the huge, curved windows of an aquarium housing dozens of sharks, sawfish, eels, and reef fishes.

After all those animal encounters, watch the humans do their stuff on water skis. Guests can observe the **Baywatch at Sea World** water show performance from the beach of Geauga Lake. **Shamu's Happy Harbor** is an adventure playland with a 50-foot, four-story climbing maze with 40,000 square feet of netting. The **Access For All Garden** is an award-winning garden that features foliage of varying scents and textures in raised planters. The garden has a hands-on water wall and two new aviaries with exotically colored cockatoos. Admission is $26 for adults and $20 for kids 3 to 11.

Getting There from Cleveland: *To reach both Geauga Lake and Sea World, take the Ohio Turnpike to Exit 13 and drive 9 miles north on Ohio Route 43.*

DAY TRIP: Canton/Pro Football Hall of Fame

Distance from Cleveland: 60 miles

Composed of four galleries, the Pro Football Hall of Fame curves around its football-shaped dome. Features include twin enshrinement halls, the pro football art gallery, and the exhibition rotunda. Also popular are the movie theater, museum store, and Super Bowl memorabilia. Adult admission is $9; kids ages 6 to 14, $4. Phone: 330/456-8207.

After perusing the Hall of Fame, stop next door at the **Canton/Stark County Tourist Information Center**. The center is open seven days a week from 9 a.m. to 5 p.m. and is staffed by friendly, helpful people.

Pro Football Hall of Fame

Pro Football Hall of Fame

If you enjoy American history, your next stop should be the **McKinley National Monument** in 23-acre Monument Park, 800 McKinley Monument Drive N.W. From the Hall of Fame, head south through Canton city park system's Stadium park on Stadium Drive to Memorial Park. Follow the signs to the monument. Affectionately known as Bill on the Hill, this is the final resting place for the 25th president and his family. William McKinley was assassinated in 1901, early in his second term of office. The patio of the monument affords a panoramic view of the city.

Next door to the monument is

the **McKinley Museum of History, Science and Industry**. This 55,000-square foot museum includes an 18th-century Street of Shops, a planetarium, and Discovery World, a hands-on children's science center covering dinosaurs to space exploration. Kids especially enjoy Allosaurus, a robotic dinosaur, and "Ecosystem Island." Admission is $6 for adults, $5 for seniors, $4 for children 3 to 18. A family day pass is $18.

For an unusual look at Yankee ingenuity, check out the **Hoover Historical Center**, 2225 Easton Street N.W., North Canton. Take Market Avenue north from Canton and turn left on Easton Street. It is the only known vacuum cleaner museum in the world, but this is not just a pile of old machines. The museum is the restored boyhood home of William H. "Boss" Hoover, who pioneered the art of selling the machines door-to-door. See the historical period rooms. Look for the enormous metal knob rings that salesmen wore to rap on a customer's door. In summertime, tour the herb gardens. Open Tuesday through Sunday from 1 to 5. Admission is free. Phone 330/499-0287.

On the return trip north on I-77, stop at Exit 113 for a tour of the **Harry London Candies' Chocolate Factory**. The 1.5-hour tour through the 80,000-square-foot state-of-the-art facility includes samples of chocolates as they're being made. Admission is $2 for adults and seniors, $1 for ages 6 to 18, and free for kids under 6. Tours are available seven days a week but reservations are required. Call ahead for seasonal hours: 800/321-0444.

Getting There from Cleveland: Take I-77 south for about an hour until you reach Canton. Take Exit 107A and follow the signs.

DAY TRIP: Blossom Music Center

Distance from Cleveland: 20 miles

Blossom Music Center in Cuyahoga Falls is the summer home of the Cleveland Orchestra, which means that from Memorial Day to Labor Day this is a wonderful place to enjoy one of the world's great orchestras.

Blossom, named for members of the Dudley S. Blossom family, is an award-winning outdoor concert pavilion that seats 5,281 people. The pavilion was built at the base of a fan-shaped natural bowl, and this lawn seats an additional 13,500 people.

Couples and families like to spread a blanket on the lawn and dine al fresco on their chosen spot before a concert. The pavilion is surrounded by 150 acres of flower and tree gardens, a sculpture garden, Eells Art Gallery, picnic areas, a picnic shelter, restaurant, concession stands, and ample parking lots. The entire tract of land encompasses 800 acres and borders the Cuyahoga Valley National Recreation Area.

In addition to the orchestra concerts, Blossom stages about 35 popular music concerts, including country, rock, rap, and folk, through MCA

Concerts, Inc. If you're going to a pop music concert, don't bring any bottles or cans. Only soft-sided and Styrofoam coolers are permitted.

For outdoor theater lovers, Porthouse Theater is Kent State University's summer theater season. The 450-seat theater offers three productions that run Wednesday through Sunday from mid-June to mid-August. Call the box office at 330/929-4416.

The Blossom Ticket Office is open Friday through Sunday from 1 to 5. On orchestra performance dates, it is open from 1 through intermission. On evenings of special attractions, the ticket office opens a half-hour before gates open and closes at varying times depending upon the performance schedule. For more information, contact Blossom Music Center, 1145 West Steels Corners Road, Cuyahoga Falls, OH, 330/920-8040.

To order tickets for the Cleveland Orchestra, call 800/686-1141 from 9 to 5 weekdays. Or you can charge tickets by phone through Ticketmaster, 216/241-5555.

Getting There from Cleveland: *Take I-77 south to the Ohio Turnpike. Go east on the turnpike to Exit 12 (Ohio Route 8). Follow Route 8 south to Steels Corners Road. Turn right on Steels Corners Road and follow the signs.*

APPENDIX: CITY·SMART BASICS

EMERGENCY PHONE NUMBERS

Ambulance/Fire/Police
911

Battered Women's 24-hour Hotline
216/391-4357

Drug Abuse 24-hour Hotline
800/234-1253

Hazardous Material Spill
216/771-1365

Poison Control Center
216/231-4455

Rape Crisis Center
216/391-3914

Suicide Hotline
216/721-1115

MAJOR HOSPITALS AND EMERGENCY MEDICAL CENTERS

Cleveland Clinic
216/444-2200

Deaconess Hospital of Cleveland
216/459-6300

Fairview Hospital
216/476-7000

Marymount Hospital
216/581-0500

Meridia Euclid Hospital
216/531-9000

Meridia Hillcrest Hospital
216/449-4500

Meridia Huron Hospital
216/761-3300

Meridia South Pointe Hospital
216/491-6000

MetroHealth Medical Center
216/778-7800

Mt. Sinai Medical Center
216/421-4000

Richmond Heights General Hospital
216/585-6433

St. Alexis Hospital Medical Center
216/429-8000

St. John West Shore Hospital
216/835-8000

St. Vincent Charity Hospital
216/861-6200

Southwest General Health Center
216/816-8000

University Hospitals of Cleveland
216/844-1000

TRAFFIC INFORMATION

AAA Road Conditions
216/431-7000

Road Conditions
800/394-7623

VISITOR INFORMATION

Convention & Visitors Bureau of Greater Cleveland
216/621-5555

Hotel and ticket reservations
800/321-1004

State of Ohio Office of Travel and Tourism
800/BUCKEYE

VISITOR INFORMATION CENTERS

Tower City Center
50 Public Square
216/621-7981

Cleveland Hopkins International Airport
Baggage Claim Level
216/265-3729

West Bank of the Flats
216/623-4442

East Bank of the Flats
Old River Rd. beneath
Main Ave. Bridge
216/621-2218

CITY TOURS

Trolley Tours of Cleveland
Burke Lakefront Airport
216/771-4484

North Coast Tours and Convention Services
601 Rockwell Ave.
216/579-6160

CAR RENTAL

Alamo Rent-A-Car
800/327-9633

Avis
800/831-2847

Budget
216/433-4433

Dollar
216/267-3133

Enterprise Rent-A-Car
800/736-8222

Hertz Corporation
800/654-3131

National
800/227-7368

Thrifty
216/267-7368

DISABLED ACCESS INFORMATION

Cleveland Hearing and Speech Center
216/231-8787

Empowering People with Disabilities
216/731-1529

OTHER COMMUNITY ORGANIZATIONS

Jewish Community Federation
216/566-9200

Lesbian/Gay Community Service Center Hotline
216/861-5454

Northeast Ohio Chapter of Stepfamilies
216/349-2412

Ohio AIDS Hotline
800/332-2437

Urban League of Greater Cleveland
216/622-0999

BABYSITTING AND CHILD CARE

Center for Families and Children
216/861-0492

NEWSPAPERS

Plain Dealer
216/999-5000

Call and Post
216/451-2890

Sun Newspapers
216/524-0830

Free Times
216/321-2300

MAGAZINES

Cleveland Magazine
216/771-2833

Crain's Cleveland
216/522-1383

TV STATIONS

WKYC TV-3, NBC
WEWS TV-5, ABC
WOIO TV-19, CBS

WVIZ TV-25, PBS
UPN TV-43, independent
WBNX TV-55, independent
WJW TV-8, FOX

RADIO STATIONS

WBWC 88.3 FM/College
WUJC 88.7 FM/College
WCSB 89.3 FM/College
WNCX 98.5 FM/Classic rock
WGAR 99.5 FM/Country
WDOK 102.1 FM/Adult contemporary
WZLE 104.9 FM/Inspirational
WNWZ 107.3 FM/Jazz
WENZ 107.9 FM/Alternative rock
WEOL 850 AM/Jazz
WJTB 1040 AM/Adult contemporary
WOBL 1320 AM/Country
WELW 1330 AM/Adult contemporary
WSLR 1350 AM/Country

BOOKSTORES

Appletree Books
12419 Cedar Rd.
Cleveland Heights
216/791-9434

B. Dalton Booksellers
Parmatown Mall
8041 W. Ridgewood Dr.
Parma
440/888-3612

Great Northern Mall
North Olmstead
440/734-7887

Middleburg Plaza
7232 Pearl Rd.
Middleburg Heights
440/884-7020

Barnes & Noble Booksellers
5900 Mayfield Rd.
Mayfield Heights
216/473-1040

The Booksellers
Pavilion Mall
24031 Chagrin Blvd.
Beachwood
216/831-5035

Book Stacks Unlimited
1300 E. Ninth St.
Cleveland
216/861-0467

Borders Books and Music
30121 Detroit Rd.
Westlake
216/892-7667

17200 Royalton Rd.
Strongsville
440/846-1144

2101 Richmond Rd.
Beachwood
216/292-2660

Brentano's
Galleria at Erieview
1301 E. Ninth St.
Cleveland
216/621-7544

Doubleday Book Shop
230 Huron Rd.
Cleveland
216/621-6880

Oh, Books!
33637 Aurora Rd.
Solon
440/349-2665

Page Two
14879 Detroit Ave.
Lakewood
216/521-5384

Waldenbooks
411 Euclid Ave.
Cleveland
216/574-9156

Parmatown Mall
7793 W. Ridgewood Dr.
Parma
440/845-5911

Great Northern Mall
North Olmstead
440/734-8892

Southland Center
6861 Southland Dr.
Middleburg Heights
440/842-8388

Euclid Square Mall
Euclid
216/289-2514

6255 Mayfield Rd.
Mayfield Heights
440/442-2187

INDEX

ABOUT THE AUTHOR

After 10 years as a staff writer for the *Akron Beacon Journal*, Nancy Peacock began covering Cleveland as a freelance writer for a variety of magazines, including *Business Week*, *Midwest Living*, *New Choices*, *Romantic Homes*, *Cleveland*, and *Corporate Cleveland*. A graduate of the Ohio University Creative Writing Department, Peacock began her journalism career at the *Medina County Gazette*. She and her husband, Larry, have two children, Aaron and Natalie.

JOHN MUIR PUBLICATIONS and its City•Smart Guidebook authors are dedicated to building community awareness within City•Smart cities. We are proud to work with Project: Learn as we publish this guide to Cleveland.

Project: Learn enables adults to acquire the basic reading, writing, listening, and speaking skills needed to solve the problems of daily living, to take full advantage of citizenship, and to participate fully in the affairs of the community.

Project: Learn provides English as a Second Language tutoring, pre-GED classes, workplace skills training for manufacturing employees, basic-level classes for inmates, comprehensive library services designed especially for new readers, literacy centers in neighborhoods, and computer-assisted learning instruction. All of these services have one fundamental aim—to provide basic-level students with whatever help they need in realizing their goals.

For more information, please contact:
Project: Learn
2728 Euclid Avenue, Suite 200
Cleveland, OH 44115
216/621-9483